WE BELIEVE
CORE TRUTHS FOR CHRISTIAN LIVING

We Believe: Core Truths for Christian Living

Rev. Randall A. Bach, General Editor
Dr. David L. Cole, Theological Editor
Rev. Andrea P. Johnson, Copy Editor

Copyright © 2015 by OBC Publishing
Published in Des Moines, Iowa, by OBC Publishing

ISBN 978-0-9608160-3-3
Library of Congress Control Number: 2015901973

All rights reserved. No portions of this book may be reproduced, stored in a retrieval system, or transmitted in any form by any means – electronic, mechanical, recording, or any other – except for brief quotations in reviews or articles, without the prior permission of the publisher.

Scripture quotations are from the Holy Bible, New International Version, unless otherwise indicated. Copyright © 1973, 1978, 1984 by International Bible Society.

Book and cover design by Greg Roberts

Printed in the United States of America
First Edition 2015

Contents

Preface		V
Acknowledgments		VII
Introduction		1
Chapter 1.	The Book of Books: The Bible	3
Chapter 2.	Our Heavenly Father: God	29
Chapter 3.	Our Redeemer: The Person and Work of Jesus Christ	49
Chapter 4.	Our Comforter: The Person and Work of the Holy Spirit	71
Chapter 5.	Creation, Humanity, Sin, Angels, Demons: His World	89
Chapter 6.	People of God: The Church	113
Chapter 7.	Relating to Each Other: Community Life	137
Chapter 8.	His Future for Us: Next Things	161
Chapter 9.	New Life in Christ: Salvation and Sanctification	183
Chapter 10.	Celebrating God's Grace: Water Baptism and the Lord's Supper	205
Chapter 11.	Experiencing Renewal: Baptism in the Holy Spirit and Spiritual Gifts	223
Chapter 12.	Our Great Commission: Evangelism and Missions	245
Glossary		277

Preface

When you committed to follow Christ for life, did you wonder what your next steps should be? Did you think your life would automatically become perfect? What does being a "good" Christian look like anyway?

Maybe you still have lots of questions about the Christian faith and have yet to decide whether or not you are ready to commit your life to Christ. Open Bible Churches published *We Believe: Core Truths for Christian Living* to provide answers to these types of questions, to provide a solid foundation for those new to or still considering the Christian faith.

The material for *We Believe* can be studied independently or in a group setting. If studying independently, we suggest reading one chapter per setting, taking time to contemplate the questions at the end of the chapter. We also suggest using a journal or notebook in which to write your answers to the questions and other thoughts or observations.

As a companion piece to the main text, the *Leader's Guide* is meant to assist churches and ministry leaders who would like to present the material in a classroom or small group discussion setting. Working through the material as a group can strengthen relationships between students as you grow together in Christ.

The guide includes a class outline for each chapter of *We Believe*. The outline includes five main divisions: Introduction, Impressions, Investigation, Interaction, and Integration. There are also video introductions for each chapter, PowerPoint slides that present main points and positions, plus lists and links of additional resources. You may view or download the *Leader's Guide* and other resources at

WeBelieveOBC.com

Each class session is formatted to be approximately 45 to 60 minutes long, although actual length may vary according to the discussion generated. Leaders should allow time for the material to be pondered and applied as participants discuss and share from their hearts, instead of simply working to "get through" the information.

Whichever method of study you choose, this book will help you establish a firm foundation – whether you have recently decided to embrace the Christian life or are needing some questions answered before making a decision.

It is our prayer that you will encounter the teaching ministry of the Holy Spirit afresh as you interact with the material and integrate it into daily life.

Randall A. Bach, David L. Cole, and Andrea P. Johnson

Acknowledgments

We appreciate you! If you are reading this, you are making an effort to become more like Christ by studying His words and applying them to your life. That act gives Him great pleasure. He inspired His disciple John to write, *"I have no greater joy than to hear that my children are walking in the truth"* (3 John 1:4).

At Open Bible Churches, we believe it is imperative to read, study, and apply the Word of God to our lives. Too many people base life decisions on incorrect assumptions because they do not have an understanding of truth. For that reason we felt the need to offer *We Believe: Core Truths for Christian Living*. *We Believe* can be studied independently or within the context of a classroom setting. For information on how to use this book, please see the Preface.

We appreciate greatly the many people who have had a part in making this book a reality, especially the writers, experienced pastors and theologians who worked diligently to present our beliefs in layman's terms.

The writers are:

Rev. Randall A. Bach	Rev. J. Kenneth Groen
Dr. James M. Beaird	Dr. Andy Homer
Rev. Burton J. Campbell	Rev. Monte J. LeLaCheur
Dr. David L. Cole	Dr. Randall L. Loescher
Rev. Jeffrey E. Farmer	Rev. Charles R. Loftis
Rev. Dyrie M. Francis	Rev. John C. Simmons

We also greatly appreciate Trudy Kutz and Barbara Bach, who spent hours proofreading copy. And many thanks go to Burt Campbell who, in addition to writing, did an amazing job formulating contemplation questions for each chapter and providing the format for the *Leader's Guide*.

Our deep thanks goes to Edgar Figueroa, who spent hours and hours translating the entire book into Spanish, and to Lois McCarty, for proofreading the translation.

We also greatly appreciate Greg Roberts, Open Bible's Print Communications Director, for graphic design, layout, and publishing research, and Nate Beaird and Nicole Fultz for their assistance as members of our office staff.

We especially want to thank our Open Bible pastors, faithfully serving their congregations and our Lord, who make sure to teach their congregations to understand and apply God's Word, the Bible, to their lives.

Randall A. Bach, David L. Cole, and Andrea P. Johnson

Introduction

Did Beethoven begin playing beautiful concertos the first few weeks he sat at a piano? Not at all. But Beethoven did eventually make great contributions to the world of music as he developed his gifts. And he did so by giving himself wholeheartedly to the study of music and applying what he learned when he sat down to the piano.

The same principle applies to the Christian life. Without taking time to learn and study the core truths of the Bible, the Christian's handbook, it will be very difficult to maximize your growth and fulfill your destiny as a Christian. But we believe God intends for your life to become a beautiful masterpiece. And we trust that *We Believe: Core Truths for Christian Living* will help you in that process.

Some people think the ultimate goal is to "give our lives to Christ," as if once we give our lives to Christ we have "arrived" and need nothing else. However, we must advance through the different stages of development, to learn how to walk and talk, to move toward the full maturity of adulthood. Even the name "Christian" addresses our ultimate goal: to become Christ-like. One of the best descriptions of God's expectations for us emphasizes the importance of Christian maturity:

> *… until we all reach unity in the faith and in the knowledge of the Son of God and become mature, attaining to the whole measure of the fullness of Christ. Then we will no longer be infants, tossed back and forth by the waves, and blown here and there by every wind of teaching and by the cunning and craftiness of men in their deceitful scheming* (Ephesians 4:13-14).

The more we become like Christ, the closer we come to understanding and fulfilling God's purpose for our lives. It is important then to learn as much as we can about Him. This effort to know Him is a lifelong process that involves the Bible and the Holy Spirit. The Bible, God's Word, His Truth, is our textbook and the Holy Spirit is our teacher. God gave us His Word so that we could know Him better. He sent the Holy Spirit to help us understand His Word and apply it personally to our lives. Even Bible scholars who have studied God's Word for years find the Holy Spirit teaches them something new each time they open the Scriptures.

The name Open Bible Churches declares our belief, not only in the Bible, but also in the imperative of opening it in order to read, study, understand, and apply what God says to us through its pages. In fact, we are instructed in 2 Timothy 2:15 to, ***Do your best to present yourself to God as one approved, a workman who does not need to be ashamed and who correctly handles the word of truth.*** As you journey through *We Believe: Core Truths for Christian Living*, may you delight in becoming approved in handling God's Word.

Randall A. Bach, President
Open Bible Churches

CHAPTER 1

The Book of Books:
The Bible

CHAPTER 1

The Book of Books:
The Bible

> **❝** We believe the Bible is the inspired Word of God and the only infallible guide and rule of our faith and practice. **❞**

IS THE BIBLE A MIRACLE?

More than words on a page, the Bible is actually a living entity with the power to change lives, as evidenced by the following true story:

> Dr. Joseph Conlee, who had pastored one of the largest congregations on the Pacific Coast in the late 1800s, had become a drunken castaway – shuffling around in rags, lying in the gutter, and cursing God.
>
> Joseph bade his family goodbye and boarded a steam ship to the Yukon, Alaska, where he was surrounded by prospectors searching for gold. Before long he accepted an offer to maintain a gold claim on the Forty-Mile Creek. His pay was housing in a log cabin and all the food and whiskey he wanted.
>
> One October night, when the temperature was forty degrees below zero, another cold and hungry loner, Jimmy Miller, knocked at the door, wanting to join the former pastor, followed two weeks later by Wally Flett, also in search of shelter.
>
> The three men spent the next few months partying and telling vulgar stories, but eventually the close quarters got on their nerves. Jimmy became ill and needed a doctor but the roads

were impassable. Joseph reached for his medicine chest. When he opened it a little black book fell out, a Bible his daughter had given him. Joseph opened the stove to burn it but Wally objected. "We have nothing else to read in this God-forsaken place," he said.

While recovering, Jimmy read the Bible aloud. The whiskey barrel went down more slowly and the trio seemed to be cursing less. Christmas came; they read about Christ's birth. In January, the Gospel of John. February 14 was Valentine's Day – a day of miracles.

Joseph, missing his daughter, started to cry. Wally admitted he wanted to pray, but was afraid the others would laugh. He wondered if the Bible were true. In an amazing transformation the three men knelt and poured out their hearts before God. By 2:00 a.m. they rolled the whiskey barrel out the door, broke it open with a hatchet, and praised God as they watched the alcohol trickle out into the snow (adapted from *Lonely Cabin on the Forty Mile*, a tract written by Charles S. Price in the 1940s).

The three men who entered that cabin in the Yukon came out of it miraculously transformed. Wally Flett, Jimmy Miller, and Joseph Conlee each dedicated the rest of their lives to ministry upon returning from Alaska. Joseph Conlee became one of the founders of the Bible Standard Training School (now New Hope Christian College) in Eugene, Oregon. It was the "Book of books," the Bible, that brought about the transformation. What is it about the Bible that causes it to contain such power?

What is this book that so changed the lives of these men?

What is the Bible?

The word *Bible* comes from the Greek *ta biblia*, which means "the little books." Though the Bible is a single book, it is also a library, a collection of 66 books.

As we have it today the Bible is divided into two sections: the Old Testament (OT) and the New Testament (NT). The word *testament* means "covenant," for the Bible is the story of God's covenant (pledge or agreement) with His people whom He loves and for whom He died. There are 39 books in the OT and 27 books in the NT. In the year 1250 A.D. the books of the Bible were divided into chapters, and 300 years later each chapter was divided into verses. The chapters may have anywhere from two verses (Psalm 117, the shortest chapter in the Bible) to 176 verses (Psalm 119, the longest chapter in the Bible).

This library was written by about 40 different people, most of whom were not contemporaries. Some authors wrote hundreds of years before or after others did their writing. Some were separated by more than 1,000 years, such as Moses who wrote the first book of the Bible (Genesis) and the Apostle John who wrote the last book of the Bible at the end of the first century (Revelation).

A Miracle in Literature

There are no other books like those that compromise the Bible. The writers not only lived in different times, but they also came from different walks of life; they were fishermen, shepherds, royalty, priests, prophets, and princes. One was a royal cupbearer, one a tax-collector, one a physician, one a religious zealot. They wrote in three different languages (Hebrew, Greek, or Aramaic), and in circumstances as diverse as battlefields, temples, deserts, cities, prisons, and palaces. They wrote on mountaintops and in dungeons, in poverty and in wealth.

It seems impossible that such different people could write the same book. And that's the point. They didn't. One would write history, another theology, another poetry, another a biography, another prophecy, and some even wrote personal letters. They wrote some of the world's most loved songs and stories. They wrote while in Egypt, Palestine, Arabia, Syria, and in Europe.

No one ever called a meeting and said, "Hey, let's write a book." No one on earth had a plan. There were no professional editors. No one got paid. The Bible took at least 1,600 years to write and spanned 60 generations of world history. Yet God was carefully watching over the process as the ages unfolded. And His Holy Spirit handpicked the people to do the writing. The Bible is unparalleled in literature.

A Miracle of Unity

The most significant miracle in human history is the Living Word – God becoming a man in the person of Jesus Christ. Jesus was actually God's "thoughts" to us (logos in the Greek), or His living Word to us. The Bible says, *In the beginning was the Word* (John 1:1). Then it says, *The Word became flesh and made his dwelling among us* (John 1:14). The focus of every book in the Bible is God revealing His heart to us. And His heart – His living Word to us – is Jesus, who brings unity to the Scriptures.

The second most significant miracle in human history is the miracle of the Bible – the written Word. This miracle exceeds the opening of blind eyes and deaf ears, the healing of a disabled person, or the raising of the dead. God inspired men through the Holy Spirit to author and to ultimately bring together into one Book the writings of many men who had immensely different degrees of literacy and education.

When the Bible's 66 books were compiled as one, something impossible happened. They never contradicted each other! The storylines and plots were woven together as though one author had drafted the entire text. To the natural mind it seems utterly impossible, but it is true. The 66 books of the Bible blended into a single, harmonious whole to become God's Word for all times for all peoples.

Author Gwynn McClendon Day said in *The Wonder of the Word*, "The Bible is one as God is One. One person dominates every book of the Bible – Jesus Christ. The Bible is one in prophecy; it is one in doctrine; it is one in purpose; it is one in truth; it is one in spirit." God wrought miraculous unity out of diversity.

The Book of Books

The Bible is the world's best-selling book, outpacing its nearest rival many times over. In fact, it has been the number one best-seller since the invention of the Gutenberg printing press in 1436.

The Bible has been translated into more languages than any other book, can be found in more homes, in more businesses, in more automobiles, and has been downloaded to more mobile devices than any other book. The Bible is the most published and cited book in the world. It has been quoted by more presidents and peasants, monarchs and mothers, generals and governors, soldiers and sailors, and teachers, athletes, and clergy than any other book written.

"The Bible stands alone: unapproachable in grandeur; solitary in splendor; mysterious in ascendancy; as high above all other books as heaven above earth" (Dyson Hague, in his address to Parkdale Bible Society, May 1912).

The Bible is the Book of books. And though it is thousands of years old, it is still more relevant today than the evening news, tomorrow morning's newspaper, the Google homepage, or any book downloaded to any tablet. As theologian A. Z. Conrad affirmed, "This Book outlives, out loves, out lifts, outlasts, outreaches, outruns, and outranks all books."

The Bible is a miracle! It is the only true Word of God. Other books may claim to be God's word, but none can stand beside this miraculous Book of books.

HOW DID WE GET THE BIBLE? (Origin)
Inspiration

The OT and NT Scriptures (a Latin word meaning "the writings") were written as the Holy Spirit moved on men. This process, called inspiration, resulted in original manuscripts that were "breathed" into existence by divine initiative.

Peter explains it this way: *no prophecy was ever made by an act of human will, but men moved by the Holy Spirit spoke from God* (2 Peter 1:21, NASB). The apostle Paul speaks of the miracle of inspiration to young Timothy as well: *All Scripture is God-breathed* (2 Timothy 3:16).

The exact process by which God inspired biblical writers is sometimes a matter of debate. It does not need to be, for of this we can be certain: It was not mechanical dictation, for every writer of the Bible displayed his own personality and individuality. Moses was stern, David was poetic, John was tender, and Paul was authoritative.

We can also be certain the Word of God is not the product of human intellect, enlightenment, or elevated consciousness. "All Scripture" (emphasis on *All*) is breathed into the writer by God and transcends human thought or opinion. The Bible does not merely contain the Word of God, but it is the Word of God by God's direct involvement, by the "inbreathing" of His words to the writer. God gave more than ideas and thoughts to biblical writers. He gave them words (see 1 Corinthians 2:10-13, especially verse 13).

This biblical view of the Bible's origin is called the plenary verbal inspiration of Scripture. It simply means even the choice of words was inspired by the Holy Spirit. Many biblical writers claimed this was their personal experience: **My Spirit ... is on you, and my words ... I have put in your mouth** (Isaiah 59:21). Jeremiah attests to this as well: **Then the Lord...touched my mouth and said to me, "Now, I have put my words in your mouth"** (Jeremiah 1:9). The early church fathers believed the Holy Spirit gave more than ideas or thoughts, but actual words in the writing of the Bible. Clement of Rome in 90 A.D. said, "The Scriptures are the true **words** of the Holy Ghost."

The Bible came to us in the clothing of human language but inspired by the Spirit. It took a few dozen men more than 1,000 years to complete the Hebrew OT. By contrast, the New Testament was virtually an overnight phenomenon, written primarily in Greek by fewer than eight men in about 50 years.

The Canon

Not everything written by godly men was authoritative as a guide for the Jewish and Christian faiths. Someone had to decide which writings qualified to be Scripture and which ones did not. A permanent standard had to be established and agreed upon.

The word *canon* originally meant "measuring rule," and in discussion of the Bible means those books accepted by Jewish leaders and Christian leaders as inspired and authoritative.

According to R. Laird Harris in Zondervan's *Pictorial Bible Dictionary*, the OT canon of Scripture was ultimately based on evidence of prophetic authorship. "Those who spoke the word of God to Israel were prophets," he declares. Harris references Numbers 12:6 (KJV) and Hebrews 1:1 in defense of this widely held position: *If there be a prophet among you, I the Lord will make myself known to him,* and *God...spoke...through the prophets.*

By the second century the books of the OT were agreed upon. A millennium had passed since Job wrote the oldest book of the OT and Malachi concluded it. Protestants and Jews receive as authoritative the same 39 books of the OT. Divided into five major sections, they include the first five books of the Bible called the "Pentateuch," followed by twelve books which fit into a category called "history." There are five "wisdom and poetry" books, the five "major prophets," and twelve "minor prophets."

In contrast to the marathon it took for the OT to be written and come together, compilation of the NT was a short fifty-yard dash. There was early widespread agreement among Christians regarding the NT canon of Scripture.

Composed of 27 books, it includes what are called the four "Gospels" (the good news of Jesus Christ – His birth, His life and ministry, His death and resurrection), the history book of Acts (the birth of the Church and three missionary journeys of Paul), 21 letters (epistles) written by apostles of the Lord Jesus to Christian believers and leaders of the Church, and the book of Revelation (a prophecy of end-time events given by Jesus and written by the Apostle John).

Manuscripts

During the ancient centuries before Christ, the oldest books of the Bible were written on leather scrolls. Author Andrew Conrad illustrates the destructive process of time on leather by considering what happens to an old pair of shoes left in the attic. "Leather ultimately reverts to dust," he explains, and "the same drying and crumbling held true for ancient biblical scrolls, in spite of the great care given them" ("How the Bible Came to Us," *Guideposts*, 1983).

After the beginning of the Christian era, the OT and NT manuscripts were copied onto papyrus, a paper made from bulrush plants that grow primarily in the Nile Delta. Starting around 700 A.D. scribes used vellum, a refined form of leather parchment prepared from animal skins.

Conrad explains that "most papyrus and vellum biblical manuscripts were destroyed by moisture, temperature change and the rigors of much use."

Although we hear about "original manuscripts," the fact is there is not a single one in existence, either of the OT or NT. This reality does not compromise the authority of our faith, for there are in existence today thousands of early Hebrew and Greek manuscripts which were carefully and meticulously copied by ancient scribes.

Regarding copies of Hebrew manuscripts, author Sidney Collett says "Jewish scribes exercised the greatest possible care…counting not only the words, but every letter, noting how many times each particular letter occurred, and destroying at once the sheet on which a mistake was detected" (*All About the Bible,* Revell, 1966). According to Collett, the scribes had to pronounce aloud each word they copied to maintain their focus. Determined to safeguard the accuracy of successive copies of Scripture through the ages, two rules applied: No scroll could be used once the text started to fade, and scribes were not allowed to erase a mistake to make a correction. Even if an entire passage or a full day's work was nearly complete, the scribe had to discard it and start over.

Amazing Discoveries

Manuscript evidence for the NT in the Greek language is overwhelming. No ancient literature has a parallel. The volume and accuracy of the ancient manuscripts supporting the NT exceed any other writings on earth.

Biblical studies scholar Carl Cosaert provides these amazing numbers in the *Ministry* journal (September 2011): 2,907 **minuscule** manuscripts, written between the ninth and eighteenth centuries in small cursive script, are in existence. There is a second category of manuscripts called *lectionaries*, copies of NT Scriptures read as part of a worship service, dating back as early as the fifth century, of which there are 2,449. Finally, there are 321 *majuscule* manuscripts, the third and oldest category, dating from the fourth to ninth centuries, which derive their name from the old style large block Greek letters.

The oldest majuscule manuscripts were discovered in the mid-nineteenth century by a 29-year-old German scholar at an ancient monastery in the Sinai Peninsula, St. Catherine's. He noticed 43 leaves of parchment in a wastebasket ready to light the monastery oven. He realized to his amazement that they were part of the Greek OT, and immediately rescued them. He later returned to the monastery, where he acquired several other manuscripts, the oldest of which dates back to 350 A.D. and contains a copy of both the Greek OT and NT. This manuscript is referred to as **Codex Sinaiticus** (from the Latin *caudex*, meaning "stem" or "tree trunk").

In 1897 two young Oxford scholars, Bernard Grenfell and Arthur Hunt, stumbled upon 40,000 pieces of ancient documents in an Egyptian town called Oxyrhynchus. They had been searching for copies of Greek classics that had disappeared over the centuries. After digging unsuccessfully for three weeks, they decided to try the city dump. Their second spade of dirt turned up the oldest copy of the gospel of Matthew ever found. Since then over 50 pieces of NT papyri have been identified there, which has led to a number of other papyri discoveries across Egypt.

The Rylands Papyrus (or fragment), the oldest existing piece of NT Scripture, was found in the 1920s. This fragment, about half the size of a dollar bill, includes five verses from the gospel of John dated around 125 A.D. John wrote his gospel late in the first century, which means this portion of Scripture (called Papyrus 52) narrows the gap between the original manuscript and copies to less than 50 years!

What about the OT? In 1947 Bedouin herdsmen were driving their goats to the Bethlehem market near the Dead Sea in southern Israel. A shepherd boy looking for a lost goat passed a cave and tossed in a stone. The sound of breaking pottery lured him into the darkness. There he found numerous clay jars containing ancient scrolls. When scholars completed their research, the scrolls, preserved in clay jars by the dry desert heat, were declared to be over 1,900 years old. The most notable scroll was a complete copy of the OT book of Isaiah. It was 24 feet long and had been transcribed sometime between 150 and 50 B.C. Additional scrolls with biblical text were found in 11 other caves. Together they are known as the **Dead Sea Scrolls**.

Just as the **Codex Sinaiticus** gives assurance that the integrity of the NT has been well guarded through the centuries, the **Dead Sea Scrolls** verify the accuracy of OT transcriptions. Leather may crumble and ink may fade, but the Word of God is eternal and will not perish…though many have tried to destroy and discredit it.

HOW HAS THE BIBLE SURVIVED? (Eternal)
Fierce Opposition

Because the Bible is the inspired Word of God, it has powerful enemies. It is the most loved Book of the ages; it is also the most hated. Yet it stands! *The word of the Lord stands forever* (1 Peter 1:25).

Imagine – how could anyone oppose the Bible? God's Word gives life, joy, and peace. It provides hope, comfort, and freedom. The Bible causes one's heart to sing and feet to dance. It is the wisdom of the ages. The Bible is good news! Yet through the centuries it has been in the crosshairs of Satan – a primary target for destruction and elimination. When the devil has been unable to destroy it, he calls on critics to discredit it.

The survival of the Bible through tumultuous centuries and civilizations is clear evidence of its inspiration and divine origin. God has protected and promoted this Book of books against fierce opposition. It has been burned and banned. It has been attacked and annihilated. It has been outlawed and confiscated. Possessing it or distributing it has been a crime punishable by torture and death. Relentless and bitter persecutions have been waged against Christians who remained faithful to it.

Yet it stands. *Your word, O Lord, is eternal; it stands firm* (Psalm 119:89). Isaiah also declares the eternal nature of God's Word: *The grass withers and the flowers fall, but the word of our God stands forever* (Isaiah 40:8).

Famous Attacks

Jehoiakim, a king of Judah, attempted to destroy the Word of God in about 600 B.C. (Jeremiah 36:21-32). He was infuriated about Jeremiah's warnings, so he cut the scroll in pieces and threw it into the fire. But the writing was reproduced at God's command, and we still have Jeremiah's book today.

In 303 A.D. the Roman Emperor Diocletian sought to eliminate all Bibles. Every copy that could be found was burned. Thousands upon thousands of Christians were martyred for their faith and for possessing Bibles. After two years of slaughter, Diocletian erected a victory column over the embers of a Bible and declared Christianity and the Bible extinct. Little did he know twenty years later his successor, the Roman Emperor Constantine, would embrace Christianity. Constantine's dream was to place a copy of the Bible in every church in his empire. Within 24 hours fifty copies of the Bible were brought out of hiding and presented to the emperor.

During Medieval times the Church of Rome refused to trust people with the Scriptures. Martin Luther said he was a grown man before he saw his first Bible. Edicts, councils, and papal bans resulted in innocent Bible readers being subject to persecution, torture, and painful martyrs' deaths.

In recent history countries in the Soviet Union and Asia opposed Christian believers and forbade possession of or the reading of the Bible. Russia, Korea, China, and Japan, to name a few, were nations closed to the Scriptures. During this repression smugglers, at great risk of life, carried Bibles behind the Bamboo and Iron Curtains.

Believers in underground churches gathered at night, often in forests or barns, to worship the one true God and His Son Jesus Christ. They made hand copies of the Scriptures or committed whole chapters and books to memory. Today millions of Bibles are in circulation in these same countries as thousands upon thousands come to a saving faith in Jesus through the teaching and preaching of God's Word.

Truth Prevails

Skeptics and scoffers also sought to undermine the authority and inspiration of the Bible by so-called "enlightened rationalism." For instance, the eighteenth century French philosopher Voltaire attempted in vain to overthrow the Word of God. An agnostic, Voltaire dared to predict that within one hundred years the Bible would be a forgotten book, found only in museums. Before a century was up, however, Voltaire's home was owned by the Geneva Bible Society, from whose efforts millions of Bibles have gone around the earth.

The noted American agnostic Robert Ingersoll once held a Bible in his hand and declared, "In 15 years I will have this book in the morgue!" In 15 years, however, Ingersoll was in the morgue, and the Bible was alive and well.

The Test of Time

Time is the ultimate test of literature. The older a book, the less likely it is to be read. Most books barely survive a year. Those fortunate enough to last longer are dead within a hundred years. The few exceptions that do exist, such as the classics, are still forgotten by the general public and soon forgotten by students.

The Bible alone has survived the test of time. Daily it is read by children and adults, by the rich and the poor, and by people of all nationalities. The very existence of the Bible is proof it was not written by men alone, but by God's Spirit.

HOW CAN I KNOW THE BIBLE IS TRUE?
(Authority)

Hard Questions

Is the Bible trustworthy? Is it true? Should its principles and commandments have authority over my beliefs and conduct? How can something written thousands of years ago have any significance today? Can I be totally committed to and enthusiastic about the Bible's complete authority? Is the Bible reliable as it relates to disciplines like science and history?

These penetrating questions find themselves at center stage in the drama of biblical authority. Surrounding these issues are related subjects such as biblical inerrancy, biblical infallibility, biblical criticism, and biblical inspiration. These are heady concepts, but when you express them in everyday language they come back to the simple question: "Is the Bible true, can it be trusted, and should it have final say in my life?" Happily there is irrefutable evidence to document the authority, reliability, and infallibility of the Book of books.

God Himself

David Dockery, writing about the authority of the Bible in *SBC Life*, explains: "Any approach to the subject of biblical authority must begin with God Himself, for in God all authority is finally located. God is His own authority. There is nothing outside of Him on which His authority is established."

Said another way, if God is the Bible's author, and the Bible is to be believed and accepted as trustworthy, then one must begin by believing God Himself. That is, "We believe the Bible is truth because we believe God is truth."

When we think of authority in our human world, we think of a badge, or a title, or a position. Examples might include a policeman's badge, a judge's title, or the position of president. Each has authority in his or her own context, the right and the power to require obedience. And while it is true the policeman, the judge, and the president can demand our obedience, it is also true they cannot demand our acceptance and belief. That comes by earning trust and respect. So here is the problem: At some point we human beings who are born in sin will fail. Always. Therefore, human authority cannot and never will be the foundation on which truth stands.

God's truth and authority is ultimately sovereign and final. His context is the universe – everything created and existing. He has established His eternal reign over humankind and the events of history by ruling from heaven. A Babylonian king named Nebuchadnezzar lived a life of arrogance and luxury. When God frightened him with a dream, a young prophet named Daniel was called to interpret. God's message to the human king was stern: You will be punished until *"you acknowledge that the Most High is sovereign over the kingdoms of men. ...Heaven rules"* (Daniel 4:25, 26). God Himself rules and reigns and has all authority.

Revelation

So who is God? Moses, Israel's deliverer from Egyptian bondage, asked God that very question. God simply answered, "I am."

You're probably thinking, "I am what?" What God means is that He is. He has always been and will always be. Who God is can only be known by His self-disclosure or what we call "revelation." Imagine God completely opening up and revealing all of Himself to you, and you will begin to understand revelation, or the self-disclosure, of God. The living Word (Jesus) and the written Word (the Bible) assist; they remove the mystery and "reveal" the nature, character, and being of God Himself so you can start a relationship with Him.

The magnitude of God's authority is His revelation of Himself.

At a time when Abraham and his wife were old and well past childbearing years, God made an unbelievable promise to this chosen couple: "**Sarah your wife shall have a son**" (Genesis 18:10). This was hard for Abraham and Sarah to believe. So God made the promise to them in the form of a pledge or covenant. But since there was nothing or no one outside of God Himself upon whom He could swear, He pledged by His own name (Hebrews 6:13), for there was nothing greater. When Sarah did give birth to a child in her old age, the couple then trusted God's word as being true and reliable.

Centuries later God revealed Himself in the person of Jesus Christ (John 1:1-18), who was called the living Word of God. Jesus obeyed and even fulfilled the OT scriptures and appealed to them as authoritative. Just before He died and ascended back to heaven, He said, *"All authority in heaven and earth has been given to me"* (Matthew 28:18). Jesus then deposited His authority in chosen disciples/apostles, who became the foundation of the Church (Ephesians 2:20 and 3:5). These are the men who wrote the NT Scriptures under the anointing and guidance of the Holy Spirit.

And so God's Spirit inspired the words of the prophets and the apostles, whose writings became recognized as authoritative. The Bible is Truth, completely trustworthy and able to speak to us today. Three significant witnesses come forward to affirm the truth, authority, and infallibility of the Scriptures. They are the Bible's internal accuracy of history, accuracy of prophecy, and accuracy of science.

Archaeology and History

The historical accuracy of biblical accounts is beyond dispute. Dates and details, kings and kingdoms, people and places, stories and structures have all been unearthed by excavation of sites located in Bible lands.

Archaelogical digs that corroborate Scripture have been conducted by secular scientists, biblical scholars, and even treasure hunters.

Here are a very few examples of exciting archaeological finds. Old Testament scholar and archaeologist E. A. Speiser discovered an "Adam and Eve seal" depicting a naked man and woman bowed down with a serpent being driven out. This Sumerian seal, dated about four millenniums before Christ, confirms the creation story in Genesis.

Exodus 5:7, written some 3,500 years ago, details how Israelite slaves in Egyptian bondage were forced to make bricks without straw. When Pithom, the treasured city of the Egyptian Pharaoh Ramesses II was excavated, archaeologists found houses made of sunbaked bricks, some with straw and some without, exactly as the Bible indicates.

The Bible refers to a people known as the Hittites, but prior to the 19th century we had no secular history to affirm they ever existed. For this reason, for centuries the Hittites were considered "biblical mythology" by skeptics. But the discovery of an ancient library in central Turkey by A.H. Sayce and Hugo Winckler firmly established the historicity of the Hittite nation.

The list of OT archaeological finds is nearly endless. Respected scholar Dr. J. O. Kinnaman declared, "Of the hundreds of thousands of artifacts found by archaeologists, not one has ever been discovered that contradicts or denies one word, phrase, clause, or sentence of the Bible" (*The Signature of God*, by Grant Jeffrey, 1998).

New Testament discoveries abound as well. Some of the most famous are the house of Peter at Capernaum (Matthew 8:14), Jacob's well (John 4), the Pool of Bethesda in Jerusalem (John 5: 1-14), the Pool of Siloam (John 9:1-4), the theater at Ephesus (Acts 19:29), and Herod's palace at Caesarea (Acts 23:33-35). The testimony of archeological discoveries keeps providing conclusive evidence as to the historical accuracy of Scripture.

Prophecy and Fulfillment

Prophecy is telling history before it happens. Men and women in the Bible described future events before they took place. It wasn't magic, fortune-telling, or practicing the occult. There were no crystal balls. It was the power of the Holy Spirit coming upon individuals whom the Lord used to announce His plans before they occurred.

God states, *"I am God, and there is none like me, declaring the end from the beginning, and from ancient times the things that are not yet done"* (Isaiah 46: 9, 10, KJV). This is one of the most majestic wonders of the Bible: things declared centuries before they happened. Where in literature can people find anything comparable to the predictions and fulfillments of prophecy? Prophecies about nations like Edom, Moab, Egypt, Israel, Assyria, and Babylon are so specific and definite that their later fulfillment has silenced skeptics.

Daniel's prophecy in chapter two reaches beyond human comprehension, for his interpretation of the king of Babylon's dream actually foretells the rise and fall of empires in chronological order before they happen; such as Babylon, Medo-Persia, Greece, and Rome.

Jeremiah knew in advance that the Babylon captivity of Judah would last exactly 70 years; Joel prophesied the great outpouring of the Holy Spirit in Acts 2 during the feast of Pentecost; and Malachi foretold the coming of John the Baptist 400 years before he appeared.

At the summit of prophetic utterance and fulfillment is the OT's amazing collection of prophecies about Jesus Christ. Numbering over 300, the prophetic details surrounding Jesus' earthly life are staggering – His birth, ministry, rejection, suffering, resurrection, and ascension – all were written before He was born and all have been fulfilled to the letter. They were not written by one author, but by at least twenty different authors. Who could have known He would be born of a virgin (Isaiah 7:14)? Or His birthplace would be Bethlehem (Micah 5:2)? Or the price of His betrayal (Zechariah 11:12)? Who could have known He would be subjected to brutal physical punishment (Isaiah 53:5), or crucified between thieves (Isaiah 53: 2), or that soldiers would cast lots for His garments (Psalm 22:18)?

The answer is clear: only the Holy Spirit, for **prophecy never had its origin in the will of man, but men spoke from God as they were carried along by the Holy Spirit** (2 Peter 1:21). Fulfilled prophecies of Scripture are unimpeachable evidence that the Bible is the Word of God.

Science and the Bible

Science, which means "knowledge," deals with discovery – seeking laws and principles in our universe that are reliable and repeatable based on systematic observation, measurement, and experimentation. Skeptics suggest the Bible cannot coexist with science because the two oppose one another. They argue science can be taught only on a naturalistic basis with no reference to God or the supernatural.

The Bible, however, actually precedes science. It deals with revelation and inspiration, both of which come from God. Since God was before all things and created all things, and since by Him all things exist and hold together (Colossians 1:16, 17), it should not be a surprise to learn true science has its foundation in the knowledge of God.

The founding fathers of science understood and believed this and found their inspiration for scientific research in Scriptures such as these: ***The fear of the Lord is the beginning of knowledge*** (Proverbs 1:7). *[In Christ] are hidden all the treasures of wisdom and knowledge* (Colossians 2:3). Jesus answered, *"I am the…truth"* (John 14:6). In fact, John 1:3 makes it clear that not one thing exists that God didn't create. If Jesus is Truth, and the Bible is true, then it is impossible for true science to be in conflict with God.

The list of early scientists who believed in God, creation, and the Bible is impressive. These include Pasteur, Pascal, Kepler, Newton, Ray, and Boyle, to name only a few. These men of Christian faith went into their laboratories expecting to discover what God had already created and designed in His universe. The Bible often informed their research, for in its fathomless depths can be found a treasure trove of scientific truth.

Not mentioned in the list above is Dr. George Washington Carver, a scientific genius who often stated his achievement came directly from God and the Scriptures. Born the child of slaves and rejected by a university because of his color, Carver went on to achieve great influence and prestige in the scientific world. He is best known for his work with the peanut, from which he invented 300 valuable products. Besides securing an appointment to the U.S. Department of Agriculture in 1935, his honors include the Roosevelt Medal for distinguished service in the field of science, the honorary degree of Doctor of Science from the University of Rochester, and an award from the Thomas A. Edison Foundation for the Advancement of Science and Education.

The secret of Dr. Carver's success is related in his own words in the 1943 biography, *George Washington Carver*, by Rackham Holt: "I can do all things through Christ…with my prayers I mix my labors, and sometimes God is pleased to bless the results…I never have to grope for methods; the method is revealed at the moment I am inspired… . Without God to draw aside the curtain I would be helpless."

People outside of the Christian faith are still surprised to hear that many scientific laws of the universe were revealed in the Bible centuries before science "discovered" them. Biblical writers had no idea, for example, they were disclosing scientific laws of botany, anthropology, zoology, astronomy, and geology…but God did. In Isaiah 40:22 (NKJV), written about 700 B.C., the prophet refers to God as: **He who sits above the circle of the earth.** At the time that was spoken, common belief was that the earth was flat. In fact it was 22 centuries later in 1522, when the explorer Magellan's expedition completed the circumnavigation of the globe, that people finally agreed the earth was round.

U.S. Navy officer Matthew Maury, a Bible-loving Christian, was in charge of the Depot of Charts and Instruments of the Hydrographic Naval Office from 1841 to 1861. While reading Psalm 8 one day, he was captivated by verse eight. There it declares that God gave mankind dominion over **the fish in the sea, and all that swim the paths of the seas.** The Spirit of God inspired Maury with this thought: "There must be paths, or currents, or rivers in the seas just like in the atmosphere." With confidence in the accuracy of the Bible, and accompanied by his charts and books, he set out to "discover" those ocean paths. And he did – the Gulf Current, the Japanese Current, the California Current, and others. Before he was done, ships could reduce their ocean crossings by as much as three weeks.

The Bible is filled with scientific insights, divinely inspired and recorded long before science discovered them. Others include the reliability of nature (Genesis 8:22), the circulation of the atmosphere (Ecclesiastes 1:6), the hydrological cycle (Isaiah 55:10), the weight of air (Job 28:24, 25), the second law of thermodynamics/entropy (Psalm 102:25, 26), light before the sun (Psalm 74:16), the filtering of the ozone layer (Amos 9:6), the conducting path for lightning (Job 28:26), and the knowledge of germs (Leviticus 13:1-6).

Christians do not need to choose between science and the Bible. Science was developed in the womb of a Christian/biblical worldview. True science always supports the authority and inspiration of Scripture, and that includes the creation account in Genesis and the mystery of the dinosaurs, which is really no mystery at all.

HOW DOES THE BIBLE APPLY TO ME? (Application)
A Biblical Worldview - It Works!

What good is your smart phone if it doesn't work, or your computer if the battery is dead? If your car in the garage or a toaster in your kitchen doesn't work, you can't use it. The big question is this: Does the Bible work today?

The answer is a resounding "Yes!" The Book of books still speaks today, touching every issue of life. The Bible's truth is unchanged by culture, whether it is ancient or modern, and has proven to be the best guide in aiding with things like decision-making and values formation. A worldview shaped by the Bible will give you the absolute best foundation on which to live.

What is a worldview? A worldview is a set of beliefs from which you view reality and make sense of the world. A biblical worldview means you believe the Bible and allow it to be the filter for your decision-making and actions. The Bible becomes the foundation of everything you say and do. It matters not what you say you believe, but it's your decisions and actions that determine what you really believe.

God's Holy Spirit works through the Bible to lift a person from being a victim to the cares of this world to becoming a victorious overcomer in this world. He does this through the promises and the power of the Word of God.

The Bible's Promises

The Bible is filled with promises from God to you. Rev. Dick Mills, known for memorizing these promises and giving them as prophetic utterances to people, often said there are 8,800 promises in the Bible – 7,700 of which are personal words from God to you.

Not one of these promises has ever been broken. King Solomon stated, *"Not one word has failed of all the good promises he gave"* (1 Kings 8:56). God Himself said through Isaiah, *"So is my word that goes out from my mouth: It will not return to me empty, but will accomplish what I desire and achieve the purpose for which I sent it"* (Isaiah 55:11).

Nearly all of God's promises have a condition, clearly stated or at least implied by the context of the verse. Examples would include promises conditioned by prayer, or purity, or faith. When these conditions are met, the promises hold true.

Two Greek words in the Bible for "word," *logos* and *rhema*, can be used to distinguish the more objective word of God found in all of Scripture *(logos)* from the more occasional, personal *(rhema)* words from the Lord which come to individuals to provide guidance, heal diseases, or give wisdom, hope, and peace. These and more are promised in the Bible:

- *"I am with you and will watch over you wherever you go…. I will not leave you until I have done what I promised you"* (Genesis 28:15).

- *The Lord will open the heavens, the storehouse of his bounty… to bless all the work of your hands* (Deuteronomy 28:12).

- *Do not let this Book of the Law depart from your mouth…. Then you will be prosperous and successful* (Joshua 1:8).

- *For he will command his angels concerning you to guard you in all your ways* (Psalm 91:11).

- *My God will meet all your needs according to his glorious riches in Christ Jesus* (Philippians 4:19).

- *If any of you lacks wisdom, he should ask of God, who gives generously to all…and it will be given to him* (James 1:5).

True testimonies of God's promises fulfilled give us hope. Entire armies have been saved, sick and broken bodies have been healed, heavenly "windows" have been opened with material and spiritual blessing, leaders and laity have received wisdom and guidance, parents have seen their prodigal children return to God and reconnect with fellow believers, and other prayers have been miraculously answered.

All the resources of God's throne and His kingdom are at work to uphold His Word. He cannot violate His promises any more than He can cease to be God Himself. Every single promise in the Word of God has been tested myriads of times throughout the ages, and proven to be true. *He who promised is faithful* (Hebrews 10:23). *For no matter how many promises God has made, they are "Yes" in Christ* (2 Corinthians 1:20).

The Bible's Power

Assume you have reached a dead end. You have come to a mountain you cannot climb, to a relationship you cannot mend, to an assignment that appears impossible. Life buries you and you cry to Jesus for strength and power beyond yourself.

How will the Holy Spirit speak to you? Where do you turn? You turn to the Bible. *The voice of the Lord is powerful* (Psalm 29:4). *The Son of God holds everything together with his powerful word* (Hebrews 1:3, NCV).

Imagine it. Like a nuclear adhesive the Word of God holds everything together. Love and embrace the Word of God, and "just as a shout in the mountains can start an avalanche, so a single word spoken in God's way and in his time can have a seismic effect" (Russian writer and dissident Aleksandr Solzhenitsyn).

Age upon age the Word of God has demonstrated a power unparalleled in human history. It has the power to turn sinners into saints, to transform entire cities and nations, to repel demons, to raise the dead, to silence the boastful and proud, to open prison doors, and to set captives free.

The Bible "can bring plenty out of poverty, and praise out of pain…. It can change darkness into light, failure into success, and incompetency into adequacy. No other book, whether of religion, philosophy, psychology, science, biography, poetry, or any other subject, can substantiate a claim to one small fraction of the wonder-working power of the Bible" (G. M. Day).

We Believe

Pentecostal statesman and author Jack Hayford writes that God's Word has been revealed "in both the Scriptures and in His incarnate Son – Jesus Christ." He continues, "There is no such thing as health or growth in Christian living, apart from a clear priority on the place of the Bible in the life of the individual. The Scriptures are the conclusive standard for our faith, morals, and practical living and are the nourishment for our rising to strength in faith, holiness in living, and effectiveness in service. The Holy Spirit who comes to fill us is the same Person who has given us the Book to guide and sustain us" *(Spirit-Filled Life Bible)*.

We will never believe more than we know, and we will never live higher than what we believe. If we believe the Bible, the Book of books, we should study it (2 Timothy 2:15), memorize it (Psalm 119:11), and live by it (Matthew 4:4). As Jesus said, **"Man does not live on bread alone, but on every word that comes from the mouth of God."**

Related Scriptures:

Psalm 119:89; Matthew 24:35; 2 Timothy 2:15, 3:16-17; 2 Peter 1:19-21

For Further Reading

Free, Joseph P., revised by Howard F. Vos. *Archaeology and Bible History, Revised Edition,* Grand Rapids, MI: Zondervan, 1992. (Extensive illustrations and bibliography)

Lightfoot, Neil R. *How We Got the Bible.* Grand Rapids, MI: Baker Books, 2003).

Hitchcock, Mark. *The Amazing Claims of Bible Prophecy.* Eugene, OR: Harvest House Publishers, 2010.

Stone, Larry. *The Story of the Bible*. Nashville, TN: Thomas Nelson, 2000.

www.carm.org/bible-inspired (Christian Apologetics & Research Ministry)

Time to Interact

Take some time to interact with the following questions. Consider writing your answers in a journal and/or discussing them with a fellow believer for deeper reflection and insight.

1. How has the Bible made an impact on your life? Are there particular passages that have brought transformation to you? What are they? How are you different because of them?

2. Why do you think the early believers and scribes took such care to safeguard the words and even the individual letters of the Bible? What does this suggest to you about the reliability and accuracy of the Scriptures? Does this help you to better trust the Bible as the Word of God? In what way?

3. Throughout history and in many countries today access to the Bible has been hindered by those in authority. Many Christians are overjoyed just to find fragments and mere portions of the Bible in their own language. What has been your attitude toward the Scriptures? Why do you think that some believers tend to take the Bible for granted? What could help overcome the development of such a casual and ho-hum mindset regarding the Scriptures?

Time to Integrate

Knowing about how the Bible was formed and the impact it has had on countless generations in numerous fields is both interesting and inspiring. Beyond that, however, we are meant to become partakers in its wonderful truths and to discover the joy of the transformation it brings. Consider the following application steps for integrating the Bible into your everyday life experience.

1. Develop a regular, intentional plan for reading the Scriptures. Will you read every day? How much will you read? Some people make it a goal to read through the Bible in a year. How will you embrace

the Bible as a regular aspect of your life? Numerous reading plans are available online. Check out:

- www.bible.com/reading-plans
- www.biblegateway.com/reading-plans
- www.biblestudytools.com/bible-reading-plan
- www.ewordtoday.com/year
- www.oneyearbibleonline.com

2. Can you spend at least 15 minutes a day reading the Bible? As you do, take these steps:

- Ask the Holy Spirit to speak to you and reveal His heart as you read.
- Pick a single book or epistle (letter). Work to read through that book completely, a chapter or two at a time (perhaps over several days) rather than just skim through multiple random passages. Envision the life situation reflected in the passage. Who are the main characters? What is the setting? What is the thought being emphasized? What does the passage reveal about the nature of God?
- Which verses seem to speak right to your heart? Can you memorize key verses that bring truth, peace, hope and direction?
- What truths can be applied to your life? What steps can be taken to act on the teachings and examples found in the Word?
- Is there any aspect of the reading that could be used to strengthen, encourage, or comfort someone else? How might the Holy Spirit want you to be a carrier of the Scriptures to minister life to another?

CHAPTER 2

Our Heavenly Father:
God

CHAPTER 2

Our Heavenly Father:

God

GOD THE FATHER

> We believe in God the Father, the co-Creator with the Son and the Holy Spirit, who is the eternal, all powerful, all knowing, everywhere present, and unchangeable Creator of all."

GOD

> "We believe there is one God. In the unity of the Godhead there are three persons, Father, Son, and Holy Spirit, equal in every divine perfection and attribute, fulfilling distinct, but complementary roles in the great work of redemption.

We believe in the almighty God and Father of all created things, who existed before time began. By His power and wisdom He created and sustains everything that exists for His own glory. The Westminster Shorter Catechism, 1648, found at *http://confessionsoffaith.org/downloads/westminster_shorter_catechism.pdf,* provides a comprehensive definition of God: "God is a Spirit, infinite, eternal and unchangeable in His being, wisdom, power, holiness, justice, goodness and truth. Although sovereign, God seeks to cultivate an intimate relationship with man" (Genesis 1:1; Job 38-40; Isaiah 40:10, 26-28; 57:15; Malachi 2:10; Ephesians 1:5, 2:10; 1 Peter 4:19).

The Bible does not set out to provide a series of proofs of the existence of God, but the Scriptures are replete with statements pointing to the fact of God's existence. Man is charged to approach God through the gateway of faith and believe that God is. *And without faith it is impossible to please God, because anyone who comes to him must believe that he exists* (Hebrews 11:6).

Psalm 14 addresses as "fools" people who say in their heart there is no

God. These godless people believe they can put God out of their minds simply because they choose not to include Him in their lives. They belong to a group called *practical atheists*, who live as though God does not exist. Another group, *theoretical atheists*, hold the intellectual belief that God does not exist. It has been pointed out that the statement, "There is no God," really means that God does not interfere in the affairs of the world. Therefore counting on His absence, men become "corrupt," contemptible in their actions (*Jesus Among Other Gods*, by Ravi Zacharias, pp. 47-53).

THE EXISTENCE OF GOD

We believe that God has clearly revealed His existence to His creation through the pages of the Bible, through nature, and through history (Genesis 1:1; Exodus 3:13-15; Psalm 19:1; Isaiah 40:21-23; Hebrews 1:1-2).

For generations skeptics have questioned God's existence. The religious leaders of Jesus' time demanded miraculous signs to prove His authority/divinity (John 2:18). Tradition supports two lines of arguments, naturalistic and biblical, to demonstrate the existence of God. In the naturalistic line are four possible philosophical explanations for the existence of God:

The first is the **cosmological argument**, which is based on the fact that a cosmos, or world, exists. There has to be an original cause for the world to exist. Paul Enns, a pastor and biblical scholar, illustrates this point with the analogy of a man who wears a Bulova wristwatch. Although he has never seen a watchmaker, the fact of the existence of the wristwatch suggests there is a Swiss watchmaker who made the watch. The cosmological argument says that every effect must have a cause. Therefore since there is a world, there must be a Creator.

The second argument is the **teleological argument**, from "teleos," meaning "design or purpose." It relates to the design or purpose that can be observed in creation. There are those who argue that an orderly universe came into being through the process of natural selection (by chance). However, it is considered quite unlikely that random "by chance" actions would result in the highly integrated organizations which are evident in the world. Although possible, it would require a great deal of faith to believe (*A Survey of Bible Doctrine*, by Charles C. Ryrie). On the other hand, the Psalmist declares that the magnificence of the universe testifies to the existence of a God who created the universe for a purpose

(Psalm 8:3-4; 19:1-4; *The Moody Handbook of Theology*, by Paul Enns).

The third argument, the **anthropological argument**, relates to the nature of humankind. In all cultures, people commonly demonstrate the presence of an active conscience and possess a moral nature, intelligence, and mental capacities (Genesis 1:26-28; Colossians 3:10). Some argue that these qualities are the result of the evolutionary process and occur totally by chance. However, this argument does not explain conscience or humanity's natural desire to connect with or believe in a higher being. Romans 2:14-15 relates the case of Gentiles who had no revelation of the law, yet their consciences guided them into doing the right thing because God placed a moral witness within them.

The question could be asked: "Does the very existence of man point to the existence of a personal God?" The Apostle Paul addressed this question with the philosophers of Athens, saying *"Since we are God's offspring, we should not think that the divine being is like gold or silver or stone – an image made by man's design and skill"* (Acts 17:29). The very idea of good and bad, or right and wrong, in the culture leads some to conclude that man's quest for moral ideals points to the existence of a God who makes those ideals a reality.

The fourth argument is the **ontological argument**. The term *ontological* comes from the Greek verb "to be" and means "being" or "existence." The ontological argument is more philosophical than inductive and reasons that "if man could conceive of a perfect God who does not exist, then he could conceive of someone greater than God Himself, which is impossible. Therefore God exists." The basis of the argument rests on the fact that since universally human beings have an awareness of God, then God must have placed the idea in them. This idea began in the 11th century with Saint Anselm of Canterbury, a Benedictine monk, philosopher, and theologian.

Biblical Arguments for the Existence of God

We believe the Bible provides sufficient evidence of the existence of the true and living God who created the heavens, the earth, and everything that exists and is active in the universe. Throughout the pages of the Bible the existence of God is assumed and at times directly argued. Genesis 1:1 opens the Scriptures with the words, *In the beginning God*

... . David clearly records in Psalm 19 that God has revealed His existence to the entire world through His creation. *The heavens declare the glory of God; the skies proclaim the work of His hands. ... There is no speech or language where their voice is not heard, their voice goes out into all the earth* (Psalm 19:1, 3-4).

The prophet Isaiah chided the backslidden people who made and worshipped idols to consider whether or not their man-made idols could fashion such a world as ours. *Lift your eyes and look to the heavens: Who created all these?* (Isaiah 40:26). The apostle Paul argued before a non-Christian audience that God sent the rain and the change of seasons, both of which testify to His existence (Acts 14:17).

God conveys truth about Himself to humankind through general revelation. In this regard He unveils aspects of His nature so that all humanity becomes aware of His existence. Psalm 19 emphasizes the general revelation of God in the universe and in nature. Romans 1:18-21 also highlights the general revelation of God and man's accountability to God.

In addition, God has revealed Himself to humanity through His provision and power, and people should respond to this gracious God (Matthew 5:45; Acts 14:15-17). God has also revealed Himself to humanity through their conscience (Romans 2:14-15).

Another way God conveys the truth about Himself is through special revelation. Unlike general revelation that is open to all mankind, God reveals Himself through dreams and visions to specific people. He speaks audibly to some, and to others He has presented Himself in visible form (called a *theophany*).

God revealed Himself through the Scriptures and through Jesus Christ, His Son. The Apostle Peter wrote that *No prophecy of Scripture came about by the prophet's own interpretation. For prophecy never had its origin in the will of man, but men spoke from God as they were carried along by the Holy Spirit* (2 Peter 1:20-21).

This infallible record (the Bible) gives man the truth about God and the most accurate picture of the Almighty God. It provides understanding of God's person and works. It also reveals Jesus Christ, and Christ in turn has revealed God the Father to mankind (John 1:18).

GOD'S ATTRIBUTES
Natural Attributes

We believe in the only true and all-wise God, infinite, holy, almighty, full of power and glory, who existed before time began and will live and reign forever.

God reveals Himself in the Scriptures in ways that are comprehensible to humankind. For instance the names of God express His whole being, while His attributes indicate various aspects of His character. God's attributes are to be distinguished from His works. His attributes do not "add" anything to Him; they reveal His nature.

Theologians classify His attributes in a variety of groups, but for this purpose God's attributes will be considered in two groups: natural attributes and moral attributes. His natural attributes are unique to Himself, not shared by humans. For example, He is infinite. His moral attributes show characteristics similar to those humans possess. For example, God is just. (Man can be just.)

Sovereign

We believe that God is sovereign. He created and owns everything and has the absolute right to govern and dispose of His creatures as He pleases. The word sovereign means chief, highest, or supreme. When God is addressed as sovereign, it means that He is the number one Ruler in the universe. The title possesses authority. Therefore God has total and absolute authority over the universe. Yet He does not rule His universe as a dictator because of the exercise of His attributes (such as goodness, mercy, love, and justice) acting harmoniously together (Isaiah 41:1-4; Daniel 4:35; Matthew 20:15; Romans 9:21; Ryrie, page 25).

David caught a glimpse of the sovereign Lord as he asked and then answered the question: *Who is this King of glory? The LORD strong and mighty, the LORD mighty in battle. Lift up your heads, O you gates; that the King of glory may come in. Who is he, this King of glory? The LORD Almighty – he is the King of glory* (Psalm 24:8-10).

Spirit (Job 11:7; John 1:18; 4:24)

We believe that God is a spirit with personality; He thinks, feels, and speaks. He can communicate directly with the creatures made in His image. He is the source of all life. As a spirit, God is not subject to limitations as are human beings with physical bodies. He is invisible to the natural eyes and other senses. God, as a spirit, is not without form since Jesus refers to God's form in John 5:37. Human mind and language are inadequate to grasp or describe the nature of God. God the Father told Moses, *"You cannot see my face, for no one may see me and live"* (Exodus 33:20).

Although God is Spirit, He can manifest Himself in a way that can be understood by man. At the baptism of Jesus Christ, the Spirit of God descended like a dove and landed on Him (Matthew 3:16). God also describes His infinite personality in language understood by finite minds. The Bible speaks of God's hand, arm, eyes and ears, and describes Him as seeing, feeling, hearing, repenting, and more. In spite of this revelation, God remains incomprehensible to mankind.

Self-Existent

We believe that God exists in Himself and is independent in His being and His virtues, decrees, and works. Although He is a living being, He has no needs. He created everything to depend on Him (Psalm 104:10-30). In response to Moses, God declared His self-existence with the words, *"I AM WHO I AM"* (Exodus 3:14). The use of the verb of being (I AM) emphasizes that He has continual existence in Himself. John 5:26 declares that the Father has life in Himself. God has so created His creatures that every living thing is dependent on someone or something else – the unborn needs its mother's support, all animals need their surroundings, the trees need sun and rain for life. But God is independent and existent in Himself (Acts 17:28).

Source of Life

We believe in the promises of God the Father who, as Jesus told Nicodemus, *"so loved the world that He gave His one and only Son, that whoever believes in him shall not perish but have eternal life"* (John 3:16). God the Father has life in Himself and has granted this life to Jesus

Christ His Son (John 1:4, John 5:26). God is described as the fountain of life (Psalm 36:9) and the spring of living water (Jeremiah 2:13). All life originates with and flows from God and His Son.

The word *life* is very popular in the epistles of the Apostle John. The Gospel of John has 36 references to the word *life*. 1 John refers to life 13 times and Revelation references the word 15 times. Life does not exist on its own accord. It exists in God. Jesus Himself gives eternal life to all who believe in Him (John 3:15-16, 36, 4:14, 5:24, 20:31).

There is marked contrast between the wages of sin, which is death, and the gift of God, which is eternal life (Romans 6:23). Eternal life is more than existence. It signifies favor and fellowship with the eternal God. Believers who are in fellowship with God experience this favor and fellowship in the present time. Eternal life can also be described as future since the future life of those who believe in God's Son yields perfect fellowship with God (Romans 6:22; Titus 1:2). He gives abundant life (John 10:10) and resurrection life (John 11:25).

Infinite

We believe in an infinite and eternal God who cannot be confined to space or time. He is without limitations as humans are limited. In relation to space, God is characterized by immensity. His presence fills everywhere, making an impact on all of space and everything that exists. Only in heaven is His presence and glory more revealed than elsewhere in the universe (1 Kings 8:27).

There is a vast difference between the Creator God and His creation. Dr. Bill Bright stated in his book *God: Discover His Character* that this difference is as great as the difference between the potter and the vessel he created. Just as the potter could not be confused with the clay vessel he created, God is distinct in nature and substance from His creation and is far above it in every way. Yet in this example both the potter and the vessel are finite while God is infinite and is incomparable to His creation.

In relation to time, God is eternal (Exodus 15:18; Deuteronomy 33:27; Nehemiah 9:5; Psalm 90:2; Jeremiah 10:10; Revelation 4:8-10). With God there is no distinction between the present, past, and future. All things are equally open to Him. God has existed before time and will continue to exist. Being eternal, God is unchangeable. He is the same yesterday, today, and forever (Hebrews13:8).

We believe in an all-knowing (or omniscient) God who is perfect in knowledge. He needs no teacher or counselor (Isaiah 40:13-14; Romans 11:33). His knowledge at any given moment is past, present, and future. He knows what is unknowable to anyone else (1 Corinthians 2:11). The Psalmist David acknowledged the omniscience of God when He said God knew his actions, words, and innermost thoughts even before they were formed (Psalm 139:1-4). Believers can have peace no matter the nature of their circumstances because *"your Father knows what you need before you ask Him"* (Matthew 6:8).

Some of the controversy surrounding the omniscience of God concerns His knowledge of who will be saved or lost. Nonetheless, even though God knows who will be saved or lost, He allows an individual to exercise his or her own free will and make that choice. He does not force anyone to accept Jesus Christ as Lord and Savior (John 1:12). In other words, God foresees but does not predetermine.

Immanent and Transcendent

We believe the holy and righteous God is highly exalted above His creation, even though His infinite love and goodness cause Him to approach the humble and contrite man. Transcendence means that God is separate from and exalted above the world and man (Isaiah 6:1).

Some biblical writers and characters had visions of God that demonstrated this attribute of transcendence. For instance, the prophet Isaiah (6:1) saw Him high and exalted. He further wrote, **For this is what the high and lofty One says – he who lives forever** (Isaiah 57:15).

The immanence of God speaks of His presence in the world and nearness to man (Acts 17:28; Ephesians 4:6). God is separate from the world, yet He is in the world. He sent His only begotten Son, the Lord and Savior Jesus Christ to be with humanity. Then Jesus fulfilled His promise to send "another Comforter," the person of the Holy Spirit, to be in everyone who receives forgiveness of their sins by receiving Jesus Christ as their Lord and Savior.

Daniel had a vision of God that left him without strength. As he beheld

God's glory and awesome appearance, he lost all stamina and was speechless on his face as if in a deep sleep (Daniel 10:4-9). Similarly Moses hid his face in fear of looking at God (Exodus 3:1-6) while Abraham prostrated himself as God spoke with him (Genesis 17:1-5). Gideon feared that he would die after encountering the Angel of the Lord because he felt that no human being could see God and remain alive (Judges 6:17-23).

The Apostle Paul, speaking in Athens to pagan worshipers, declared of the true God, *"'For in him we live and move and have our being.' As some of your own poets have said, 'We are also His offspring'"* (Acts 17:28). In another epistle, he continued that there is *one God and Father of all, who is over all and through all and in all* (Ephesians 4:6).

Immutable

We believe in the unchanging and unchangeable God of the Bible (Malachi 3:6; Isaiah 46:9-10). Unlike the unpredictable characters of many of the gods of false religions, the God of the Bible is the only unchanging Supreme Being. He has never changed in His holiness or love. The Bible presents Him as the same from eternity to eternity. Theologians call this consistency and dependability God's immutability (Bright, pp. 272-273). This does not mean God is lacking in variety, for a glance at His creation reveals a variety of life forms in shape, size, color, complexity, and adaptability. For example, each human fingerprint is completely unique; no two snowflakes are alike. A whale is quite vast compared to a tiny mosquito.

Consider the variety of flowers and trees, from the delicate rose to the mighty oak tree. Yet God is constant in every aspect of His being, His perfections, purposes, and promises. He does not change the principles and the character that underlie the variety and creativity present in the universe. God's plans are always for people to conform to the image of His Son.

Since God is absolute in perfection, it is impossible for Him to improve or deteriorate. James 1:17 states that there is no variation or shifting shadow with God. In spite of changes in the world, God does not change in His person or in His response to His creatures. It is reassuring to note that because God remains unchanging, His love and His promises will never change. He is trustworthy.

The principles throughout the Old and New Testaments remain the same. The Scriptures reveal that Abram (Abraham) believed God and was credited with righteousness because of his faith (Genesis 15:6; Romans 4:13). Those who believe in His Son Jesus Christ can hold to the promise of John 3:16, *"that whoever believes in Him shall not perish but have eternal life."*

Moral Attributes

We believe in a holy, loving, righteous, and just God. Nothing escapes His gaze. He sees and knows everything.

Goodness (Psalm 25:8; Acts 14:17; Psalm 68:10; Lamentations 3:22)

"The goodness of God is that attribute by which He imparts life and other blessings to His creatures" (*Knowing the Doctrines of the Bible*, by Myer Pearlman). God models goodness by providing for the righteous as well as the unrighteous (Matthew 5:45). The Lord's goodness leads Him to be compassionate and gracious (Psalm 145:9). **The Lord is good, a refuge in times of trouble** (Nahum 1:7). God is good to sinners and desires them to repent of their sins. His goodness leads sinners to repentance (Romans 2:4).

God is inherently good and created a perfect universe. Noticing the existence of evil and sufferings in the world around them, some people have difficulty believing that God is good. A commonly asked question is "Why did a God of love create a world with so much suffering?" The truth is that God is not responsible for evil in the same way that the manufacturer of a piece of equipment would not be liable if the workman were careless in handling it.

Second, God, who is almighty, permits evil to occur. The reason is not always evident or understandable. The Apostle Paul wrote, **His ways [are] past finding out** (Romans 11:33, NKJV). Third, God is so powerful He can overrule evil for good. For example, Joseph's brothers sold him as a slave but God turned around his circumstances and he eventually became second in command to Pharaoh, ruler in Egypt (Genesis 41:41-44). It has also been noted that many Christians come out of the "fires" of suffering with transformed character and strengthened faith. They drew near to God because of their suffering.

Another contributing factor to suffering in this world is that God has arranged the universe according to natural laws. Violation of these laws can result in accidents. For instance, if someone carelessly or deliberately steps off the edge of a cliff, he will no doubt suffer the consequences of violating the laws of gravity.

Last, in response to the question of why evil is allowed, we must remember that God's timing is not the same as ours. While we endure suffering in this imperfect world we know God's justice will prevail in due season (Luke 18:7-8).

Love

We believe that God first loved us and gave His Son to die in our place in order to pay the full price for our sins. His love is unconditional, unsolicited, and unwavering. Love is the attribute of God that causes Him to desire a personal relationship with mankind whom He has created in His own image and likeness. God's love is balanced and He desires obedience in the objects of His love. His love causes Him to be immeasurably interested in humankind's welfare. However, the depth and extent of His love is incomprehensible to our finite minds. Who can fathom why God would send His Son to suffer a cruel and shameful death in order to pay the price for the sins of the world? (Zephaniah 3:17; John 3:16; Romans 5:5; 1 John 4:9).

Another definition of the love of God is "that perfection of the divine nature by which God is eternally moved to communicate Himself. It is not merely emotional, but rational and voluntary affection based on truth and holiness and exercised in free choice." The Greek term *agape*, translated "love," is often used to denote God and His response to humanity (*The Moody Handbook of Theology*, by Paul Enns; John 5:42; Romans 8:35, 39; 1 John 4:8, 10, 11; Revelation 1:5). The use of the word agape implies that this love is reason-based rather than emotionally-based, a love in which the object is loved regardless of its worth, even if the love is not reciprocated.

God loves the world and desires sinners to be saved. He also commands believers to love one another, for demonstrating such love will convince the world that those who love are His disciples.

Holiness

The holiness of God means His absolute moral purity; He can neither sin nor tolerate sin. Holiness pervades all the other attributes of God and is considered all He is and does. The basic meaning of holiness is "set apart" or "separation." Exodus 15:11 explains that in His holiness God is matchless and awesome. He is **high and exalted** (Isaiah 57:15). He commanded the people in Leviticus 11:44, **"Be holy, because I am holy."**

One can conclude that holiness is the attribute which guards the distinction between God and His creation. Holiness is the divine nature itself. The seraphim describe the radiance which flows from God as they cry, **"Holy, holy, holy is the Lord Almighty"** (Isaiah 6:3).

Men are said to sanctify God when they honor and reverence Him as divine (Leviticus 10:3; Numbers 20:12; Isaiah 8:13). When God's commandments are violated, men dishonor Him and "profane" His name. This dishonor conflicts with "hallowing" His name (Matthew 6:9), or responding to a holy God with reverence. Only God is holy in Himself.

Justice

We believe in the justice and righteousness of God, the perfect "Judge" and "Lawgiver" of all the earth (James 4:12). The word justice is sometimes discussed alongside the righteousness of God. God's justice is based on His holiness, truthfulness, and righteousness. The justice of God means that God is entirely correct and fair in His dealings with humanity. His justice acts in accordance with His law. His justice therefore relates to His response to man's sin. Since God's law reflects God's holy standard, then God is righteous and just when He judges humankind for their violation of God's revealed law. He is fair in His judgments and is no respecter of persons (Genesis 18:25; Psalm 7:11; 2 Corinthians 5:10).

Moses observed that God is just and fair. He is **a faithful God who does no wrong** (Deuteronomy 32:4). God cannot be bribed or corrupted because His judgments are grounded in integrity. He searches the heart and tests the mind and hands down just sentences (Jeremiah 17:10).

TRINITY

Deuteronomy 6:4 declares that God is one, and beside Him there is no God. This concept of unity (and yet three personalities) is known as the doctrine of the Trinity. Before finite creatures were created, there existed the Divine Unity, a compound unity of three distinct persons cooperating with one mind and purpose. We believe in the doctrine of the Trinity, outlined in our Statement of Faith, which speaks of the unity of God: "in the unity of the Godhead there are three persons, equal in every divine perfection and attribute, executing distinct, but complementary roles, in the great work of redemption."

The word *trinity* derives from the Latin phrase "tri unitas," meaning three in one. Even though the concept is implied in Scripture on occasion, and is evidenced in passages that refer to the Father, Son, and the Holy Spirit, the term trinity does not appear in the Bible (Matthew 28:19). For example, the Hebrew word *Elohim*, which is the word for "us," was used in Genesis 1:26 when God said, **"Let us make man in our image, in our likeness."** The plural personal pronoun indicates the work of trinity in creation. Other Scripture passages reflect the harmonious function of the Trinity, such as in the events at Jesus' baptism (Matthew 3:16-17) and the benediction spoken in 2 Corinthians 13:14.

The Trinity is an eternal fellowship, but the work of man's redemption necessitated its historical manifestation. The Father creates, the Son redeems, and the Holy Spirit sanctifies; yet in operation the three are present. The Son took to Himself human nature and entered the world in a new way, and then was given a new name, Jesus. The Holy Spirit entered the world in a new way as the Spirit of Christ, embodied in the Church. Yet all three worked together. The Father testified of the Son (Matthew 3:17) and the Son testified of the Father (John 5:19). The Son testified of the Spirit (John 14:26) and later the Spirit would testify of the Son (John 15:26).

THE PERSON AND WORK OF THE FATHER
The Particular Relationships of the Father

(Please note that here we are focusing on the person and work of the Father and not the other two members of the Trinity. Later chapters

contain specific emphases on the person and work of Jesus Christ and the person and work of the Holy Spirit.)

We believe in the scriptural representation of God the Father as supreme Creator of the universe (Genesis 1:1; Romans 4:17; Hebrews 11:3). Both Old and New Testaments employ the term Father. Broadly speaking, Father describes God as the producer of all things and creator of man. He created man in His own image and likeness to rule His creation (Genesis 1:26, 27). God's fatherhood has several dimensions.

1) All people are called the offspring of God (Acts 17:29). In a sense, God is Father of all in His relationship as creature-Creator. This is not a spiritual relationship.

2) God is the Father of the nation Israel (Exodus 4:22). The relationship was both spiritual, involving those who believed, and governmental, encompassing the entire nation (believers and non-believers).

3) God is the Father of the Lord Jesus Christ (Matthew 3:17).

4) God is the Father of all who believe in Christ as Lord and Savior (Galatians 3:26).

The Particular Works of the Father

Since almost everything God does involves in some way all the members of the Trinity, focus will be on those things which seem to be the special prerogative of the Father.

1) The Father was the author of God's plan (Psalm 2:7-9).

2) The Father was involved in the election of men and women into the family of God (Ephesians 1:3-6).

3) The Father sent the Son to this world (John 5:37).

4) The Father is the one who disciplines His children (Hebrews 12:9).

God's vastness, magnificence, and complexity of the universe testify to His exceeding great power and wisdom (Psalm 19:1). The Lord merely spoke and the heavens and earth were created. God has more power than all the forces of nature. The combined energy of earth's storms, winds, ocean waves, and other natural forces do not equal a fraction of God's omnipotence, His unlimited power.

God is the sustainer of life (Acts 17:28; Hebrews 1:3). One school of thought (Deists) holds that God created the universe but relinquished its maintenance to a kind of clockmaker deity who makes a world that can run on its own. The Scriptures do not support this line of reasoning since Hebrews 1:3 states, **The Son is the radiance of God's glory and the exact representation of his being, sustaining all things by his powerful word.**

God has the power to judge sin and rebellion, as evidenced in the destruction of Sodom and Gomorrah (Genesis 19:15-28) and in the destruction of the people in the flood while Noah and his family were saved in the Ark (Genesis 7; Psalm 50:6; 58:11). God justly exercises ownership and rulership over the universe (Genesis 24:3; Isaiah 37:16; 54:5).

God the Father is unrelenting in pursuing a personal relationship with humankind. He is compassionate and gracious, slow to anger, and abounding in faithfulness (Exodus 34:6). God the Father assured His people of His unending love by reminding them that even if it were possible for a mother to forget her nursing child, He would never forget His people (Isaiah 49:15). It is God the Father who sent His Son, the Lord Jesus Christ, to pay the ultimate price for the sin of mankind, so that we might become children of God (John 1:12, 13).

Knowledge of the true God comes from His revelation of Himself in the Bible and not from human imagination or calculation. The knowledge of God is critical to accepting and believing that the true God who has been revealed is capable of doing what He claimed He did, including performing miracles, giving us an inspired Bible, becoming incarnate, and advancing His Kingdom in the world.

Related Scriptures

God the Father -
Deuteronomy 32:6; Psalm 103:13; Isaiah 63:16; Matthew 6:9; John 1:3, 5:19-23, 17:1-11; Acts 17:28; Romans 8:14-16; Ephesians 4:6

God -
Genesis 1:26; Matthew 3:16-17; 2 Corinthians 13:14; 1 Timothy 1:17; 1 John 5:7

Further Reading

Bright, Bill. *God: Discover His Character*. Orlando: New Life Publications, 1999.

Enns, Paul. *The Moody Handbook of Theology*. Chicago, IL: Moody Press, 1989.

Pearlman, Myer. *Knowing the Doctrines of the Bible*. Springfield, MO: Gospel Publishing House, 1937.

Ryrie, Charles C. *A Survey of Bible Doctrine*. Chicago, IL: The Moody Bible Institute, 1972.

Zacharias, Ravi. *Jesus Among Other Gods*. Orlando: World Publishing, 2000.

Time to Interact

Take some time to interact with the following questions. Consider writing your answers in a journal and/or discussing them with a fellow believer for deeper reflection and insight.

1. How did you come to know that God exists? What or who helped you to realize He was there? How does God continue to make His presence known to you?

2. This chapter discusses the many attributes of God. Which ones stand out to you? Why do you think that is? What might God especially want you to know about Him in this season of your life?

3. With the Trinity, we come to know and experience the divine mystery of three persons (Father, Son, and Holy Spirit) who are equal and altogether God. Do you find that you are more comfortable embracing one than the others? Why do you think that is? What steps can you take to draw close to God in the fullness of who He is?

Time to Integrate

An intellectual or theological understanding of God is important, but is not the same as actually knowing Him. As you reflect on this chapter, work through the following as you deepen your relationship with Him.

1. There are numerous biblical names and titles for God. Jesus invited us to call God "Father." How does this understanding of Him affect your life? What might you say to someone who struggles with seeing God as Father because they have had a difficult experience with their earthly father?

2. Examine your own heart for areas of wounding or disappointment concerning the concept of "father." What needs to be healed or restored? Confess those areas of brokenness and hurt to Father God. Thank Him that He is perfect in His love for you and ask Him to complete a cleansing and healing work in you. Expect to find rest and joy in your experience of God as Father!

3. An old adage says "like father, like son." Although His natural attributes (such as sovereignty, infinity, and immutability) are certainly reserved for Him alone, God's moral attributes (such as love, goodness, and holiness) are intended to be reflected in us. Which of these attributes do you believe God might be working to develop in you right now? How is He doing that? Make a list of His moral attributes (perhaps reflect on the fruit of the Spirit in Galatians 5:22-23) and invite the Father to reproduce His nature in you with each one.

CHAPTER 3

Our Redeemer:
The Person and Work of
Jesus Christ

CHAPTER 3

Our Redeemer: The Person and Work of
Jesus Christ

GOD THE SON

" We believe in God the Son, co-Creator with the Father and Holy Spirit, who took upon Himself human form, being conceived by the Holy Spirit, born of the Virgin Mary, and given the name Jesus. His death by crucifixion and bodily resurrection reconciled the human race to God. He ascended to heaven where He is seated at the right hand of the Father making intercession for us as the King of kings and Lord of lords."

GOD

"We believe there is one God. In the unity of the Godhead there are three persons, Father, Son, and Holy Spirit, equal in every divine perfection and attribute, fulfilling distinct, but complementary roles in the great work of redemption."

RESURRECTION

"We believe the resurrection of our Lord Jesus Christ assures the believer of bodily resurrection and eternal life. "

Each of the first three sentences in the above Statement of Faith addresses a particular aspect of the nature, mission, and ministry of Jesus. The first sentence articulates both the divine and human natures of Jesus. The second sentence speaks of His main mission and primary purpose in our salvation. And the third addresses His post-resurrection ascension and continuing role in our lives as believers.

These three sentences contain various phrases that identify particular aspects of what the Bible teaches about the person and work of Jesus. The following explanations focus on each of these phrases and show how they are derived from the biblical account.

Throughout the history of the Church, many statements of faith concerning Jesus have been written. Two of the earliest of these are the Apostles' Creed and the Nicene Creed. Both contain a descriptive account of how the early church fathers documented what they understood the Bible to say about Jesus and how the believing Church should respond to those truths in their confession of Jesus as Lord. While Open Bible Churches is not "creedal" in nature, it is certainly helpful to examine these and other historic statements to grasp how the early church fathers addressed their belief in Jesus.

Of course, there is much additional biblical material on Jesus that is not covered in this chapter. Some of this, such as His promised return or what is commonly referred to as the Second Coming and His commission to the Church to continue His ministry on earth until He comes again, are dealt with in other sections of this book. The focus of this chapter is the issues concerning His deity and humanity, His birth and incarnation, some aspects of His earthly ministry, His death and atonement or saving grace, His victory over death and the grave by His resurrection, His ascension into heaven, and His sovereign lordship over all creation.

HIS DEITY AND HUMANITY– THE GOD/MAN

The first article in the Open Bible Churches Statement of Faith concerning what we believe about Jesus clearly articulates both the divine and human natures of Christ.

> We believe in Jesus Christ, **God the Son, co-Creator** with the Father and Holy Spirit, who took upon Himself **human form, being conceived by the Holy Spirit, born of the Virgin Mary**, and given the name Jesus.

The Son of God

What is meant by the divine nature or deity of Jesus is that He always was, is, and always will be fully God. The first few verses of the first chapter of the gospel of John clearly demonstrate that Jesus was with God the Father at the beginning of creation. John's gospel intentionally uses the same first three words to begin the account of Jesus as were used in Genesis creation account, *In the beginning* … . The Genesis answer to what was before the heavens and the earth were created is simply "God." That is to say, *In the beginning God* ... . John echoes this truth concerning the divine nature of Jesus at the opening of his gospel account when he writes, *In the beginning was the **Word**, and the **Word** was with God, and the **Word was God**. He was **with God in the beginning**. Through him all things were made; without him nothing was made that has been made. In him was life, and that life was the light of men* (John 1:1-2).

When John used the term "Word" he was, of course, referring to Jesus. In verse 14 this is clarified when John continues this concept in his prologue, *The **Word** became flesh and made his dwelling among us. We have seen his glory, the glory of the **One and Only**, who came from the Father, full of grace and truth.*

To further establish the divine nature of Jesus as fully God, John says that *all things were made through him, (and) without him nothing was made that was made.* This includes not only the created world as we know it, but also all life as well. *In him was life, and that life was the light of men*. And so as Genesis identifies God as the Creator and the Originator of all life and light, John tells us that Jesus Himself is one with the God of creation and the originator of all life and light.

John also refers to the deity of Jesus when he records in the book of Revelation these words from Jesus Himself to John, *"I am the Alpha and the Omega," says the Lord God, "who is, and who was, and who is to come, the Almighty"* (Revelation 1:8). In the Greek language commonly spoken during the days of Jesus and the early church, "alpha" is the first letter of the alphabet, and "omega" is the last letter. So here Jesus declares that He is the beginning (***Alpha***) and the end (***Omega***); He supersedes time *(is, was, and is to come),* and He alone is the one without contenders *(the Almighty).* These descriptive words can mean only one thing: Jesus is God.

But perhaps the most telling passage of Scripture concerning the deity or divine nature of Jesus is the prophetic name *Immanuel*. Speaking through the prophet Isaiah seven hundred years prior to the human birth of Jesus, God said, *"Therefore the Lord himself will give you a sign: The virgin will be with child and will give birth to a son, and will call him Immanuel"* (Isaiah 7:14). It was this prophetic word that the angel spoke to Joseph to console and encourage him in preparation for the human birth of Jesus (Matthew 1:22-23). Since the name or title *Immanuel*, meaning "God with us," was prophetically assigned to Jesus seven hundred years before His human birth, this can mean nothing other than Jesus is God.

This is a foundational truth about Jesus: He always was and is and always will be fully God. His being, His existence was and is eternal. He preceded creation, joined the Father in creation and the bringing forth of life, and is Himself without beginning and without end. He is the second member of the triune Godhead: Father, Son, and Holy Spirit. And that is why the early church fathers wrote in the Nicene Creed that he is "the only Son of God, eternally begotten of the Father, God from God, Light from Light, true God from true God, begotten, not made, of one Being with the Father. Through him all things were made...."

The statement "We believe in Jesus Christ, God the Son, co-Creator with the Father and Holy Spirit" affirms that Jesus Christ is fully God. He was with God prior to and during the very creation itself, yes, before time, and is therefore the Eternal One along with the Father and the Holy Spirit.

The Son of Man

Open Bible's Statement of Faith concerning Jesus does not end by identifying only the divinity of Jesus. It also recognizes and affirms His humanity in these very human words: "who took upon himself **human form**, being **conceived** by the Holy Spirit, **born** of the Virgin Mary, and **given the name** Jesus." Again the words in the prologue to John's gospel identify the humanity of Jesus when he writes, *the Word became flesh and made his dwelling among us* (John 1:14). In the contemporary language of *The Message* Bible this verse is rendered, ***The Word became flesh and blood, and moved into the neighborhood.*** This particular reading focuses our attention on the full humanity of Jesus. We think of Him moving into our neighborhood, perhaps even next door. Notice the emphasized words in the above statement about His human nature. He took upon Himself *human form*, was *conceived, born,* and *named Jesus*. Humanity, conception, birth, and the naming of a newborn – these are all terms of human experience.

There are, of course, many Scriptures that reveal the true humanity of Jesus, a few of which are referenced here.

Three of the common titles for Jesus in the Bible are Son of God, Son of Man, and Son of David. It is obvious that the first of these expresses His divine nature as God, and the latter two His human nature as one of us. The term "Son of Man" is used in the four gospels approximately eighty times. It was the term by which Jesus frequently referred to Himself, as when He asked His disciples, *"Who do people say the Son of Man is?"* (Matthew 16:13).

Another telling reference to the humanity of Jesus in Matthew's gospel is in chapter 13:53-56. Following a season of His powerful teaching and healing ministry, Jesus returned to His hometown and began teaching the people in their synagogue. Matthew writes that **they were amazed: *"Where did this man get this wisdom and these miraculous powers?" they asked. "Isn't this the carpenter's son? Isn't his mother's name Mary, and aren't his brothers James, Joseph, Simon and Judas? Aren't all his sisters with us? Where then did this man get all these things?"*** The issue here is that they understood that Jesus was fully human. They had no trouble accepting His human nature. They knew Him well as the boy Jesus. They knew His family and had watched Him grow up. He had indeed "moved into their neighborhood" and they had no trouble accepting His role as one of them.

The account of the temptation of Jesus by the devil prior to the beginning of His public ministry further substantiates the humanity of Jesus. The account in Luke 4:1-13 makes clear that the devil is trying to exploit the incarnation, Jesus having come to earth to live among us as a man. Observe the devil's strategy; it gets straight to the heart of what it means to be human. Everyone can identify with the three aspects the devil deployed in his strategy. We humans need or strongly desire food for the stomach, safety and well-being in the face of danger, and personal power and authority. It is safe to say then that even the devil recognized that Jesus was fully human.

These examples from the Scriptures plainly show that Jesus' human nature was recognized by Jesus Himself, the four authors of the gospel accounts of Jesus' life, His hometown friends and family, and even the devil.

Finally, three particular scriptural references masterfully combine the divine and human natures of Jesus. First, Paul writes at the beginning of his letter to the Romans, *Paul, a servant of Christ Jesus, called to be an apostle and set apart for the gospel of God – the gospel he promised beforehand through his prophets in the Holy Scriptures regarding his Son, who as to his* **human nature** *was a descendant of David, and who through the Spirit of holiness was declared with power to be the* **Son of God** *by his resurrection from the dead: Jesus Christ our Lord* (Romans 1:1-4).

Second, the author of Hebrews combines these two natures of Jesus: *Therefore, since we have a great high priest who has gone through the heavens, Jesus the Son of God, let us hold firmly to the faith we profess. For we do not have a high priest who is unable to sympathize with our weaknesses, but we have one who has been tempted in every way, just as we are* [His human nature] *– yet was without sin* [His divine nature] (4:14-15).

Perhaps the most compelling section of Scripture dealing with the blending of the two natures of Jesus, the God/Man and the divine/human, is in the Apostle Paul's beautiful poem in his letter to the Philippians (2:5-12).

> *Your attitude should be the same as that of Christ Jesus:*
> *Who, being in very nature God,*
> *did not consider equality with God something to be grasped,*
> *but made himself nothing,*
> *taking the very nature of a servant,*
> *being made in human likeness,*
> *And being found in appearance as a man,*
> *he humbled himself*
> *and became obedient to death –*
> *even death on a cross!*
> *Therefore God exalted him to the highest place*
> *And gave him the name that is above every name,*
> *that at the name of Jesus every knee should bow,*
> *in heaven and on earth and under the earth,*
> *and every tongue confess that Jesus Christ is Lord,*
> *to the glory of God the Father.*

TWO COMMON HERESIES

The word *heresy* is defined in the *Random House College Dictionary* as "religious opinion or doctrine at variance with the orthodox or accepted doctrine." Throughout the history of the Church, many doctrinal errors or heresies have arisen concerning the person of Jesus. The two that are most common in our culture today are that Jesus is not God and that Jesus cannot be the only source of salvation.

The Historical Jesus

The first of these, that Jesus is not God, stems from a misunderstanding of His human nature and a rejection of the doctrine of the Incarnation. Briefly stated, the Incarnation is the doctrine that the second person of the Trinity assumed human form in the person of Jesus Christ and is completely both God and man. Those who reject this doctrine will sometimes speak of the "historical Jesus," and by this they mean that Jesus existed as a person in history but could not possibly have been divine. He was a good man, even a holy man, an excellent teacher, yes, and even a prophet. He taught us how to be people of peace, how to love one another, and how to honor God; but to suggest that He was God, they say, is an absurdity beyond reason.

This "historical Jesus" notion denies the classical and traditional understanding of the Incarnation as seen in the previously cited Scriptures of John 1:14, Isaiah 7:14, Matthew 1:23, Romans 1:1-4, and Philippians 2:5-12. These passages teach us that God came to earth in the person of Jesus Christ and that God was "incarnate" in the human body of Jesus. The "historical Jesus" notion also denies the virgin birth of Jesus as recorded in Isaiah, Matthew, and Luke. And it follows that His death meant only His demise and that His resurrection is simply a myth.

These denials are based on the idea that Jesus was a real man in history, but the accounts here aforementioned are metaphorical or mythological and not historical. In order to arrive at the conclusion that Jesus is not God and to deny His divinity, it is necessary to reconstruct the biblical narrative in a manner that accepts the historical Jesus as a person and rejects any notion of Incarnation. This view then, of course, also rejects the doctrine that the biblical authors were divinely inspired by God, a topic that was covered in an earlier chapter.

Pluralism

The second heresy or false teaching that is prominent in our day is that Jesus is not the only way to salvation and cannot be the only way to the promise of a blessed eternal life at the end of our earthly existence. This belief has become more popular in recent times due to the emphasis on pluralism and inclusiveness that is prevalent in our social structures today. The view that faith in Jesus is the only way for people to be saved and to avoid eternal punishment, we are told, is outdated and irrelevant in the modern and globally aware world of the 21st century.

The concept that Jesus is the only way to be saved or that Christianity is the only true religion and the Bible is the only true scriptural source for divine truth is considered by many to be arrogant, intolerant, and downright ignorant.

But Jesus Himself claimed to be the only way to God when He said, *"I am the way and the truth and the life. No one comes to the Father except through me"* (John 14:6). Likewise Peter, in answer to the religious leaders of his day who were questioning him concerning how a lame man was healed, stated, *"Salvation is found in no one else, for there is no other name under heaven given to men by which we must be saved"* (Acts 4:12).

The *NIV Life Application Study Bible* provides an excellent instructive footnote to Acts 4:12:

> *Many people react negatively to the fact that there is no other name than that of Jesus to call on for our salvation. Yet this is not something the church decided; it is the specific teaching of Jesus himself (John 14:6). If God designated Jesus to be the Savior of the world, no one else can be his equal. Christians are to be open minded on many issues, but not on how we are saved from sin. No other religious leader could die for our sins; no other religious teacher came to earth as God's only Son; no other religious teacher rose from the dead. Our focus should be on Jesus, whom God offered as the way to have an eternal relationship with himself. There is no other name or way!*

Both of the above heresies or teachings are at variance with what Open Bible Churches believes about Jesus because the teachings deny His divine nature. The Incarnation – that God dwelt bodily in the person of Jesus – is the cornerstone of Christianity.

HIS WORK AND MISSION

The next two sentences in the statement of faith regarding our beliefs about Jesus Christ deal with His work, His earthly existence and ministry, and His ultimate and central mission.

The second sentence says, "His death by crucifixion and bodily resurrection reconciled the human race to God." This takes us to the heart or the central core of His mission here on earth and introduces us to the two most critical aspects of His earthly existence and ministry: His death and resurrection. Unless our focus is on these two critical aspects of Jesus' life on earth, we miss the intent of the biblical presentation concerning the life, the work, and mission of Jesus Christ.

The third sentence in the statement says, "He ascended to heaven where He is seated at the right hand of the Father making intercession for us." This statement addresses Jesus' post-resurrection ascension into heaven and His continuing role and ongoing ministry in our lives as believers. It also speaks of His ultimate sovereign lordship over all creation, present and future.

When thinking about the works of Jesus, we sometimes think only in terms of His miracles and teachings. While these are certainly a great part of His earthly work, they are not all encompassing. That is because in addition to His miracles and teaching, His death and resurrection and ascension are also vital aspects of His work on our behalf.

The works of Jesus are intricately connected with the person or nature of Jesus. His works are a statement or a manifestation of His nature. Sometimes we hear it said about a naturally gifted athlete, "You can't teach that; it's a gift of nature." And so it is with Jesus. He is the God/Man. His works are an extension of His nature as both God and Man.

His Earthly Ministry

Any attempt to discuss the earthly work or ministry of Jesus must begin with His miraculous birth. Born to a virgin, He was given the names Immanuel (Matthew 1:23) and Jesus (Matthew 1:21 and Luke 1:31). These two names alone specify a great deal about the ministry Jesus was about to embark upon during His earthly journey. As has already been discussed in the above section on the two natures of Jesus (divine and human), the name Immanuel means "God with us." It is, therefore, a statement of His divine nature and introduces us to the doctrine of the Incarnation.

Upon greeting Mary, who was to be the virgin mother of Jesus, the angel Gabriel prophesied to her that she was to name her son Jesus. Earlier Joseph had been told in a dream that the child who was to be born to Mary was to be given that same name, Jesus, *"because he will save his people from their sins"* (Matthew 1:21). Matthew continues by telling us that Joseph followed through with the angel's directive by giving Mary's newborn son the name Jesus (1:25).

Both these birth names, Immanuel and Jesus, are instructional for our primary understanding of Jesus' earthly work, ministry, and mission. In both cases they introduce us to the truth that His mission on earth was to supersede that of all other human beings. He was "God with us," the God/Man who came to "save us from our sins."

From the angels' visits with Joseph and Mary, to Mary's visit with Elizabeth, to the journey to Bethlehem, to the angels' announcement to the shepherds, to the visit by the Magi, to the escape to Egypt and the return from Egypt to Nazareth, to the ceremonial presentation of Jesus in the temple on the eighth day, the full accounts of the birth of Jesus (as recorded by Matthew and Luke) are filled with this truth: the birth of this child was above and beyond any other human birth. And subsequently, as was previously spoken by the prophets, this child was to be the Christ, the promised Messiah sent by God.

The earliest account we have of the earthly work of Jesus is when He was just twelve years old. He was *in the temple courts, sitting among the teachers, listening to them and asking them questions. Everyone who heard him was amazed at his understanding and his answers.* Upon being discovered there by Joseph and Mary and questioned by them concerning their anxiety about Him having been missing from their party for several days, He asked them this piercing question, *"Didn't you know that I had to be in my Father's house?"* (Luke 2:41-49).

Looking at the earthly ministry of Jesus from that first event at twelve years of age, to His crucifixion on a Roman cross, to His resurrection and ascension into heaven, we can easily discern that He always pointed us to God and clarified for us that His mission was to be about his Father's business.

Three aspects of His earthly work are prominent in the gospel accounts: His teaching ministry, His healing of people with various afflictions and diseases, and His miraculous works in addition to human physical healings and deliverances. All accounts of the earthly work and ministry of Jesus focus on His mission as Immanuel and Jesus, the Christ of God. He is "God with us," "the One who came to save us from our sins," and "Christ, the Messiah, the Anointed One."

When we read about Jesus' miracles like calming the stormy sea (Matthew 8:23-27) or feeding the five thousand (Luke 9:10-17) or raising Lazarus from the dead (John 11:1-44), we are seeing Him as **Immanuel, God with us**, in action. And when we read one of His excellent teachings, like the parable of the Prodigal Son (Luke 15:11-32), we are seeing Him as **Jesus, because he will save his people from their sins.** And when we hear Jesus asking His disciples, *"Who do people say I am?"* and *"What about you? ... Who do you say I am?"* we affirm Peter's response, *"You are the Christ"* (Mark 8:27-29).

The Apostle John sums up the prevalence and the purpose of the miraculous portion of the earthly works of Jesus when he writes, *Jesus did many other miraculous signs in the presence of his disciples, which are not recorded in this book. But these are written that you may believe that **Jesus is the Christ, the Son of God**, and that by believing you may have life in his name* (John 20:30-31).

When we examine the earthly work of Jesus that encompasses His teaching ministry, His compassionate healing of many people, and His miraculous works, we are introduced to the One who is both the Son of God and the Son of Man, Jesus, Immanuel, the Christ.

HIS DEATH AND ATONEMENT

When we study the earthly works of Jesus, we dare not stop with His miraculous works and healings, nor can we stop with the masterful teachings of the greatest of all teaching masters. As great as these are, as much as they give us a clear picture of Jesus, Immanuel, and the Christ, they are preliminary to the greatest of all His earthly works.

Jesus came to earth with a primary cause and an absolute agenda. His cause and agenda differed from that of every other human being. He came to die. It is true that "it is appointed unto man once to die," but none of us came into this world with our primary mission being our death. While death is our destiny, it is not our ultimate goal in life. That is different with Jesus. His goal in this life was to die, and His death, not His life on earth, was destined to be His greatest work and achievement, because as our Statement of Faith says in the second sentence, *"His death by crucifixion and bodily resurrection reconciled the human race to God."*

In his book *The Jesus I Never Knew*, Philip Yancey writes, "Of the biographies I have read, few devote more than ten percent of their pages to the subject's death – including biographies of men like Martin Luther King, Jr. and Mahatma Gandhi, who died violent and politically significant deaths. The Gospels, though, devote nearly a third of their length to the climactic last week of Jesus' life. Matthew, Mark, Luke and John saw death as the central mystery of Jesus" (187-188).

Jesus Himself knew of His coming death and resurrection. One day as He and His disciples were on their way to Jerusalem, He said to them, *"the Son of Man will be betrayed to the chief priests and teachers of the law. They will condemn him to death, and will hand him over to the Gentiles, who will mock him and spit on him, flog him and kill him. Three days later he will rise"* (Mark 10:33-34). In fact, on multiple occasions He told His disciples and others of His pending death (Matthew 12:40; Mark 8:31-33; John 2:19).

The four gospels detail the "how" and the "what" of the horrible and gruesome suffering and death of Jesus on that "old rugged cross" at Calvary. Believers need to read and re-read these details again and again – not just on Good Friday.

But it is other passages such as the "suffering servant" prophetic words of Isaiah that show us the "why" of Jesus' death. *Surely he took up our infirmities and carried our sorrows, yet we considered him stricken by God, smitten by him, and afflicted. But he was pierced for our transgressions, he was crushed for our iniquities; the punishment that brought us peace was upon him, and by his wounds we are healed* (Isaiah 53-4-5).

It is the "why" of Jesus' death that shows the heart and soul of His reason for coming to earth. He came to die for us so that we could be forgiven, to make atonement for our sins and to reconcile us back to God.

The Apostle Paul cuts to the heart of the central earthly mission of Jesus when he writes these words to Timothy, **Here is a trustworthy saying that deserves full acceptance: Christ Jesus came into the world to save sinners** (1 Timothy 1:15). Also in Romans 5:8 he wrote, **But God demonstrates his own love for us in this: While we were still sinners, Christ died for us.** And Jesus Himself said about His mission on earth, *"the Son of Man did not come to be served, but to serve, and to give his life as a ransom for many"* (Matthew 20:28).

Speaking with the Pharisees, Jesus told them that He had *"not come to call the righteous, but sinners to repentance"* (Luke 5:32). And with that calling of sinners to repentance, He also forgave them of their sin. At Simon the Pharisee's house, when He told the "sinner" woman who had anointed Him with oil, washed His feet with her tears and dried them with her hair, *"Your sins are forgiven"* (Luke 7:48), His central mission – forgiveness of sins – was wrought sharply into focus. And when Jesus said to the paralytic at Capernaum, *"Son, your sins are forgiven"* (Mark 2:5), He was taking us right to the heart of His central purpose in coming to earth – to forgive us of our sins. Of course, those who were there questioned His ability to actually forgive sins. In fact they accused Him of blasphemy because they concluded that only God could forgive sins.

And at least that part of their conclusion was correct. Indeed, only God can forgive our sins against Him. That is why the biblical doctrine of "atonement" is so critical. A working definition of atonement is "to make amends for or to satisfy or make reparations for a wrong or injury." In the Bible, the word atonement is used in direct correlation with our sin. It is because we have separated ourselves from God by our sin that atonement must be made if we are to be reconciled to God.

In the book of Leviticus God required a special day to be set aside once a year for the Israelites to "atone" for their sins. This was called the Day of Atonement. It was a day when the ancient Israelites, by following the sacrificial requirements of the law, could be assured of their forgiveness. Today the Day of Atonement, or Yom Kippur, is still considered to be the holiest day of the year among people of Jewish faith.

The Bible teaches that because of sin we are all separated from God (Romans 3:23). In order to be reconciled to God atonement is necessary. Our sin needs to be satisfied or atoned for if the wrong that has separated us from God is to be amended and we are to be put back in a right relationship with God.

The book of Hebrews explains that the sacrificial death of Jesus is God's plan for atoning for our sins.

> *In the past God spoke to our forefathers through the prophets at many times and in various ways, but in these last days he has spoken to us by his Son, whom he appointed heir of all things, and through whom he made the universe. The Son is the radiance of God's glory and the exact representation of his being, sustaining all things by his powerful word.* **After he had provided purification for sins**, *he sat down at the right hand of the Majesty in heaven* (Hebrews 1:1-3).

> *When Christ came as high priest of the good things that are already here, he went through the greater and more perfect tabernacle that is not man-made, that is to say, not a part of this creation. He did not enter by means of the blood of goats and calves; but, he entered the Most Holy Place once for all* **by his own blood, having obtained eternal redemption.** *The blood of goats and bulls and the ashes of a heifer sprinkled on those who are ceremonially unclean sanctify them so that they are outwardly clean. How* **much more, then, will the blood of Christ, who through the eternal Spirit offered himself unblemished to God**, *cleanse our consciences from acts that lead to death, so that we may serve the living God!* (Hebrews 9:11-14).

> *And without the shedding of blood there is no forgiveness* (Hebrews 9:22).

> *The law is only a shadow of the good things that are coming – not the realities themselves. For this reason it can never, by the same*

> sacrifices repeated endlessly year after year, make perfect those who draw near to worship.
>
> Therefore, when Christ came into world, he said: "Sacrifice and offering you did not desire, but a body you prepared for me; with burnt offerings and sin offerings you were not pleased. Then I said, 'Here am – it is written about me in the scroll – I have come to do your will, O God.'"
>
> And by that will, we have been made holy through the **sacrifice of the body of Jesus Christ once for all.**
>
> Day after day every priest stands and performs his religious duties; again and again he offers the same sacrifices, which can never take away sins. But when **this priest had offered for all time one sacrifice for sins**, he sat down at the right hand of God… because **by one sacrifice he has made perfect forever those who are being made holy** (Hebrews 10:1-14).

These Scriptures plainly reveal that the sacrificial death of Jesus is God's means of making atonement for our sins. And only Jesus could do this because He was the *"Lamb of God, who takes away the sins of the world!"* (John 1:29), or as Peter said it, *For you know that it was not with perishable things such as silver or gold that you were redeemed from the empty way of life handed down to you from your forefathers, but with the* **precious blood of Christ, a lamb without blemish or defect** (1 Peter 1:18-19).

And again Peter wrote about Jesus

> He committed no sin, and no deceit was found in his mouth. When they hurled their insults at him, he did not retaliate; when he suffered, he made no threats. Instead, he entrusted himself to him who judges justly. **He himself bore our sins in his body on the tree, so that we might die to sins** and live for righteousness; by his wounds you have been healed. For you were like sheep going astray, but now you have **returned** to the Shepherd and Overseer of your souls (1 Peter 2:22-25).

The biblically correct understanding of Jesus' death on the cross as the means of the atonement for our sins is perhaps best expressed in two additional verses of Scripture. The first is *But God demonstrates his own love for us in this: While we were still sinners, Christ died for us* (Romans 5:8). The second is the familiar words of Jesus in John 3:16: *"For God so loved the world that he gave his one and only Son, that whoever believes in him shall not perish but have eternal life."*

Open Bible's teaching on the doctrine of atonement offers clear scriptural parameters that avoid two opposite erroneous views, called "limited atonement" and "universalism." The limited atonement theory states that Christ died only for a few. In His Sovereign will God chose some for whom the death of Christ would atone. Those whom God chose for destruction are His created beings, but they are not included in the atoning sacrifice of the Savior. It makes no provision for the free will of man to accept or reject the atoning sacrifice of Jesus. Nor does it make provision for this truth – Christ died for all and His atonement is available to all.

The second errant view is universalism, which is the opposite of limited atonement. Universalism teaches that since God loves all (John 3:16) and *He is the atoning sacrifice for our sins, and not only for ours but also for the sins of the whole world* (1 John 2:2), and because *for as in Adam all die, so in Christ all will be made alive* (1 Corinthians 15:22); therefore, all will be included in the final restoration and no one will be shut out of God's atoning act of grace and forgiveness. Among other things, this faulty view fails to consider that only **in Christ** all are made alive and **in Adam** all die. While it is true that *He is patient with you, not wanting anyone to perish, but everyone to come to repentance* (2 Peter 3:9), it is also true that the *Lord knows how…to hold the unrighteous for the day of judgment, while continuing their punishment* (2 Peter 2:9).

HIS RESURRECTION AND ASCENSION

The death of Jesus is not the end of Jesus. He came not just to die, but to win the final victory over death. That is why our Statement of Faith refers to his "resurrection and ascension." Each of the four gospels gives an account of the resurrection and the post-resurrection, pre-ascension appearances of Jesus (Matthew 28, Mark 16, Luke 24, John 20-21).

The origins of the Christian faith following Jesus' time on earth are firmly planted in His resurrection. The resurrection of Jesus was the center and core of the faith of the earliest Christians. The Book of Acts, the account by Luke of the faith and actions of those earliest Christians following the death of Jesus, begins with an affirming statement of the resurrection of Christ: *After his suffering, he showed himself to these men and gave many convincing proofs that he was alive. He appeared to them over a period of forty days and spoke about the kingdom of God* (Acts 1:3).

Later in Acts, the main message of those early Christians was that Christ had risen from the dead and was very much alive. Peter's first sermon on the Day of Pentecost (Acts 2:14-41) proclaimed the resurrection of Jesus. That theme continues to accentuate the message of those early followers of Jesus throughout the book of Acts (Acts 3:15; 4:10; 4:33; 5:30; 7:55-56; 10:40; 13:30, 37). Paul's affirmation of the resurrection in 1 Corinthians 15 is a primary document that establishes the reality and importance of the resurrection of Jesus. In verse 14 Paul writes, *And if Christ has not been raised, our preaching is useless and so is your faith.* That is why the Nicene Creed and the Apostle's Creed, those early post-first century creeds of the church, spoke not only of the nature, the birth, and the death of Jesus, but they also proclaimed His resurrection. They were intent on affirming this truth: Christ is risen; He is risen indeed!

Nonetheless, just as the story of Jesus does not end with His earthly ministry or His death, neither does it end with His resurrection. Jesus is not yet finished. "He ascended to heaven where He is seated at the right hand of the Father making intercession for us as the King of kings and Lord of lords." This statement addresses the present and ongoing ministry of Jesus. He is now sitting at the right hand of the Father making intercession for us. This part of our Statement of Faith is based on Scripture. *Christ Jesus, who died – more than that, who was raised to life – is at the right hand of God and is also interceding for us* (Romans 8:34).

And He *is now* King of kings and Lord of lords. *Therefore God exalted him to the highest place and gave him the name that is above every name, that at the name of Jesus every knee should bow, in heaven and on earth and under the earth, and every tongue confess that Jesus Christ is Lord, to the glory of God the Father* (Philippians 2:9-11).

In the introductory comments to the book of Acts in *The Message Bible*, Eugene Peterson wrote, "The story of Jesus doesn't end with Jesus, it continues in the lives of those who believe in him. The supernatural does not stop with Jesus. Luke makes it clear that these Christians he wrote about were no more spectators of Jesus than Jesus was a spectator of God – they are in on the action of God, God acting in them, God living in them. Which also means, of course, in us" (1966).

The earthly ministry of Jesus has not ended. His death, His resurrection, His ascension – none of these has concluded the presence and ministry and works of Jesus. He is continuing His work on earth through His body, the Church. **Now you are the body of Christ, and each one of you is a part of it** (1 Corinthians 12:27). Indeed our calling is to be His continuing presence in our world, to be the hands and feet of Jesus as long as we have life and breath – to accomplish His will *"on earth as it is in heaven"* (Matthew 6:10). It must be all about Jesus all the time. And as we in the Church bend our knees to Jesus and confess that Jesus Christ is Lord, we will see Him reign as Sovereign Lord over all creation in His never-ending Kingdom.

Related Scriptures

God the Son -
Isaiah 53:1-5; Matthew 1:21-23; John 1:1-3, 11:25-26; Ephesians 1:20-23; Philippians 2:1-6; 1 Timothy 2:5

God -
Genesis 1:26; Matthew 3:16-17; 2 Corinthians 13:14; 1 Timothy 1:17; 1 John 5:7

Resurrection -
Matthew 28:1-7; Romans 6:1-10; 1 Corinthians 15:20-22; 1 Thessalonians 4:14-18

For Further Reading

Bach, Randall A. and Schmidt, Dennis M. *We Believe: Principles in Christian Living*. Des Moines, IA: Open Bible Publishers, 1992.

Copan, Paul, ed. *Will the Real Jesus Please Stand Up?* Grand Rapids, MI: Baker Books, 1999.

Life Application NIV Study Bible. Wheaton, IL: Tyndale House, 2005.

Nash, Ronald H. *Is JESUS the Only SAVIOR?* Grand Rapids, MI: Zondervan, 1994.

Peterson, Eugene H. *THE MESSAGE: The Bible in Contemporary Language.* Carol Stream, IL: NavPress, 2002.

Wright, N.T. *Simply Jesus.* San Francisco, CA: Harper One, 2011.

Yancey, Philip. *The Jesus I Never Knew.* Grand Rapids, MI: Zondervan, 1995.

Time to Interact

Take some time to interact with the following questions. Consider writing your answers in a journal and/or discussing them with a fellow believer for deeper reflection and insight.

1. Why do you think it is important to understand that Jesus is both fully God and fully man? By looking at the Lord's life and ministry, what can we learn about God? By examining His example and His interactions with others, what might we learn about humanity?

2. The names *Jesus* and *Immanuel* reflect both the human and divine natures of Christ and remind us of this truth: He is "God with us!" When did this truth come alive in you? How have you experienced Jesus as "God with us?"

3. During His earthly ministry, Jesus ministered through teaching, healing the sick, and working miracles. What teachings of Christ have made an impact on your life? In what ways have you been affected by His healing ministry? What has been your experience of His miraculous power? As you read the Gospels, which verses might give you encouragement and hope that Jesus is still ministering in this way?

Time to Integrate

As you reflect on the life and mission of Jesus, open your heart to a fresh encounter of His presence and ministry.

1. This chapter emphasizes the way in which Jesus came to call sinners to repentance. How has Jesus made Himself known to you? What has been the impact on your life? Find a friend this week and share with each other how Christ rescued you from your sins and the difference that has made in your lives.

2. Take some time to remind yourself of the sufferings of Christ and all He went through to redeem us from our sins. Write a letter expressing sincere gratitude to Him for the depths of His love and for enduring such pain and heartache on your behalf. As you read it over, consider how your choices and actions this week could reflect that same heart of thanksgiving.

3. Romans 10:9-10 says, *If you declare with your mouth, "Jesus is Lord," and believe in your heart that God raised him from the dead, you will be saved. For it is with your heart that you believe and are justified, and it is with your mouth that you profess your faith and are saved.*

   Have you made that confession? Have you surrendered yourself to the lordship of Jesus? The primary reason He came to this world and offered His life as an atoning sacrifice was to provide redemption for every single one of us and enable us to believe and place our faith in Him. If you are ready to receive Christ as your Lord and Savior, skip ahead right now to Chapter 9, "New Life in Christ: Salvation and Sanctification." Especially look for the section marked "An Invitation," and let it lead you into a saving encounter with Jesus. You will never be the same!

CHAPTER 4

Our Comforter:
The Person and Work of
The Holy Spirit

CHAPTER 4

Our Comforter: The Person and Work of
The Holy Spirit

GOD THE HOLY SPIRIT

" We believe in God the Holy Spirit, co-Creator with the Father and Son, who is now sent by the Father through the Son to convict the world of sin, lead us into all truth, and empower and equip the Church to carry on Christ's work on earth."

GOD

"We believe there is one God. In the unity of the Godhead, there are three persons, Father, Son, and Holy Spirit, equal in every divine perfection and attribute, fulfilling distinct, but complementary, roles in the great work of redemption. "

THE PERSON OF THE HOLY SPIRIT

Gaining a broad perspective on the Holy Spirit's activities *through*, *to*, and *in* the Body of Christ helps believers visualize with clarity the different personal traits and workings of the Holy Spirit so that they can gain a better understanding of the relationship of His work in their lives.

The process of getting to know someone generally includes a time of interaction wherein preferences and personalities emerge. Eventually each person makes choices as to how they will treat the other, and discovers what the other person favors and what offends them.

Scripture records many instances in which the Holy Spirit displays personality traits we can understand – almost *human* traits that indicate He can be honored or grieved. The believer's objective should be a resolve to always honor the Holy Spirit in words, actions, and attitudes. The best way to get to know a person is to consider what they say and how they act, and whether or not their actions align with their words.

Likewise, the best way to get to know the Holy Spirit and to understand His leading in one's life is to examine what the Bible says about Him and how He can be honored or grieved.

The Holy Spirit is a person. He has intellect, emotions, and will. Jesus never referred to the Holy Spirit as "it." He always ascribed traits of personality and abiding relationship when speaking about the one whom He would later call the "Comforter" or "Advocate." He told His followers that this Advocate would be with them forever: *"And I will ask the Father, and he will give you another Advocate, who will never leave you"* (John 14:16, NLT). The Holy Spirit of God became the influence the Father chose to utilize in the world system after the death and resurrection of Jesus Christ the Son.

Human-Like Traits

He speaks:

> *He who has an ear, let him hear what the Spirit says to the churches. To him who overcomes, I will give the right to eat from the tree of life, which is in the paradise of God* (Revelation 2:7).

The Holy Spirit speaks to the listening ear and the receptive heart. He promises a sure pathway to those who acknowledge His efforts to provide guidance and counsel to people in the midst of an unsure situation. Revelation 2:7 indicates that the only prerequisite for receiving instruction from the Holy Spirit is our willingness to listen.

Having a listening ear does not necessarily mean that we will hear God's voice audibly. As a matter of fact, that is a rare occurrence for most Christians. But when we are listening and receptive, the Holy Spirit will indeed speak to us – sometimes as a verse of Scripture stirs us, sometimes as the word of a friend encourages us, sometimes as we are moved during times of prayer. The Holy Spirit speaks, and as we sense His presence we are often provided with His guidance and direction.

Prayer becomes the channel through which the Holy Spirit speaks to the listener. He communicates His thoughts to the human heart and imparts direction in seemingly hopeless situations. He teaches that prayer becomes a two-way conversation in which the listener gains valuable insight while learning to express the needs present in his or her life. When the believer gains direction and counsel, it is because that person heard the heart of the Father through the work of the Holy Spirit. Jesus' words to His disciples are His words to each of us today. Our Advocate still listens and guides us through the demands of life.

He provides instruction and directives about how to execute the will of the Father. He gave instructions to identify and set apart Barnabas and Saul for a special work (Acts 13:2). He touches hearts with a message from the Father. Since He and the Father are one, He always communicates perfectly what the Father desires to accomplish in the lives of obedient followers of Jesus Christ.

He intercedes:

> *In the same way, the Spirit helps us in our weakness. We do not know what we ought to pray for, but the Spirit himself intercedes for us with groans that words cannot express* (Romans 8:26).

As our Advocate, He interprets to the Father the groaning of our hearts when we simply do not know how to pray during a difficult time. He knows perfectly the will of the Father and how to communicate our pain to a loving heavenly Father who then reciprocates by providing mental or spiritual relief during a time of deep anguish. Since we have only the human perspective of our situation, we see **through a glass darkly** (1 Corinthians 13:12). But He sees the big picture. He knows our hearts are so heavy that we cannot feel anything except the pain of the circumstance. This verse literally means that it is God who is praying for us. Can you imagine a better process? God, who has the answer, is also the one praying for us. He stands on our behalf as our Advocate.

He teaches:

> *"But the Counselor, the Holy Spirit, whom the Father will send in my name, will teach you all things and will remind you of everything I have said to you"* (John 14:26).

Perhaps as a new Christian you have wondered how in the world you could ever grasp all that the Bible teaches. Here's the remarkable answer: We have a personal instructor, a "Holy Tutor," who is not only able to help us understand the unchangeable truths of the Word, but who will also help us apply those truths to our

THE HOLY SPIRIT

lives, to our situations. The Holy Spirit is a great teacher!

He influences:

> *"When he comes, he will convict the world of guilt in regard to sin and righteousness and judgment: in regard to sin, because men do not believe in me; in regard to righteousness, because I am going to the Father, where you can see me no longer; and in regard to judgment, because the prince of this world now stands condemned"* (John 16:8-11).

Jesus tells us the Holy Spirit will "convict" or "convince" the world with regard to sin, righteousness, and judgment. You became a Christian because the Holy Spirit was at work, convicting you of your sin and your need to respond to God's offer of love and forgiveness.

He testifies:

> *"When the Counselor comes, whom I will send to you from the Father, the Spirit of truth who goes out from the Father, he will testify about me"* (John 15:26).

As a court of law examines evidence to either support or disavow a claim, a credible witness helps provide a realistic baseline for the proceedings. Once the credibility of the witness is confirmed, the closing arguments for both sides must incorporate information provided by the witness in making their final pleas before the jury. The jury then weighs their arguments based on the testimony of that witness.

The Holy Spirit testifies to the veracity of the claims of Jesus – God the Son. We are then called to make a decision based on the evidence provided. The Holy Spirit of God has the ability to touch our hearts with truth. Since that truth is eternal, the testimony lives on in the hearts and lives of those who decide in favor of Jesus Christ. The Holy Spirit continues to testify to our hearts daily about the goodness and love of the Father, forgiveness of sins, and decisions that are too weighty for us to make alone. He provides the connection to the human heart and continually testifies of the victory Jesus won in a cosmic court to restore us to our rightful inheritance from God.

He leads:

> *The Spirit told Philip, "Go to that chariot and stay near it"* (Acts 8:29).

While life's road contains many twists and turns, the Holy Spirit always leads us in the path of protection and purpose. In Philip's case, the Holy Spirit had a divine appointment for him. A man seeking to know the Scriptures openly invited Philip to explain to him the Holy Scriptures, giving Philip the opportunity to explain God the Father's plan was for all humankind.

Likewise, the Holy Spirit of God desires to transform believers and lead them in the paths of God the Father's providence, protection, purpose, provision, and power. God's immutability (remaining unchangeable over a long period of time) provides confidence in the believer's heart. The Holy Spirit will never lead us astray. He will lead us only in the will of the Father. As we submit to His leading, He constantly demonstrates His faithfulness.

He commands:

> *Paul and his companions traveled throughout the region of Phrygia and Galatia, having been kept by the Holy Spirit from preaching the word in the province of Asia. When they came to the border of Mysia, they tried to enter Bithynia, but the Spirit of Jesus would not allow them to* (Acts 16:6-7).

Someone once said, "God has the right to order our steps and our stops." There are times when our course of action would end in disaster or failure. It is then that the Holy Spirit can reveal the proper course of action (or inaction). The Holy Spirit shuts some doors and opens others. Since He alone really knows the heart of the Father, His course of action is always correct. He will prevent us from pursuing certain agendas so that the will of the Father might be accomplished. He sees the big picture and knows how and when we can proceed without falling off the mission.

The more we rely on the Holy Spirit, the more sensitive we become to His promptings. We trust where we once questioned His motives – thinking that we had misinterpreted His signals. We gain confidence in our utter reliance upon God to lead us through the working of the Holy Spirit. Since victory comes to the obedient heart, we have the opportunity to always walk in victory by listening to His voice and following His lead.

He guides:

> *"But when he, the Spirit of truth, comes, he will guide you into all the truth. He will not speak on his own; he will speak only what he hears, and he will tell you what is yet to come"* (John 16:13).

When a mountain climber undertakes the adventure of climbing a high mountain, he must become a part of a team that has already climbed the mountain or hire a guide who knows the terrain. The individual climber cannot simply show up at Mount Everest's base one day and declare his adventure as a lone wolf to be underway. He must secure the talent and experience of someone who has been there before and knows the inherent dangers and pitfalls of such a climb.

Likewise, the Holy Spirit knows the "terrain." He already knows the dangers ahead. He knows the spiritual battles that await the child of God. He knows the expressions of counterfeit faith and will guide us to truth. His mission is to keep us in the Father's will and may even give us a glimpse of what is ahead – particularly if we become tempted to stray into the counterfeit expressions of God's chosen path. He will help us know beyond a doubt that He knows what is ahead, He has a plan, and He will keep us safe.

He appoints:

> Paul told the elders at Ephesus, *"Keep watch over yourselves and all the flock of which the Holy Spirit has made you overseers. Be shepherds of the church of God, which he bought with his own blood"* (Acts 20:28).

Author A. W. Tozer said that the man who aspires to leadership disqualifies himself from it. The Holy Spirit touches the heart of a potential leader and assures him or her of a divine call into the service of the King of kings. A person cannot simply decide to become an overseer or shepherd. Rather, the Holy Spirit alone executes the will of the Father in calling anyone into His service.

The Bible is clear that as Christians we are all ministers, yet God calls certain ones to fulfill the role of shepherd or overseer. Receiving the call of God on one's life is not dependent on the results of a personality test or a gifts assessment, although these tools may serve as confirmations of that call. The call represents an impartation of divine power and authority to keep the Church of Jesus Christ from wandering into dangerous territory. Since the Holy Spirit knows the heart of man, He knows whom He can trust with such a task and He appoints (calls) certain individuals to abandon the life of a follower and embrace the life of a leader.

The Holy Spirit helps those He appoints to guard their hearts and minds. He grants them an understanding of what is at stake in the awesome responsibility of helping Him guide the formation of less mature Christians or seekers. His appointment carries with it the conviction necessary to become single-minded leaders, intent only on doing the will of the Father.

He can be lied to:

> Then Peter said, *"Ananias, how is it that Satan has so filled your heart that you have lied to the Holy Spirit and have kept for yourself some of the money you received for the land? Didn't it belong to you before it was sold? And after it was sold, wasn't the money at your disposal? What made you think of doing such a thing? You have not lied just to men but to God"* (Acts 5: 3-4).

The early Church was an exciting place to be in the first century. However, one of its first crises was about money. A prominent couple in the church decided to sell property and donate the money to the church. Between the time of the sale and the time of the monetary gift to the church, the couple decided to keep a part of it for themselves but asserted that they were giving it all.

Peter confronted them. He asked them why they had allowed Satan to enter their hearts and hold some of it back. Then he told them, *"You have lied to the Holy Spirit."* Imagine everyone's surprise when the two dropped dead right in front of everyone. Whether their motive was greed or ambition or both, the Holy Spirit knew their hearts and abruptly revealed their deceit.

He can be insulted:

> *How much more severely do you think a man deserves to be punished who has trampled the Son of God under foot, who has treated as an unholy thing the blood of the covenant that sanctified him, and who has insulted the Spirit of grace?* (Hebrews 10:29).

The author of Hebrews mentions those who have made the conscious decision to walk away from the grace that was extended to them for salvation. He speaks of those who experienced the wonderful deliverance from sin yet chose to return to it. The author states that the person guilty of turning away from the faith literally tramples underfoot the Son of God and insults the Spirit of grace.

He can be sinned against:

> *"And so I tell you, every sin and blasphemy will be forgiven men, but the blasphemy against the Spirit will not be forgiven. Anyone who speaks a word against the Son of Man will be forgiven, but anyone who speaks against the Holy Spirit will not be forgiven, either in this age or in the age to come"* (Matthew 12:31-32).

Jesus spoke these words to a group of Pharisees who ascribed His power and authority to Satan rather than to the Spirit of God. Bible teachers sometimes have interpreted these words from Jesus about a sin against the Holy Spirit that is not forgiven as referring to an "unpardonable sin," one in which a person's heart has become so darkened that they actually see the words and actions of the Holy Spirit as coming from Satan himself. Since it is the Holy Spirit who convicts a person of sin, if you fear you have committed the "unpardonable sin" and feel concerned about it, you have not. If you feel conviction in your heart about something you have said or done, the Holy Spirit is still at work in your life and has not been withdrawn from you.

He can be grieved:

> *And do not grieve the Holy Spirit of God, with whom you were sealed for the day of redemption* (Ephesians 4:30).

Any parent knows the pain associated with a rebellious child. A parent feels profound disappointment when a child's behavior goes counter to the instructions for life given by the faithful parent. Likewise, we can grieve the Holy Spirit by actions and attitudes capable of producing and living in sin. This verse states that we are **sealed with the Holy Spirit for the day of redemption.** Yet our unrepentant hearts can actually foul the atmosphere shared with the Holy Spirit.

He has a mind:

> *And he who searches our hearts knows the mind of the Spirit, because the Spirit intercedes for the saints in accordance with God's will* (Romans 8:27).

The Bible indicates that the Holy Spirit is a thoughtful Person. He has a mind, and knows how to use it. He is a thinking being who is fully capable of bringing about resolutions to human situations that seem like dilemmas to us.

He has a will:

> *All these are the work of one and the same Spirit, and he gives them to each one, just as he determines* (1 Corinthians 12:11).

The Holy Spirit determines which gift fits each believer. He can also determine which gifts can do the best for God's Kingdom and who will be responsible to develop those gifts. Gift distribution is not some arbitrary exercise by someone or something not capable of knowing the potential in each believer. It is the Holy Spirit who knows and then decides to give the gifts of the Spirit.

Each of these emotions and acts are characteristics of a person. The Holy Spirit is not an impersonal force like gravity or magnetism. He is a *person* with all the attributes of personality.

THE DIVINE NATURE OF THE HOLY SPIRIT

Throughout the Bible it is clear the Holy Spirit is God. Evidence is found within the Holy Scriptures to indicate that His attributes are those of God Himself.

He is eternal:

> *How much more, then, will the blood of Christ, who through the eternal Spirit offered himself unblemished to God, cleanse our consciences from acts that lead to death, so that we may serve the living God!* (Hebrews 9:14).

The Holy Spirit did not come into existence after the creation of the world, during the crucifixion of Jesus Christ, or at the establishment of the primitive church. He has always been and will always be. God has always existed as God the Father, Son, and Holy Spirit.

He is omnipotent:

> *The angel answered, "The Holy Spirit will come on you, and the power of the Most High will overshadow you"* (Luke 1:35).

The Holy Spirit is also all-powerful. As part of the Trinity, He participated in the creation of the earth. The Holy Spirit is an agent of creation (Genesis 1:1; Job 33:4; Psalm 104:30). He is called the **Spirit of life**, who sets you *free from the law of sin and death* (Romans 8:2). He is stronger than all the might of humankind: *" 'Not by might nor by power, but by my Spirit,' says the Lord Almighty"* (Zechariah 4:6).

He is omnipresent:

> *Where can I go from your Spirit? Where can I flee from your presence?* (Psalm 139:7).

King David realized the awesome truth that the Holy Spirit is everywhere present. He has no spatial boundary. Equally comforting is the understanding that the Holy Spirit knows no boundary of time. *How much more, then, will the blood of Christ, who through the eternal Spirit offered himself unblemished to God, cleanse our consciences from acts that lead to death, so that we may serve the living God!* (Hebrews 9:14).

He is omniscient:

> *However, as it is written: "No eye has seen, no ear has heard, and no mind has conceived what God has prepared for those who love him" – but God has revealed it to us by his Spirit.*
>
> *The Spirit searches all things, even the deep things of God. For who among men knows the thoughts of a man except the man's spirit within him? In the same way no one knows the thoughts of God except the Spirit of God* (1 Corinthians 2:9-11).

Just as God the Father and Jesus the Son are omniscient, so also is the Holy Spirit. The Spirit of God is all knowing. In 1 Samuel 2:3, Hannah says, *"The Lord is a God who knows."* The Holy Spirit is God and knows everything there is to know.

He is called God:

> Then Peter said, "Ananias, how is it that Satan has so filled your heart that you have lied to the Holy Spirit and have kept for yourself some of the money you received for the land? Didn't it belong to you before it was sold? And after it was sold, wasn't the money at your disposal? What made you think of doing such a thing? You have not lied just to men **but to God**" (Acts 5:3-4).

> And we, who with unveiled faces all reflect the Lord's glory, are being transformed into his likeness with ever-increasing glory, which comes from the Lord, **who is the Spirit**" (2 Corinthians 3:18).

He is the Creator:

> Now the earth was formless and empty, darkness was over the surface of the deep, and the Spirit of God was hovering over the waters (Genesis 1:2).

> By the word of the Lord were the heavens made, their starry host by the breath of his mouth (Psalm 33:6).

THE DOCTRINE OF THE TRINITY

God *does* teach the reality of the Trinity, both in the Old and New Testaments. He unfolds His revelation of Himself in the Bible progressively. There are indications from the very beginning of the book of Genesis that God subsists in three persons: the Father, the Son, and the Holy Spirit.

Who is more important? Why is the Holy Spirit always mentioned last? It has to do with function. We pray *to* the Father, *through* the Son, *in the power* of the Holy Spirit. The order has nothing to do with equality. Instead, function and chronology are the focal points of understanding this complex issue.

THE HOLY SPIRIT IN THE OLD TESTAMENT
As Creator

The Scriptures appear to indicate that the Holy Spirit was clearly active in at least three aspects of creation. Genesis 1:2 involves the Holy Spirit in the creation of the heavens and the earth. Genesis 1:26 states, *"Let us make man,"* which indicates His participation as a member of the Godhead in the creation of man. (Also review Genesis 2:7 and Job 33:4.) Finally, Psalm 104 (especially verse 30) describes His role in the creation of the animal kingdom. Other Scriptures include:

> *In the beginning God created the heavens and the earth* (Genesis 1:1).

> *Then God said, "Let us make man in our image, in our likeness, and let them rule over the fish of the sea and the birds of the air, over the livestock, over all the earth, and over all the creatures that move along the ground"* (Genesis 1:26).

> *And the Lord God said, "The man has now become like one of us, knowing good and evil. He must not be allowed to reach out his hand and take also from the tree of life and eat, and live forever"* (Genesis 3:22).

> *The Lord said, "If as one people speaking the same language they have begun to do this, then nothing they plan to do will be impossible for them. Come, let us go down and confuse their language so they will not understand each other"* (Genesis 11:6-7).

As Prophet

The Holy Spirit seems to have ministered in very specific ways in the Old Testament era, coming upon particular people for a particular purpose. This happened often in the case of the prophets. When we think of the prophets, we usually focus on the eschatological aspects of their ministry, those things that deal with the last days. Certainly the Holy Spirit inspired men and women in this way so that they could "see" into the future (Ezekiel 8). But the role of the prophet was also to declare the present will of God with clarity and authority. Here, too, the Holy Spirit played an important role in calling, encouraging, and inspiring the prophets (Isaiah 6).

THE HOLY SPIRIT IN THE NEW TESTAMENT

More light is shed on the Holy Spirit in the New Testament. Jesus had to establish an understanding for His continued presence.

> *Then Jesus came to them and said, "All authority in heaven and on*

earth has been given to me. Therefore go and make disciples of all nations, baptizing them in the name of the Father and of the Son and of the Holy Spirit, and teaching them to obey everything I have commanded you. And surely I am with you always, to the very end of the age"* (Matthew 28:18-20).

He promised a Helper in His absence. He did not leave His followers without hope or direction.

"And I will ask the Father, and he will give you another Counselor to be with you forever – the Spirit of truth. The world cannot accept him, because it neither sees him nor knows him. But you know him, for he lives with you and will be in you" (John 14:16-17).

The Apostle Paul also made reference to the Holy Spirit's abiding presence:

May the grace of the Lord Jesus Christ, and the love of God, and the fellowship of the Holy Spirit be with you all (2 Corinthians 13:14).

THE HOLY SPIRIT IN THE LIFE OF THE CHRISTIAN

Once the Holy Spirit has brought spiritual birth to one's heart, He doesn't leave the believer to wonder if he or she really can be assured of salvation. Romans 8:16 offers the marvelous promise: **The Spirit himself testifies with our spirit that we are God's children.** Not only that, but a follower of Christ is also then sealed by the Holy Spirit. Using a real estate transaction as a metaphor, He Himself becomes the "earnest money" that promises our full redemption.

And you also were included in Christ when you heard the word of truth, the gospel of your salvation. Having believed, you were marked in him with a seal, the promised Holy Spirit, who is a deposit guaranteeing our inheritance until the redemption of those who are God's possession – to the praise of his glory (Ephesians 1:13-14).

The Apostle Paul gives valuable insight into the Holy Spirit's defense system for the maturing believer. In his letter to the Galatian church, he writes, ***But the fruit of the Spirit is love, joy, peace, patience, kindness, goodness, faithfulness, gentleness, and self-control*** (Galatians 5:22-23). As the new Christian grows, these fruits should become more and more evident.

The Holy Spirit is infinitely practical in His ministry. He sets us in the "kingdom of light," then gives us the tools to stand in victory. Even beyond that, He offers the means by which we can find satisfaction and fulfillment in service to others on His behalf. The ability to serve is found in power. The Holy Spirit is our source of power. He baptizes and fills us so that we might have power for service. ***"But you will receive power when the Holy Spirit comes on you; and you will be my witnesses"*** (Acts 1:8).

To study the Holy Spirit is not to study only the past power of the Church, but also the *present potential* that lies unleashed within the Body of Christ. We must move from theory and theology to reality and revelation concerning the essential empowerment by the Holy Spirit of God. As we embrace and receive the power of the Holy Spirit in our lives, we will experience the fulfillment of God's design and desire for us.

Related Scriptures

God the Holy Spirit -
Genesis 1:2; John 14:26, 15:26, 16:8; Acts 1:8

God -
Genesis 1:26; Matthew 3:16-17; 2 Corinthians 13:14; 1 Timothy 1:17; 1 John 5:7

For Further Reading

Bach, R. A. Bach & Schmidt, D. M., eds. *We Believe: Principles in Christian Living*. Des Moines, IA: Open Bible Publishers, 1992.

Time to Interact

Take some time to interact with the following questions. Consider writing your answers in a journal and/or discussing them with a fellow believer for deeper reflection and insight.

1. What misconceptions have you held or observed in others regarding the Holy Spirit? How did this chapter help your understanding? What truths stood out to you? What new questions were created?

2. In what ways have you heard the Holy Spirit's voice? How did you

know the voice was His? What did you do after hearing Him? What was the result?

3. Of the many descriptions of the Holy Spirit mentioned in this chapter (including Intercessor, Advocate/Helper, Counselor/Teacher, One who convicts, Testifier, Leader) how have you encountered Him? In what role do you need Him right now?

4. Have you ever been concerned that you had grieved or sinned against the Holy Spirit? If so, how can you be made right with Him? How will you live out your repentance?

Time to Integrate

As you yield to the presence and power of the Holy Spirit, invite Him to make Himself known in and through your life in stronger measure.

1. How has the Holy Spirit possibly empowered you to serve? Ask Him to reveal His heart for the people in your sphere of influence and to show you how He wants to better connect them to the love of God. For each face He brings to mind, choose to depend on His power to make a difference by serving them with some practical steps.

2. We are meant to grow in relationship with the Holy Spirit. What is your next step? What apprehensions do you have? Spend some time in prayer, asking the Holy Spirit to make Himself known to you in greater ways. Ask Him to open your eyes to teachable moments and sudden encounters in His presence.

3. Consider what it might look like to keep a deliberate record of the work and ministry of the Holy Spirit in your life. Write in a journal what you sense Him saying. As you evaluate what you feel He is saying to you according to the Scripture and begin to incorporate His voice into your daily decisions, what is the impact? How does your ability to discern His voice improve?

CHAPTER 5

Creation, Humanity, Sin, Angels, Demons:
His World

CHAPTER 5
Creation, Humanity, Sin, Angels, Demons:
His World

GOD
> We believe in God the Father, the co-Creator with the Son and the Holy Spirit, who is the eternal, all-powerful, all-knowing, everywhere-present, and unchangeable Creator of all."

THE FALL OF MANKIND
> "We believe the human race is fallen from its original, created goodness because of the sin of Adam and Eve in the Garden of Eden."

CREATION

Does it really matter whether God created the universe or whether it exists and is sustained by some unseen force called *evolution*? It matters completely, because the answer is brought to bear on how one will approach every facet of life as a matter of philosophy. Would there be societal order in the absence of a justice system's creation or anarchy, as individuals choose their own course to rectify what they consider wrongs?

Critics of scientific creationism warn, "Beware of predetermined scientific conclusions dressed in the garb of religious conviction" while critics of evolution warn, "Beware of predetermined religious conclusions dressed in the garb of scientific convictions."

Adherents to either philosophy usually begin with a theological premise – most often, "God exists" or "God does not exist." Believers in both philosophies attempt to make the facts fit their premise.

Open Bible Churches believes, however, that science and Scripture, the heavens and the earth – even the existence of the human conscience and its drive to find truth – speak for themselves: Everything living has its origins in something that was living.

Original Design

In the beginning God created the heavens and the earth (Genesis 1:1). Evidence of a Creator abounds everywhere, every day, in the 360,000 childbirths a day, at tens of thousands of architects' drawing boards, at thousands of easels and art galleries, on factory assembly lines (mechanized or not), in church planting.... **Life comes from life; organization from an organizer; design from a designer.**

Has anyone seen a building constructed by a hurricane? How about an organism assembled by an explosion? The answer is *never* and the science is settled. Disorder does not produce order. Life comes from living things.

God's original intent for all of nature, for all of humanity's experience regarding relationship to and with Him, was one of harmony. Moreover, Scripture reaffirms the biblical account in Genesis by describing the origins of all things as a work of creation and ascribing it all to a Creator (Nehemiah 9:6; Job 12:7-10; Psalm 19:1-4; 24:1-2; 33:5-6; 89:11; 104:24-25; 145:9, 13; 148:1-6; Matthew 19:4, Mark 10:6; John 1:1-4; Romans 1:20; 8:19-21; Colossians 1:15-16; 1 Peter 4:19; Revelation 4:11).

Evolutionists assert that *nothing* except random chance, in connection with survival of the fittest, produced the human brain. What are the odds that nothing produced something? Since **survival of the fittest** does nothing but remove changes that were created by chance, it is chance and chance alone that is supposed to create the changes in the first place. This line of reasoning is circular.

Compare, Contrast, Conclusion

Is the God of the Bible an absentee landlord who constructed a system and then gave its governance over to a force that would take all things in an upward spiral, as most agnostics believe? If evolution as a guiding principle and force is true, then why does science demonstrate that all systems are in a state of degradation or simplification?

Evolution – and increase in complexity and diversity – being the force that governs natural systems is not observable, measurable, conclusive, or repeatable. However, that order, complexity, design and life originate from order, complexity, design, and life is clearly observable, measurable, conclusive, and repeatable.

God's Hallmark in Creation: Humanity

When God created all things, He spoke the words (Genesis 1:3, 5, 6, 8, 9-10, 11, 14-15, 20, 22, 24). In an age where talk is all around us 24/7 – and "cheap" – it is comforting to know that when God speaks, tremendous things happen!

What Distinguishes Man from the Rest of Creation?

The pinnacle of all creation's work was announced in these words: *"Let us make man in our image, after our likeness ... ."*

Consider this from the narrative of Genesis (1:26-28; 2:7-8, 15-17, 18-25):

- Humankind is the expression of God's special creation made in His image.

- Humankind is the expression of God's creation specifically mentioned as having directly received life by God's breath.

- No other creature is given responsibility for the rest of creation like humankind was.

- No other creature was given stewardship to tend the earth for its wellbeing.

Does this mean God doesn't care what happens to animals? No, of course not. It means quite the opposite (Proverbs 12:10; Matthew 6:26). Humankind holds the highest place of privilege *and* responsibility for stewardship of the earth. God created it and then appointed humankind its manager (Genesis 1:26-28).

Why is this? What is it that distinguishes humans from the rest of creation? Several things:

Genetics:

- Many with an evolutionary bent become very excited at the genetic similarities between humankind and animals, going so far as to suggest that the similarities are evidence that humans and animals spring from the same primordial origins. However, genetics are God's delivery system for each species to produce after its own kind. It is genetic distinction (of a few percentage points) that dictates that humans come from humans, apes from apes, earthworms from earthworms, canines from canines, and so forth.

Cognitive Functions:

- Reason – Humankind's ability to ponder our role and purpose in the universe is self evident. Reason is also the primary component in the ideas of logic, problem-solving, and mathematics – three of the most important distinctions humans enjoy in contrast to the animal kingdom. Nature demonstrates that any ecosystem's predators will at best tolerate one another's presence until there is conflict for prey. Humans, on the other hand, demonstrate a distinction from animals in an ability and willingness to enter into contracts with one another for each party to benefit in economic purposes.

- Conscience – Humankind demonstrates the ability to distinguish between right and wrong, declare what is good or evil, determine what is moral and immoral, and decide guilt or innocence. Humankind is the only species on the planet that has institutionalized the idea of civic responsibility based on moral obligations to others in public and private entities.

- Creative abilities – Animals have proven they have the ability to be trained. Primates have been trained to paint and build fires, birds to mimic language, canines to do tricks and obey commands, porpoises to soar out of the water and jump through hoops. However, humans demonstrate an innate sense of creativity and the ability to engineer and construct on a significant scale that distinguishes us from animals.

Communication:

- Can plants and animals communicate with one another? Science has determined this is possible for plants (for example, same-species signaling through release of organic compounds). For animals, this happens inside and outside of their respective species by nonverbal communication. (For example, after enduring the pain of hundreds of quills in their muzzles young mountain lions learn that a bristling porcupine is communicating, "Back off!"). Nonverbal communication is certainly a shared communication between animals and humans.

Animals, like humans, can also communicate verbally. Their calls are signals to others in their species that there is food nearby to be consumed or that the one bugling, hooting, and/or howling is ready to mate. Communication is an essential part of animal survival. Even the marvelous and numerous dolphin species of the world seem to have an ability to express their apparent happiness to the delight of camera-toting humans at water's edge. That said, has one ever deciphered – much less, discovered – an alphabet created by dolphins?

What distinguishes humans from the animal and plant kingdom is our ability to communicate in *language*, both written and verbal. Can a human of Hispanic descent learn to communicate verbally with another human of Chinese descent who speaks Mandarin? Yes, of course. And while a moose understands the primal communication in a gray wolf's howl (having to do with survival), humans communicate at the deepest levels through language both written and verbal. Through these means we can connect to another's very heart, soul, mind, and spirit.

Composition:

Do humankind and animal share facets of being? The answer is yes. Let's compare and contrast two schools of thought concerning man's composition.

Trichotomy is the belief that human beings are composed of three parts: a spirit, soul, and body (1 Thessalonians 5:23). Briefly, let's elaborate on each of these three. The soul is the seat of one's personality on earth; the eternal self that will, redeemed, exist forever to dwell rewarded in God's presence or will, unredeemed, exist forever to be punished in hell for rejecting His offer of salvation (Luke 16:19-31). The body is the material housing for one's spiritual components and the physical vehicle by which one experiences life through sensory perceptions. The spirit, mankind's immaterial self, discerns and decides to reflect the character of sin, Satan, or the Savior; the seat of human will and cognition.

The Apostle Paul, writing to the church at Thessalonica, identifies three distinct parts of mankind: spirit, soul, and body (1 Thessalonians 5:23). As well, the author of Hebrews declares the soul and spirit distinguishable (Hebrews 4:12).

Dichotomy is the belief that humans are made of a material self and a spiritual self because only two distinct parts, the body formed of the dust of the earth and the breath of God, are mentioned in Genesis 2:7. Soul and spirit are inseparable and the term is used interchangeably (John 12:27, 13:21).

It has been said that all living creatures have souls, but only mankind has a spirit; however, scholars assert that Scripture attributes both soul and spirit to the animal kingdom (Ecclesiastes 3:21; Psalm 104:25-30). Regardless whether humankind and animals share the same composition – body, soul, and spirit (whether in trichotomist or dichotomist arrangement) – humans are distinguished from animals by the *quality of our faculties*, not their number.

Comparatively, one may ask, then, "If the number is the same, and only the quality different, don't animals need to be saved from sin?" The answer is no because Scripture is clear that while all of creation exists under the curse of sin, only humankind needed to be redeemed from sin as it was brought into the world through an act of the first man's will (Genesis 3; Romans 5:12-21).

THE FALL OF HUMANKIND AND ITS CONSEQUENCES

God's original design for humankind was relational at its core. Note in the Genesis account of creation that God actually came into Eden to interact with Adam and Eve. *Then the man and his wife heard the sound of the Lord God as he was walking in the garden in the cool of the day* (Genesis 3:8).

This passage indicates that Adam and Eve were familiar enough with the Lord's presence and manner that they knew it was Him moving through the garden. It also indicates that God, who could have easily spoken to

Adam and Eve from His throne, actually chose – perhaps even preferred – to be in their immediate proximity. And because Adam and Eve had already disobeyed His commands and thus fallen into a sinful state, this clearly demonstrates that God's preference for relationship with the pinnacle of His creation is to be near rather than relate through distant pronouncements. This preference was repeated later on Mount Sinai when God came down to Moses personally and gave humanity the Ten Commandments written by His own finger (Exodus 31:18).

The Fall and Its Meaning

When Adam and Eve plunged the human race into a sinful state, they created a spiritual barrier for humankind that severed our direct access to relationship with our Creator.

An important doctrinal point in the story of creation's plunge into sin's curse is clearly on display for all to see and understand: humankind cannot satisfy the justice necessary to atone for (cover) our sinful state. We cannot penetrate that barrier on our own.

Note that just prior to God coming down to be with Adam and Eve, now shamefully aware of their physical nakedness, they made clothes out of fig leaves to cover themselves in an attempt to alleviate their embarrassment (Genesis 7).

The lesson? Humankind's attempts to fix our fallen spiritual state fail to satisfy the laws of a holy Creator God. Concerning any of our good works, there is no quantity or quality sufficient to earn a place before a perfect God. Our attempts to penetrate the barrier separating us directly and personally from God's presence are in vain.

Perhaps the mostly widely-known verse in the Bible (that even the unchurched can quote) is John 3:16: *"For God so loved the world that he gave his one and only Son, that everyone who believes in him shall not perish but have eternal life."*

Why is this verse quoted so often? Because it explains the very heart of the Christian gospel: God loves humanity so much that He authored the plan to purchase us back from the guarantee of sin's eventual end, which is eternal separation from God.

The Role of Free Will

One may ask, "If God loves humankind so much, how did He let us fall into such a state and destiny?"

The answer to that question cuts right to the issue of humanity's creation with a "free will," the ability to choose the path we prefer to travel in life. It was by the exercise of their free will that the first two humans were responsible for each of us being born in an innately fallen spiritual state, or simply, why we're born into sin – its conditions, effects, and eventual payday.

But our loving God, of His own will, created a fix for humankind's fallen state. We're privileged to see the very first demonstration of responsibility He would take to remedy the problem of original sin (the sin of Adam and Eve in the Garden of Eden) – not because it is His fault, but because, as God, He is able to conquer the law of sin's consequences.

The Consequences of Sin

Everything costs something – every action and every inaction.

Burning a gallon of fuel results in a loss of energy. Harsh words spoken to a loved one result in relational harm. Failure to maintain a building results in its degradation. Infidelity costs trust. Government spending costs revenue generated from taxpayers. It even costs calories to get up off the couch and flip the light switch on or off. Philosophically and literally, this is in keeping with laws of physics.

Separation

Adam's sin, which is also our sin, cost us the human race's immediate right standing with God (Genesis 3:6; Romans 5:12). The evidence of righteousness lost is found in Genesis 3:7, **Then the eyes of both of them were opened, and they realized they were naked.**

God, by His all-knowing nature (omniscience), knew Adam and Eve had sinned before He arrived in the garden, before He inquired as to their location. In their answers to God's questions found in Genesis 3:8-11, we find evidence that humans are now separated from a nature they once enjoyed.

Shame

When our eyes open to the guilt of our sinfulness, the immediate result is shame. Unlike the quality of *modesty*, this sort of shame is related to embarrassment and remorse.

Note in the Genesis account (3:8) Adam's and Eve's attempt to hide from God. Their feeble attempt to cover their physical nakedness didn't satisfy God.

This narrative carries a deep message: humankind can do much to change their outward appearance, but can do nothing in their own power to genuinely liberate their inclination to sinfulness (a bent for breaking God's commands). The response to that inability produces shame in our hearts before a holy God.

The Holy Spirit attempts to turn the eyes of an honest sinner toward a gracious Savior. Humans' sinful nature attempts to do something else entirely.

The initial human response to our sinfulness can be seen as history's first example of "passing the buck." It was the scene played out in Genesis 3:12-13 when, confronted by God for his disobedience, Adam immediately shirked his responsibility for sin's entrance into the human race by blaming Eve. When God turned to Eve for an explanation, she, without hesitation uttered humanity's first "the devil made me do it" defense, shirking her responsibility too for exercising her free will.

Since that day humankind has made an art of shifting blame onto others for our own sinful choices in an attempt to cope with sin's second consequence of shame. Somehow the human heart and mind figures that if blame can be assigned elsewhere the pain of sin's shame will be assuaged.

Humans are well noted for wanting the pleasure of sin's practice without the price of sin's pain. It is curious how so many people remain committed to that proposition to this day.

Death

The most disastrous of effects felt after humankind's fall was death and its curse upon nature. God had warned Adam and Eve about the consequences of eating from the tree of knowledge of good and evil when He said, *"for when you eat of it you will certainly die"* (Genesis 2:17). Nonetheless Adam and Eve ate fruit from the tree.

As God had promised, the two were exiled from Eden, from the tree of life, and from God's direct presence. And they now had knowledge of evil and death. Scripture identifies death in three categories:

- Physical Death. By definition, physical death is the separation of one's soul from one's body at the time when that body ceases all biological functions necessary for sustaining a living organism. God announced this as humankind's eventual end as a consequence of sin (Genesis 3:19).

  Adam did not physically die right away, of course, but having exchanged eternal life for disobedience, he eventually died at 930 years of age because the processes of mortality were instituted by his sin (Romans 5:12).

- Spiritual Death. Spiritual death is relational separation from God in this temporal age. All unbelievers are alienated from God by sin (Ephesians 2:1-3, 5). The difference between spiritual death and spiritual life is this: having one's spirit remain dead and unresponsive to the things of God as opposed to being alive and discerning of those things because Christ's resurrection power has regenerated one's spirit unto life (Ephesians 2:2, 5; 4:18; 5:14; Colossians 2:13).

- Eternal Death. Eternal death is the destination and state of those separated from God's presence to abide in hell forever. Eternal death is the paycheck for the terminally unbelieving, unrepentant, and disobedient (Romans 6:23; 2 Thessalonians 1:7-10).

  Eternal death is also referred to as the "second death." After an unbeliever's physical death, they are carried away to languish in hell until the end of the future thousand-year reign of Christ, when at the Great White Throne, unbelievers will be resurrected to face judgment for their evil works and consignment into the lake of fire (Luke 16:19-31; Revelation 20:11-15).

Results of the Fall

First, God pronounced His judgment upon the serpent (Genesis 3:14-15). He assured him of his humiliating position in history when He said, *"You will eat dust all the days of your life"* (Genesis 3:14).

Satan's humiliation was foretold in what scholars have deemed the *protoevangelium*, "the first gospel." These verses contain the first Messianic promise, *"And I will put enmity between you and the woman, and between your offspring and hers; he will crush your head* [eventually fulfilled at an empty grave], *and you will strike his heel* [Jesus' suffering and death at Calvary]" (Genesis 3:15).

Second, God pronounced judgment upon Eve; she would experience pain and sorrow in child birthing (Genesis 3:16). Evidently, prior to the fall, God designed females to enjoy a gestation and birth process that was completely joyous and painless.

Third, God pronounced judgment upon man. That judgment was not, contrary to popular belief, labor in general. To engage gainfully and honestly in labor is actually one of God's great gifts and blessings.

The judgment God specified for Adam was "painful toil." What would have been an otherwise enjoyable and highly fruitful endeavor was now to change. Instead of managing land that worked easily and in harmony with Adam and his descendants, the land would be cursed to not work so easily (Genesis 3:18-19). In fact the work changed from *simple* to *sweaty*.

The Plan of Redemption

Our natural state of sinfulness separates us from relationship with God. But note that after humans' first demonstration of sin's effects, God did something that is often overlooked because it is misunderstood. To demonstrate His love while still satisfying a law to be revealed later, God made a way of redeeming humans back into relationship with Him by the shedding of blood and then covered Adam and Eve with the product of the dead animal.

> *The Lord God made garments of skin for Adam and his wife and clothed them* (Genesis 3:21).

In John 3:16 we see this very same act: God so loves us that He gave His only begotten Son, Jesus, to sacrifice His life and shed His blood so that, for those who will believe in Him (place their trust in His work at Calvary as being sufficient to satisfy God's law) that original design for direct relationship with our Creator can be reestablished.

Original and Continuing Sin

It's a rather modern question with quite ancient roots: "Are we born innately sinful or are we born innately good and then corrupted by our environment?"

Many secularists, social scientists, and adherents to New Age religious philosophy believe the latter: that we are born in a state of mental, emotional, and spiritual perfection, each with a spark of the divine within. Each of us can choose to stifle that inner divinity on the path to godhood through failure to deal with life's imperfect situations and people. The alternative is that we can enjoy personal divinity through mastering our souls, hearts, and minds.

According to Eastern mystical and New Age thought the aim of life is to nurture that divine spark through all means possible and look within the human heart for life's answers. In actuality New Age is Old Age. The very first lie of New Age philosophy ever told was spoken by Satan in the Garden of Eden:

> *"You will not certainly die," the serpent said to the woman. "For God knows that when you eat from it your eyes will be opened, and you will be like God, knowing good and evil"* (Genesis 3:4-5).

Satan promised Eve the same thing New Age promises the human race today: "You can be a god," or – even more outlandish – "You can be God."

The mainstream teaching of Judeo-Christian thought concerning the basis of where trouble for the human race begins is the exact opposite. It states clearly:

- The human race's primary problem is of a spiritual nature with which we're inherently born.

- That spiritual problem needs to be fixed, and that fix comes from outside of humankind.

Jesus dubbed Satan the "father of lies" for good reason (John 8:44). While the devil was correct when he told Eve that the opening of her and Adam's eyes would make them like God in the sense that they would then know what good and evil is, the deception was in the impression he gave that such knowledge would put humanity on par with God. Satan is masterful in promising spiritual inches that he turns into eternally destructive miles.

Are humans really born with divinity in their hearts and then brought lower by environmental factors such as discouraging voices or unloving people? The answer is self-evident: A God or god (perfect and unequaled in strength by nature) could never be deceived or brought down. But that's the New Age movement's constant aim, to convince others that they are gods and can overcome.

It's also self-evident that the Judeo-Christian tradition identifies and addresses the real trouble for the human condition: we are born sinners and we need God to fix the problem.

When we speak of ***original sin***, we do so with two thoughts in mind. The first thought is in reference to Adam's first act of disobedience (Genesis 3:6). The second thought is in reference to the effect of the first act of sin passed down from Adam onward, every human's sinful nature.

This sinful nature is what theologians call "depravity." It consists of four conditions with which every human is born:

- We lack the righteous standing Adam and Eve originally enjoyed before the fall (Job 15:14, 16; Psalms 14:1; 51:5; 53:1; Romans 3:10).
- The natural inclination of our hearts, minds, souls, and spirits shows no affection toward God (Jeremiah 17:9; Romans 1:25; 2 Timothy 3:2-4).
- Our sinful actions begin inside, then manifest in our actions (Mark 7:15, 21-23).
- We demonstrate a natural bent toward evil things (Isaiah 53:6; Romans 3:11-18).

Depravity as an idea doesn't mean that individuals aren't born with some innately admirable human qualities or that they are prone to commit every sin imaginable (Matthew 23:23; Mark 10:17-21). It simply means that every human is born into a sinful state without the love of God necessary to fulfill His law (Deuteronomy 6:4-6; Matthew 22:34-39; 2 Timothy 3:2-4) *(Lectures in Systematic Theology,* by Henry C. Thiessen).

Take babies, for example. They are adorable. They long to be loved and that is compelling. When they become toddlers, they begin to do and say amusing things. Then they discover their free will and one of the first words they learn is "no." Normally this "no" is used in defiant response to being told what to do for their own good.

Who taught that child disobedience? What environmental factors instructed the child to be defiant? Mom? Dad? The television? Would it help if the family lived in a better house and had more money?

Original sin is clearly on display in children at early ages in every economic class, type of family, ethnicity, religion, and culture.

The Battle We Face with Continuing Sin

The New Testament discusses both "sin," referring to our inherited sinful nature that we are born into (Romans 3:23; 5:12; 6:12, 23), and "sins," which are expressions of that sin nature as we carry out acts of disobedience to God's commandments (John 8:34; Romans 7:8-9).

First, let's address an erroneous belief. Some teach that when we are saved from sin we will no longer commit sins. In essence, salvation through Jesus means being made new and completely liberated from any capacity for temptation to sin. If this were accurate, then Scriptures calling us to avoid practicing sinfulness in the New Testament would serve no purpose whatsoever to the function of Christ's Body, the Church. Scripture is clear that sins may be committed by both unbelievers and believers, all of whom are harmed by them and in need of God's grace.

The Holy Spirit offers this warning to Christ's followers (not unbelievers) through Peter's pen:

> B*e self-controlled and alert. Your enemy the devil prowls around like a roaring lion looking for someone to devour. Resist him, standing firm in the faith* (1 Peter 5:8-9).

And, again, through Paul's words: *and do not give the devil a foothold* (Ephesians 4:27).

And, yet again:

> *And what I have forgiven – if there was anything to forgive – I have forgiven in the sight of Christ for your sake, in order that Satan might not outwit us. For we are not unaware of his schemes* (2 Corinthians 2:10-11).
>
> *Be very careful, then, how you live – not as unwise but as wise* (Ephesians 5:15).
>
> *Therefore do not let sin reign in your mortal body so that you obey its evil desires* (Romans 6:12).
>
> *The acts of the sinful nature are obvious…. I warn you, as I did before, that those who live like this will not inherit the kingdom of God* (Galatians 5:19-21).

Why would the Lord caution us in His word about the activities of Satan if our capacity for temptation and to be deceived had been removed at salvation? Like physical buildings our "spiritual houses" require maintenance. The ravages of a sinful nature and the enemy's schemes pose a constant threat to the believer's relationship with Christ.

We should battle against sin (and sins), not because Jesus' mercy is insufficient, but because sin's continuing assault wears on our resolve to remain faithful. This is why Jesus instructed us to take up our crosses daily (Luke 9:23) and the apostle Paul exhorts us to pray *on all occasions with all kinds of prayers and requests* (Ephesians 6:18).

ANGELS AND DEMONS

Who are angels? Where did they come from? What does the Bible say about them?

Who are demons? Where did they come from? What does the Bible say about them?

Who Angels Are

Whether in the language of the original Old Testament (Hebrew: malak) or that of the original manuscripts of the New Testament (Greek:

angelos), the English word *angel* means "messenger." (*Angelos* is used 181 times in the New Testament alone.)

Vast in numbers, angels, though not eternal beings like Him, were created by God. On that Scripture is clear (Nehemiah 9:6; Psalm 148:5; Colossians 1:16). It isn't clear at what point in the creation narrative that occurred, but Nehemiah 9:6 and Job 38:4-7 offer the strongest indication that the angels' creation occurred with the rest of God's creative activity outlined in Genesis 1-2.

According to Scripture, angels are rational spirits (2 Samuel 14:20; Luke 15:10; 1 Peter 1:12). They were created lower than God, yet higher than man in form and abilities, freer in relation to time and the dimension to which we are consigned (Psalm 104:4; Luke 24:4-8; Hebrews 1:14). While angels are able to move in and out of the realm in which they live, they are not able to be in more than one place at a time (omnipresent, or all-present).

Also important to note is that while angels are normally invisible to humans they do appear to humans on special occasions. They have an ability to appear for God's special intentions, never for their own purpose, though they possess a free will just as humankind does (2 Peter 2:4; Jude 6; Revelation 12:7).

The Purpose of Angels

Angels are servants to both God and humankind.

In relation to God the Father:

- Angels' most important ministry is to give unceasing praise to God, who is worthy (Psalm 103:20-21; Luke 2:14; Hebrews 1:6; Revelation 5:11-12).

- They bring the law of God to His people (Acts 7:53; Galatians 3:19; Hebrews 2:2).

- They assist with and execute God's judgments upon His enemies (2 Kings 19:35; Matthew 13:30, 39, 49-50; Acts 12:23; 2 Thessalonians 1:7-8; Revelation 7-20).

- They will gather all of those chosen by God when Christ returns to the earth (Matthew 24:30-31).

In relation to God the Son, Jesus Christ:

- Angels were messengers announcing the birth of Jesus and of John the Baptist, Christ's forerunner, and of the many conditions surrounding both (Matthew 1:20; 2:13, 19-20; Luke 1:11-13, 26-28; 2:8-15).

- Angels ministered to Jesus after His temptation in the wilderness (Matthew 4:11).

- Jesus told His disciple Nathanael that he would see "angels of God ascending and descending" upon Himself (John 1:51).

- An angel strengthened Jesus in the Garden of Gethsemane (Luke 22:43).

- Angels could protect and deliver Jesus physically if Father God willed (Matthew 26:53)

- An angel rolled back the stone from Jesus' grave and announced His resurrection to the women who came that morning (Matthew 28:2-7).

- Angels were present and told a message of the future return of Jesus at His ascension (Acts 1:10-11).

- Angels offer Jesus the highest honor and acknowledge His lordship in His exalted state (1 Peter 3:22).

- Angels will return with Jesus at His Second Coming (Matthew 16:27; 25:31).

In relation to Christ's followers:

- They are charged to help protect us (Genesis 19:15-16; 2 Kings 6:15-17; Psalm 34:7; 68:17; 91:11-12; Daniel 6:22; Acts 12:11).

- They are charged with helping to encourage us in times of trial (Genesis 28:12-13; 32:1-2; 1 Kings 19:5; Acts 27:22-24).

- They are charged with helping give guidance and wisdom (Matthew 1:20; 2:13, 19-20; Acts 8:26; 10:3-5).

- They are charged with escorting our souls to our destination upon physical death (Luke 16:22).

- They rejoice when every soul is saved (Luke 12:8-9; 15:10).
- They long to know more about our salvation through Christ (1 Peter 1:10-12).

Angels are not the portly young cherubs portrayed in flea market figurines. They are capable, powerful, magnificent creatures whose obedience to the Lord in ministering to us is made clear in Scripture (Hebrews 1:14).

Satan is a Fallen Angel

Adam and Eve's sin was the first act of human disobedience and rebellion, but it wasn't the first sin in the universe. Credit for that falls to Satan (meaning adversary), an angel whose original name was Lucifer. It was he, in serpent form, who called into question God's commandment and tempted Eve into partaking of the fruit back in Eden (Genesis 3:1-6).

There are only three angels identified by personal name in Scripture:

- Michael – means who is like God, the Archangel (Daniel 10:13, 21; 12:1, Jude 9; Revelation 12:7-9)
- Gabriel – means the mighty one, bearer of great tidings (Daniel 8:15-27; 9:20-27; Luke 1:13, 19, 26-38)
- Lucifer – means morning star, literally, light bearer (Isaiah 14:12-17); the anointed cherub that covers (Ezekiel 28:12-19).

Lucifer is portrayed to us as the highest angel of God's creation, for Scripture goes into much more detail about his characteristics than those of the other angels. Isaiah 14:12-17 tells of his fall from heaven and the reason for it. Some have referred to it as The Five "I Wills":

- *You said in your heart, "I will ascend to the heavens"*
- *"I will raise my throne above the stars* (angels) *of God"*
- *"I will sit enthroned on the mount of assembly, on the utmost heights of the sacred mountain"*
- *"I will ascend above the tops of the clouds"*
- *"I will make myself like the Most High"*

Take note of that fifth "I will." Curiously, Satan believed this possible for himself and tempted Eve with the very same lie. Thus, the first act of disobedience and rebellion was a free will choice to declare independence from God.

The book of Revelation summarizes God's plan for redemption in beautiful allegory, including the satanic rebellion which broke out in heaven, his defeat, and eviction (Revelation 12:1-10). Of this event, Jesus said He witnessed Satan fall as lightning from heaven (Luke 10:18).

Demons

Upon his rebellious declaration of independence from God it is evident that Satan succeeded in convincing a third of the angels (referred to as stars) in heaven to side with him (Revelation 12:4, 7-9; Matthew 12:24; 25:41; 2 Peter 2:4; Jude 6). To reputable scholars this is the most plausible explanation of what demons are, fallen angels. And inasmuch as God pronounced all things He created as "good" when His work was completed (Genesis 1:31, with Genesis 2 serving as elaboration on the chapter 1 synopsis) it may be that between chapters 2 and 3 we have the best indication of when the rebellion occurred.

Demons are active in six functions:

- Opposing Christ's followers (Ephesians 6:12; 1 Thessalonians 2:18)
- Leading Christians astray (1 Timothy 4:1-4)
- Backing all idolatry (1 Corinthians 10:19-21; Revelation 9:20)
- Serving as the cause of some physical afflictions (Matthew 9:32-33; 12:22; Mark 9:18, 22; Luke 8:26-35; Luke 13:11-17)
- Being used by God as instruments of punishment against the ungodly (1 Samuel 16:14; 1 Kings 22:23; Psalm 78:49; Revelation 16:13-16)
- Being used by God as instruments of discipline for the godly (Luke 22:31; 1 Corinthians 5:5; 1 Timothy 1:20)

Demons should not be taken lightly, yet they are creatures who must respond to the authority of Jesus Christ. Christians who know their standing as followers of Christ need not fear demons or demonic activity. Jesus made clear to His followers, *"I have given you authority to trample on snakes and scorpions and to overcome all the power of the enemy; nothing will harm you"* (Luke 10:19). And the apostle Paul admonishes us, *Put on the full armor of God, so that you can take your stand against the devil's schemes* (Ephesians 6:11). Even though the devil and his demonic forces attempt to distract us from God's purposes for our lives, the apostle Peter challenges us to be self-controlled and alert. *Resist him, standing firm in the faith* (1 Peter 5:9). In the name of Jesus, we have the victory as we follow our Lord into spiritual battle and advance the Kingdom of God.

In summary, through our study in this chapter we affirm our belief in God (Father, Son, and Holy Spirit) as Creator of all things, including that of humanity (male and female) in His own image, and that He declared His creation to be "very good" (Genesis 1:26-31). We also affirm our belief that because of the disobedience of Adam and Eve in the Garden of Eden humans are born into sin and in need of a Redeemer. We acknowledge both angels and demons as a powerful force in the spiritual realm, but we are grateful for our Savior, the Lord Jesus Christ, the King of kings and Lord of lords. He has conquered evil, death, and hell and given us new life (1 Corinthians 15:24-26; Revelation 12:7-11; 19:11-16).

Related Scriptures

God the Father -
Deuteronomy 32:6; Psalms 103:13; Isaiah 63:16; Matthew 6:9; John 1:3, 5:19-23, 17:1-11; Acts 17:28; Romans 8:14-16; Ephesians 4:6

The Fall of Mankind -
Genesis 1:27, 3:1-6; Isaiah 53:6; Romans 3:10, 3:23, 5:12, 5:19

For Further Reading

http://www.creationdesign.org/english/chances.html

Thiessen, Henry C. *Lectures in Systematic Theology.* Grand Rapids, MI: Wm. B. Eerdmans Publishing Company, 1949.

Time to Interact

Take some time to interact with the following questions. Consider writing your answers in a journal and/or discussing them with a fellow believer for deeper reflection and insight.

1. This chapter reminds us that people were created by God as the pinnacle of all His creation. What does this suggest about the depth of God's love for you?

2. What evidence of mankind's fall into sin do you readily see in the world? What evidences are obvious in your own life? What are the hidden sins that are not so readily seen? How do people often try to rectify their sins? What do your observations tell you about our need for a Savior?

3. How are angels represented in popular culture? How do those images compare and contrast with what the Scripture says? How do angels function in relationship to God? How do angels function in relationship to mankind? Why might it be important to become aware of the ministry of angels?

4. Some people completely ignore demons, while others claim to recognize them everywhere. Why is it important not to be ignorant of the demonic realm? Conversely, what dangers might be found in becoming obsessed with demonic activity? How does it feel to know that Jesus has given His disciples authority over demons? What questions do you still have about angels and demons?

Time to Integrate

As you work to understand the origins and nature of sin, and the role of humankind in creation, work through the following ideas for further transformation.

1. When you consider your own heart and actions, what sins tend to persist? As someone who has surrendered to the lordship of Christ, how can you count yourself dead to those sins, and alive to Christ? Read through Romans 6. What truths stand out to you? How can you act on the passage to help you experience increased transformation and freedom?

2. Charged with the responsibility of stewardship over God's

creation, how are you rising to the challenge? What proactive steps can you take to care for this world in which we live? How does that include the people around you?

3. Often Christians speak of spiritual warfare and the importance of confronting the demonic realm. Yet Scripture also suggests that the angels outnumber the demons at least two to one. Ask the Holy Spirit to make you more aware of the ministry of angels around you. How could this awareness potentially influence how you pray and trust God in the midst of difficult situations?

CHAPTER 6

People of God:
The Church

CHAPTER 6

People of God:
The Church

> " We believe Christians should assemble regularly for edification, worship, fellowship, and proclamation of the gospel. All believers should do the work of the ministry according to their spiritual gifts and should tithe and otherwise contribute financially to their church. "

THE CHURCH'S ORIGIN

The Church was God's idea, meaning it is divine in purpose, definition, and construction, not confined to the limitations of organizational or sociological concepts. God maintains sole ownership of the Church. It exists because of Him, is intended to be an expression and extension of Him, and functions through Him. The first references in the gospels to church as an entity are found in Matthew 16:18 and Matthew 18:17. It is not until we read accounts about the Church in the book of Acts and the epistles that we begin to recognize local assemblies that functioned as churches. The historic "birthday" of the local church as we know it today is traced to Acts:

> *When the day of Pentecost came, they [believers] were all together in one place. Suddenly a sound like the blowing of a violent wind came from heaven and filled the whole house where they were sitting. They saw what seemed to be tongues of fire that separated and came to rest on each of them. All of them were filled with the Holy Spirit and began to speak in other tongues as the Spirit enabled them* (Acts 2:1-4).

From this recorded birthdate the Church's history on earth has been filled with excitement, fulfillment of God's promises, and hope. Throughout history there have been corrupt people intent upon contorting the Church from its godly mission to become an agent of manipulation and abuse. It has also been subjected to persecution in many parts of the world, virtually disappearing in some places for eras. However, churches have adapted and flourished through both good and bad times because the same power of the Holy Spirit that filled the house in Acts 2 continues to fill and enable people today to function as God's Church. In this chapter we are taking a look at what the Church is and what it does.

Definition

The Greek word that is used in the New Testament for church is *ekklesia*, meaning "the gathering of people called together for a purpose." Jesus used that term when He said, *"And on this rock I will build my church [ekklesia]"* (Matthew 16:18). Jesus also stated, *"They are not of the world, even as I am not of it"* (John 17:16). The Church is the people of God, called out from the world by Jesus to fellowship in His name and to live for Him. As the Apostle Paul wrote to the church in Ephesus, **to him be glory in the church and in Christ Jesus throughout all generations, for ever and ever! Amen** (Ephesians 3:21).

Two Dimensions

There are two dimensions to the Church in the New Testament, both of which refer to people rather than to buildings. There is the Church that incorporates all believers in Christ from previous, current, and future times on a universal scale that timelessly incorporates but also transcends geography, nationality, ethnicity, language, denomination, and culture, spanning both heaven and earth. No force can thwart or stop the Church from fulfilling God's mission for it. When Jesus said He would build His Church (Matthew 16:18), He was referring to the Church universal. Because of its immensity and divine scope, this dimension of the Church is sometimes referred to as the invisible Church, as opposed to the visible local church that meets in a building on the corner. It is this all-encompassing-scale Church to which the Apostle Paul refers in Ephesians 1:22-23, 4:4, 5:23. We capitalize this dimension of the word, Church, in order to distinguish it from the other dimension of the church, the geographically defined, local gathering of believers in Jesus. One author described the local church as a colony of heaven on earth.

This latter dimension of the local church is the one most commonly fixed in the minds of people and is referenced in 1 Corinthians 1:2 and 1

Thessalonians 1:1. A reader of the New Testament will enhance his or her insight and understanding of God's Word by seeking to recognize which dimension – Church or church – is included in a Scripture passage. While a pastor and elders may lead a church, Jesus leads the Church, not a pope or any other human being. Open Bible Churches believes it is imperative for all local bodies of believers, churches, to also understand and embrace that they are local components of the greater Church led by Jesus.

It is God's intention for both the Church universal and the local church, including its leaders, to be submitted to the leadership of Jesus. If a local church body does not recognize it is part of the Church universal, it becomes like an isolated island and fails to offer loving respect and honor to other churches as brothers and sisters in the family of Christ. Such exclusivity is inconsistent with the unity among believers for which Jesus prayed:

> *"My prayer is not for them alone. I pray also for those who will believe in me through their message, that all of them may be one, Father, just as you are in me and I am in you. May they also be in us so that the world may believe that you have sent me. I have given them the glory that you gave me, that they may be one as we are one: I in them and you in me. May they be brought to complete unity to let the world know that you sent me and have loved them even as you have loved me"* (John 17:20-23).

We are informed in Colossians 2:9 that in Christ all the fullness of the Deity lives in bodily form. Jesus emphasized that truth when He prayed **"Father, just as you are in me and I am in you,"** referring to two persons of the Trinity mentioned in Matthew 28:19: **"Therefore go and make disciples of all nations, baptizing them in the name of the Father and of the Son and of the Holy Spirit."** God is in three persons – Father, Son, and Holy Spirit – the Trinity. He is at the same time one and three. Each person of the Godhead bears distinct attributes, all distinctively contributing to the whole of who God is. Similarly, the Church and local churches are one. Local churches bear distinct attributes, individual in composition, size, passion, modes of worship, and avenues of ministry, all contributing to the whole of the Church. While this analogy is helpful in order to illustrate the Church's two dimensions in one, the analogy is limited to that illustration because God the Father, Son, and Holy Spirit are deity, perfect, without lack or shortcoming. By contrast, local bodies assembled to function as churches are comprised of people and people are imperfect, the ramifications of which we will consider later in this chapter.

CHARACTERISTICS OF THE CHURCH

Before we consider the ministry of the local church, we need to recognize its distinguishing characteristics because they are foundational to its ability to carry out its mission. We must know who we are as part of the larger Body of Christ before we attempt to do what we are called to do. Although the local church functions as an organization, it operates more importantly as a living, relational organism through Christ. What identifying characteristics of the local church separate and differentiate it from any other gathering of people? The following distinguishing characteristics of the Church are relational in nature.

The People of God

In the Old Testament God created a people, the nation of Israel, to be His people. However, when He sent His Son Jesus as the atonement, the ultimate sacrifice for sin, God opened an avenue of grace for all of mankind to choose to become His people. The promise God originally made to Israel was now extended to anyone who embraced Jesus as Savior and Lord: *And you also are among those who are called to belong to Jesus Christ* (Romans 1:6). God's promise was thus extended: *As God had said: "I will live with them and walk among them, and I will be their God, and they will be my people"* (2 Corinthians 6:16). The Apostle Paul described the change this way: *Consequently, you are no longer foreigners and aliens, but fellow citizens with God's people and members of God's household* (Ephesians 2:19). Furthermore, the privilege of being the people of God is not the exclusive domain of any nationality or ethnicity: *For we were all baptized by one Spirit into one body – whether Jews or Greeks, slave or free – and we were all given the one Spirit to drink* (1 Corinthians 12:13).

When only Jews were considered the people of God they represented a monocultural sameness. However, when God made provision for all who embraced Jesus as Savior and Lord to become His people, it was like the transformation of a picture drawn with a pencil into a picture richly brushed with watercolors. The people of God were transformed into a global and multicultural family.

When God sent Jesus to earth, He also sent a strong message about His desire to be in relationship with people: *"For God so loved the world that he gave his one and only Son, that whoever believes in him shall not perish but have eternal life"* (John 3:16). It would be in error to believe becoming the people of God elevates the local church to perfection. Paul described this gift of relationship with Jesus as treasure when he wrote, **But we have this treasure in jars of clay to show that this all-surpassing power is from God and not from us** (2 Corinthians 4:7). Jars of clay suggest human vulnerability instead of invincibility, an acknowledgement of the dependency of the people on God to function as His people. Rather than allowing this special distinction of being the people of God to become a cause for pride, the local church assumes a greater responsibility: **Be completely humble and gentle; be patient, bearing with one another in love. Make every effort to keep the unity of the Spirit through the bond of peace. There is one body and one Spirit – just as you were called to one hope when you were called** (Ephesians 4:2-4).

Is it possible to be part of the people of God without belonging to or participating in a church? Nothing in the Bible suggests a person cannot be a believer in Christ without also joining a church. Joining or attending an Open Bible church or any other church does not make a person a Christian. Becoming a follower of Jesus is a personal decision, not a group decision. The Bible clearly states, **Whoever claims to live in him must walk as Jesus did** (1 John 2:6). The Bible, however, also makes clear, as established throughout this chapter, that gathering and building relationship and functioning with a body of believers is vital to spiritual growth and development. If a person is interested in only a personal sense of escape from eternity apart from God, then church can be viewed as either unnecessary or as a membership "ticket" into heaven; this view demonstrates an incomplete understanding and an incorrect assumption about the Church as the Body of Christ. As will be discussed, the people of God are encouraged and strengthened by each other in their faith.

The Body of Christ

No understanding of the Church is complete without grasping God's prescribed interrelationship of believers with Jesus, with other believers, and with the corporate Church as a whole. The relationships of parts of a human body illustrate God's design for church relationships. This design applies to both the Church universal (Ephesians 1:22-23) and to individual congregations (1 Corinthians 12:12). The Church is scripturally referred to as the ***body of Christ*** (1 Corinthians 12:27).

Jesus Christ is the head of this body (Colossians 1:18). This makes clear the flow of authority. He is described as the *"**head over every power and authority**"* (Colossians 2:10).

Parts of the body are individual and yet dependently function with the rest of the body. Each part needs and cannot operate independently of the other parts. Each part contributes to the function of the others (Romans 12:4-5; 1 Corinthians 12:20; Ephesians 4:4). When believers join a church, they do not do so as complete and mature people. Rather, with the assistance and support of fellow believers, they begin their spiritual growth journey of becoming who and what God desires them to be. A hand cannot function apart from the body. A toe is useless if detached from the body. It is vital to understand God did not intend for believers to isolate themselves like detached toes. He intended for the church to be a channel through which believers encourage and build each other up (Ephesians 4:11-16). He stresses, ***Carry each other's burdens, and in this way you will fulfill the law of Christ*** (Galatians 6:2). ***Rather than being self-consumed, all parts of the body are called to look not only to your own interests, but also to the interests of others*** (Philippians 2:4).

David Ferguson, author and co-director of Intimate Life Ministries, had been praying about self-doubt. After reading Ephesians 1:18 he was struck by a truth concerning the church. It was like the Lord was saying to him:

> *David, some of the acceptance you need in the midst of your self-doubts, I'm longing to give you through My people. Some of the encouragement, care and affirmation you need when you're down and have grown weary in well-doing, I want to provide you through My Body. I will still be providing it, but it's coming through others. It's still My acceptance, My encouragement, My care, but I'm sharing it with you as Christ the Head expresses His glory through His Church. It's really Me in them and through them! (Kingdom Calling, Transformed by God's Love*, by David Ferguson).

The Priesthood of the Believer

A priest acts as a middleman between God and the people. In the Old Testament a priest carried out rituals and ceremonies on behalf of the people to atone, or make amends, for their sins. Only through priests did people have a means of worship and access to God. No one other than priests dared to enter the temple, which was viewed as the representative earthly residence of God. People had no direct relationship with God. He seemed fearfully distant to them. But God radically and forever altered the relational landscape by sending His Son Jesus to earth. Jesus dynamically changed what had been a distant relationship into a personal one with believers. The Apostle Peter proclaimed to the crowd that was watching and listening with amazement at the occurrences on the day of Pentecost, the Church's birth, *And everyone who calls on the name of the Lord will be saved* (Acts 2:21). Because Jesus offered Himself as an all-time single sacrifice for sins (Hebrews 9:26), the need for a clerical class of priests ended. Other sacrifices are no longer necessary (Hebrews 10:18) as a means of obtaining forgiveness from sins:

> *Therefore, since we have a great high priest who has gone through the heavens, Jesus the Son of God, let us hold firmly to the faith we profess. For we do not have a high priest who is unable to sympathize with our weaknesses, but we have one who has been tempted in every way, just as we are – yet was without sin. Let us then approach the throne of grace with confidence, so that we may receive mercy and find grace to help us in our time of need* (Hebrews 4:14-16).

Although pastors and spiritual elders provide leadership, instruction, and counsel through the church today, Open Bible celebrates the freedom of every believer to serve in a priestly function with direct access to God through the 24/7 intercessory advocacy of Jesus. Additionally, the Holy Spirit distributes gifts among members of the Body of Christ: *Now to each one the manifestation of the Spirit is given for the common good* (1 Corinthians 12:7). This direct access to God has major ramifications for the church today. Individual believers have freedom and authority to boldly come to God (Ephesians 3:12) in prayer with their needs. Instead of only knowing about and attempting to connect with a God who seems distant simply through rituals, believers are empowered to minister to each other because Christ, the Head, has granted both the authority and the enabling power of the Holy Spirit to do so. This freedom, authority, and availability of power to every believer are profoundly significant and continuously contemporary characteristics of the church.

Unity

The world is filled with thousands of churches that vary widely in size, language, expressions of worship, and approaches to ministry. Since Jesus prayerfully called for unity among believers (John 17:20-23) and we understand that gatherings of His believers constitute the Church, what does church unity look like in the midst of immense diversity and differences among churches?

One example of unity is groups of churches finding value in membership in a denomination or association of churches because of common values, biblical interpretation and application, philosophies of ministry and ministry priorities, and opportunity for both fellowship and mutual accountability. Open Bible Churches is such an association through which member churches subscribe to bylaws that fit within guidelines, policies, and combined global outreaches in faith that we are stronger and more effective together than we are by being independent of each other. We believe in the entirety of the Bible and rejoice that all the gifts of the Holy Spirit that are described and witnessed to in the New Testament actively continue today. We believe that churches independent of relationship with an association of other churches lack the protection of accountability. Accountability enables us to help each other remain faithful to the Bible, our relationships, our joint ministry commitments, and our biblically based practices that love and honor the people we serve. Open Bible subscribes to a value that the relationship between our members offers accountability without undue control.

Beyond denominational or associational unity the picture of unity among churches is subject to a range of interpretations. One view holds that unity should include the mass merging of congregations, denominations, and church associations into one denomination, like a merger of corporations. Open Bible believes this ecumenical quest is a misappropriation of the cause of unity, one that can stifle freedom for the Holy Spirit to move distinctively as He will through parts of the body of Christ. We believe such a mass merger would confine fresh worship expressions and limit church leadership in an attempt to achieve an appearance of unity. Control through broad uniformity and centralization of leadership, which could potentially subordinate core doctrines of the Bible to organizational structure, is not unity. In fact, we believe the global history of the local church reveals that the centralization of authority, even if in the name of unity, is vulnerable to abuse by authority.

Open Bible embraces and supports three other views of unity:

1. The first view of unity is demonstrated as a commitment to the spiritual unity of the Church universal under the Lordship of Jesus, which will culminate in heaven. While human imperfection makes earthly centralization of church authority in the name of unity both unwise and impractical, ultimate unity will be achieved in heaven, not by human manipulation but by God Himself. Open Bible believes it is part of the greater family of God, and any other distinction will be completely abandoned in heaven. We revere the Church while loving and respecting the church.

2. We also maintain a perspective on unity that embraces expressions of spiritual unity and fellowship between and with local congregations from other denominations whenever possible. This may involve joint ministry efforts within a community. While these efforts do not diminish individual church identities and convictions, they do communicate both to members of the participating churches and to the community that the Lordship of Jesus and the churches' commitment to faithful adherence to the Word of God transcends their dissimilarities. We are convinced it pleases God and is in at least partial fulfillment of Jesus' prayer concerning unity when we look for opportunities to collaborate with other churches for the purpose of ministering to a community for Him. This collaboration is always centered on glorifying God and obeying instruction from His Word rather than satisfying other agendas that could be competitive in nature.

3. Open Bible is also committed to participation in councils or associations wherein members mutually respect denominational identities and convictions while choosing to center fellowship and

ministry partnership efforts on the foundational biblical tenets that we share. This type of unity is sometimes referred to as conciliar. For example, Open Bible Churches of the United States is a charter member of both the National Association of Evangelicals and the Pentecostal/Charismatic Churches of North America, two groups distinguished by loving respect among their members, commitment to common causes, and their seeking a consequently stronger, united voice on behalf of Christ to a continent.

Open Bible believes that by practicing these three facets of unity with the body of Christ, we are endeavoring to be faithful to the Apostle Paul's encouragement in his letter to the church in Philippi: *If you have any encouragement from being united with Christ, if any comfort from his love, if any fellowship with the Spirit, if any tenderness and compassion, then make my joy complete by being like-minded, having the same love, being one in spirit and purpose* (Philippians 2:1-2).

THE MISSION OF THE CHURCH

We have considered the origin of the Church, some of its distinguishing characteristics, who belongs to it, and the interdependence of its people. What is the mission of the Church? What function does the local church fulfill? What is the Church, the body of Christ, supposed to do? The biblical account of the function and activities of the first New Testament church, commonly referred to as the early church, provides a model:

> *They devoted themselves to the apostles' teaching and to the fellowship, to the breaking of bread and to prayer. Everyone was filled with awe, and many wonders and miraculous signs were done by the apostles. All the believers were together and had everything in common. Selling their possessions and goods, they gave to anyone as he had need. Every day they continued to meet together in the temple courts. They broke bread in their homes and ate together with glad and sincere hearts, praising God and enjoying the favor of all the people. And the Lord added to their number daily those who were being saved* (Acts 2:42-47).

We believe the local church consists of humble servants of the Lord, empowered by gratitude, who minister to the Lord, minister the Word of God to its members, minister God's love to others, and minister the message of reconciliation to everyone. There is a basic three-fold direction to which God calls the church: upward, inward, and outward.

Upward

Although God is everywhere, upward signifies a heavenward, God-directed, focus. When Jesus was asked what is the greatest or most important commandment for people to follow, He responded, *"Love the Lord your God with all your heart and with all your soul and with all your mind and with all your strength"* (Mark 12:30). The first mission of the church is to corporately (as a group) do what every individual believer must also do, unreservedly and passionately express love to our Lord God. If we are going to love the real God we need to truly know the real God. To worship Him without knowing Him can become but a ritual or obligatory exercise that lacks life and authenticity. Expression of love for God is worship, which helps to establish and grow relationship with Him. The more believers grow in relationship with God the more they know and understand Him and the more their trust in Him grows. In fact, Jesus expressed frustration with believers who knew about Him but did not grow into a deepened relationship: *Jesus answered: "Don't you know me, Philip, even after I have been among you such a long time?"* (John 14:9). Worship is the gateway to deepened relationship with the Lord.

Although believers can and should develop a worshipful, individual relationship with God, an added relational dimension occurs when the gathered body of Christ, the church, worships together. Worship as a group (corporate) is not a substitute for worship by individuals. However, corporate worship adds to and enhances individual worship. On the birthdate of the church, in Acts 2, the **tongues of fire** that rested on individuals were preceded by the rushing wind of the Spirit that filled the whole house (Acts 2:2). The body of people in that house experienced the presence of God as a group when they gathered together for the purpose of being in His presence. The early church was also devoted to the apostles' teaching. The apostles' teaching has been given to us today in the Bible, and teaching from the Bible is also central to the church's worship, as is corporate prayer that the early church modeled.

Open Bible is passionately committed to the importance of this "in His presence" worship by the church where we praise the Lord, pray to Him, and devote ourselves to instruction from God's Word, the Bible. Worship can be expressed in multiple dimensions, including through acts of service, which will be addressed. However, service neither supplants nor is more important than worship focused on relational expressions of loving praise and prayer to the Lord and instruction from His Word. Jesus made this clear when He was more pleased with Mary, who sat at His feet and listened, than with Martha, who was instead focused on acts of service (Luke 10:38-42). *Worship is the upward mission, the first priority, of the church.*

Inward

Members of the body, the local church, are called by God to be in loving relationship and minister to each other as a community. We have been equipped with gifts from the Holy Spirit to encourage and build up each other in our faith: **Therefore encourage one another and build each other up, just as in fact you are doing** (1 Thessalonians 5:11). A vital component of this inward ministry is a Greek term *koinonia*, which means "fellowship." Early church believers devoted themselves to fellowship, to the breaking of bread (Acts 2:42), which is the Bible's way of saying they ate together. There is biblical precedent for why church gatherings often include food! People in the early church also broke bread in their homes and ate together with glad and sincere hearts (verse 46). There is good reason why church bodies are often referred to as the family of God. Loving families spend time enjoying each other's company in their homes and gathered together elsewhere, encouraging each other and "breaking of bread." It seems apparent believers in the early church understood that by making their primary relationships be with fellow believers they were strengthened to walk out their faith and service to the Lord. The many wonders and miraculous signs the early church experienced (Acts 2:43) were convincing evidence of the Spirit's presence and power. These "signs" and "wonders" stimulated and strengthened the faith among the group of believers.

Family-like fellowship is an activation of Jesus' command: "***A new command I give you: Love one another. As I have loved you, so you must love one another***" (John 13:34). In his letter to the Galatians, Paul stressed, **Therefore, as we have opportunity, let us do good to all people, especially to those who belong to the family of believers** (Galatians 6:10). Additionally, our relationships in the church family must be personal and close enough to supportively implement Romans 12:15: ***Rejoice with those who rejoice; mourn with those who mourn.***

Open Bible, as with most Protestant denominations, observes two ordinances, or biblically defined ceremonies: water baptism and Communion (the Lord's Supper), both of which are reserved for the people of God. Water baptism, a symbolic representation of a life having been cleansed of sin by Jesus, is provided by a church as often as the influx of new believers suggests. Open Bible prefers that Communion, a commemoration of Jesus Christ sacrificing His body, blood, and life on a cross, be offered not less than monthly. However, it is at a church's discretion how frequently to celebrate Communion.

A few contemporary applications of the inward focus of the church need to be examined.

1. The Acts 2 account of the early church states believers gathered daily. Luke 24:53 informs us that immediately after Jesus' ascension to heaven, they stayed continually at the temple, praising God. Are church members today supposed to get together daily, or even continuously? While respecting groups that hold to a view that the church should gather daily, Open Bible believes that what is most important is that the people of God gather with consistency and regularity, demonstrating that they identify with and have a "belonging" relationship with a local church body.

   People need time together in order to grow in relationship, but employment, availability of meeting places, family schedules, and other factors all seem to work in concert against the church gathering. Although meeting together can be challenging, it is imperative for believers to place a high value upon gathering together in order for individuals and their church to function in upward, inward, and outward relationships and roles. Life is full, but allowing relational gatherings with a local church body to be sacrificed or put on the shelf is shortsighted and short-circuits spiritual growth. Our contemporary struggle to remain committed to gathering as a local church is not new. Hebrews 10:25 speaks directly to those who had stopped trying to gather: ***Let us not give up meeting together, as some are in the habit of doing, but let us encourage one another – and all the more as you see the Day approaching.***

2. In the early church, all the believers were together and had everything in common. Selling their possessions and goods, they gave to anyone who had need (Acts 2:45). Does this mean followers of Jesus should sell all of their material possessions in order to give them to needy people? Some groups have suggested this passage of Scripture mandates that believers should live in commune-like orders where all possessions are held in common in lieu of personal property. That God's heart is sensitive to the plight of the needy is beyond doubt. We read in James 1:27, *Religion that God our Father accepts as pure and faultless is this: to look after orphans and widows in their distress and to keep oneself from being polluted by the world.*

Open Bible respects those who practice total material self-denial for the purpose of helping the needy. However, just as we do not believe Acts 2 requires followers of Jesus to gather daily or continuously, or that it is even practical to do so today, we do not believe selling and giving away all personal possessions is required by Acts 2:45. We do believe God calls us to be generous, even sacrificial, in giving from our material blessings, all of which come from Him, to help others in need and to spread the gospel. The Apostle Paul presented an example of how we should give when he described the response he received after asking for an offering for the poor from the Macedonians, who were themselves afflicted with poverty and yet astounded Paul with their hearts to sacrificially give: *For I testify that they gave as much as they were able, and even beyond their ability* (2 Corinthians 8:3).

3. Open Bible also believes we should honor the principle of Sabbath, which was modeled by God when he created the earth in six days and rested on the seventh day. Traditionally, observance of Sabbath has been honored on Sunday, a day when the church body gathers. Some church groups, called Adventist, hold to a view that Sabbath must be on Saturday. Open Bible is not interested in quarreling about when to observe Sabbath. We are called to keep the Sabbath holy and are comfortable with its normative observance on Sunday without mandating that as a legalistic declaration. Sometimes, however, life commitments necessitate observing Sabbath on days other than Sunday.

Loving one another like family also includes sacrificial humility. *Be devoted to one another in brotherly love. Honor one another above yourselves* (Romans 12:10). In addition to the inward church ministry commitment of loving ministry to each other Jesus emphasized an outward, testimonial purpose: *"By this all men will know that you are my disciples, if you love one another"* (John 13:35). Relational care and ministry to and among the people of a church is the inward mission of the church.

Outward

When the church's identity is fixed on its upward relational focus of worship to the Lord and when its inward relationships and ministry within the body are healthy in biblically defined terms, the church is strategically positioned to fulfill its third relational calling. That calling is an outward focus on the world that does not know Jesus as Savior and Lord. One of the marks of the early church was that *the Lord added to their number daily those who were being saved* (Acts 2:47). As with upward and inward ministry, an outward focus is the responsibility of both individual believers and the church as a body. The Apostle Paul explained that the reconciliation of relationship with God that believers experience becomes their responsibility to share with others: *All this is from God, who reconciled us to himself through Christ and gave us the ministry of reconciliation* (2 Corinthians 5:18). The outward focus of the church will be considered in more detail in Chapter 7, "Community Life."

In his letter to Timothy, the Apostle Paul emphasized the reason Timothy should pray for people who had not yet accepted Jesus as Savior: *This is good, and pleases God our Savior, who wants all men to be saved and to come to a knowledge of the truth* (1 Timothy 2:3-4). At the time of His ascension into heaven, Jesus left His last departing words for all believers and for all church gatherings of His body: *"Therefore go and make disciples of all nations, baptizing them in the name of the Father and of the Son and of the Holy Spirit"* (Matthew 28:19). This outward mission of the church is commonly referred to as the Great Commission. It is global in perspective: *But you will receive power when the Holy Spirit comes on you; and you will be my witnesses in Jerusalem, and in all Judea and Samaria, and to the ends of the earth* (Acts 1:8).

Nonetheless it is important to remember something Jesus said at an earlier time that affects the motivation for working to fulfill the Great Commission. It is commonly referred to as the Great Commandment. When Jesus was asked what the greatest commandment is and He responded, *"Love the Lord God with all your heart and with all your soul and with all your mind and with all your strength"* (Mark 12:30), He did not even pause before answering an unasked question: *"The second is this: 'Love your neighbor as yourself.' There is no commandment greater than these"* (Mark 12:31). *Loving people and making disciples is central to the outward mission of the church.* Open Bible believes the following regarding the upward, inward, and outward mission of churches:

1. A Great Commandment love for people must compel us to pursue fulfillment of the Great Commission. Without love, we think only in terms of conversion statistics. With love, we are eager to introduce and welcome people to a life-changing, life-giving relationship with Jesus Christ. Without love, we become mechanical and dutiful. With love, we become passionately driven by the opportunity to share Jesus Christ with unbelievers.

2. All three directions of a church's mission must be in operation to truly function as a church. Without an upward focus a church becomes simply a social service agency, having a form of godliness but denying its power (2 Timothy 3:5). Without an inward focus a church fails to equip, build up, and strengthen believers, which results in an anemic church unable to fully function as God intends. Without an outward focus a church should probably not even be called a church because it does not meet the definition of a church. It might be called a revival center or a spiritual club, especially if it has an upward and inward focus so exclusive that no one outside that group is welcomed, feels welcome, or is noticed. Strong as it may sound, to call a gathered group of people a church if they do not have an outward mission and focus is a masquerade.

3. The church functions both when gathered together and as members of the church serve as the outreached arms of Jesus to their spheres of influence outside the church body. The community ministry of the church will be considered in Chapter 7, "Community Life." The

outward mission of the church must also be obvious when the church gathers. This involves more than instruction. Planning for services will be with sensitivity to attracting and ministering to unbelievers. How we "do church" cannot be only for the purpose of pleasing the inward focus. Our facilities, our hospitality, our music, our words, and our attitudes must convey a very recognizable, outward, "Welcome!" to unbelievers.

4. It costs money to conduct the inward and outward functions of the church. This is not a new phenomenon because the Apostle Paul gave instructions to the churches he visited that they should set aside funds for when he visited to assist them: *On the first day of every week, each one of you should set aside a sum of money in keeping with his income, saving it up, so that when I come no collections will have to be made* (1 Corinthians 16:2). Open Bible believes that a principle found in Malachi 3:10 is applicable for believers today, understanding that the church is the contemporary spiritual storehouse: *"Bring the whole tithe into the storehouse, that there may be food in my house. Test me in this," says the LORD Almighty, "and see if I will not throw open the floodgates of heaven and pour out so much blessing that you will not have room enough for it."* The blessings of giving and receiving are both activated by tithing, which is when a believer gives a tenth of all the Lord has provided back to Him through His church.

FACES OF THE CHURCH'S MISSION

While every church must have a three-fold ministry direction, each church must also prayerfully and individually tailor the specific elements of its ministries for maximum effectiveness toward the community and culture in which it resides. We could refer to that as the church's footprint (reach, position, and influence) in its community. Open Bible Churches has also prayerfully identified the distinctive elements of the mission we believe God has called us to pursue as an association of churches. Those elements also translate to all local, affiliated churches without conflicting with local churches' ministries. We believe the purpose for which God brought Open Bible into existence as a family of churches and ministers is to glorify God and bring people to Jesus Christ, ministering to spiritual, emotional, physical, and social needs. Understanding that neither an association of churches nor an individual church can minister in every possible manner, Open Bible has prayerfully determined that God's assignment to us, our global mission, is to make disciples, develop leaders, and plant churches. All affiliated churches are invited and challenged to collaboratively participate in the fulfillment of that mission in local communities, the nation, and the world (Acts 1:8).

THE LEADERSHIP AND GOVERNMENT OF THE CHURCH

We have established that Jesus is the Head of the Church universal and of local churches. The Lord also chooses and anoints, or empowers, leaders to serve the church under and accountable to His authority: ***While they were worshiping the Lord and fasting, the Holy Spirit said, "Set apart for me Barnabas and Saul for the work to which I have called them"*** (Acts 13:2). Every organism and organization needs some form of government through which leaders serve God and minister to the people. History is full of a range of governance examples, all of which can be classified by the extent of authority or power that is vested in leaders and by who holds the leaders accountable. Most forms of church government fit into one of these classifications:

Episcopal – Authority resides in a bishop who answers to God and who governs many churches with authority that may be delegated through a hierarchical system of spiritual leaders, including church pastors, who are bishop-appointed. Church property is owned by the episcopal authority.

Presbyterian – A representative denominational form of church government with officers and elders, usually selected by the people of churches, who conduct the affairs of churches according to rules established by joint assemblies of the people and church elders of local churches. Authority is understood to be delegated by the members to the elders, one of whom usually serves as pastor. Church property is usually owned by the assembly or denomination.

Congregational – Decision-making authority rests with the members of the local church, including the selection of a pastor. In some forms of congregational government the church may belong to an association or fellowship of churches while other churches with congregational government are entirely independent entities that answer to no one outside that body. All major decisions of the church, such as the calling of a pastor, are made by members.

Nongovernment – Some groups deny the church has a need for a visible form of governance and endeavor to not have any governmental structure or leadership. Their premise is that the Holy Spirit will lead and guide independent of structure. Frequently, churches with nongovernment forms of leadership are small, extended families by blood relationship. Who owns church property can be difficult to ascertain.

There are also blends of these primary forms of church leadership and government. Which form is the correct or best version? Open Bible Churches does not claim its governmental structure is superior to others. It is simply what we believe the Lord has led us to develop in the pursuit of balance over generations of leadership. As an association of churches we do not commonly refer to ourselves as a denomination, and we exhibit a blend of Presbyterian and Congregational forms of government.

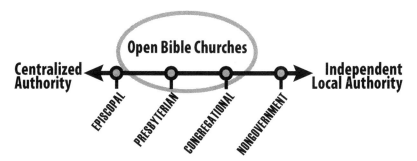

Affiliated Open Bible church bodies normally select their own pastors, but under guidelines and requirements agreed to by member church representatives and Open Bible credentialed ministers. Pastors of Open Bible churches must be credentialed Open Bible ministers who are accountable for fulfilling requirements as stated in the Open

Bible Manual. Local churches own their properties, but bylaws call for ownership to transfer to Open Bible Churches if churches should go out of existence. Affiliated churches can select from a range of approved government structures that are more Presbyterian or more Congregational in nature. All affiliated churches must operate under bylaws that meet minimal guidelines established by Open Bible Churches and must be approved by Open Bible. Ministers and church delegates alone select the president of Open Bible Churches, approve the association's bylaws, Statement of Faith, and Position Statements.

THE TRANSFORMED AND TRANSFORMATIONAL CHURCH

It is imperative for the local church to demonstrate (or live) what it teaches; if it does not, the culture in which it dwells will marginalize the church, dismissing its proclamations as removed from public life as a monastery or convent. Ralph Waldo Emerson, 19th Century American poet and essayist could have been directing his famous statement to the church: "Who you are speaks so loudly I can't hear what you're saying." Who we are must confirm and validate what we say we are.

Churches impart biblical doctrine, proclaiming Scripture-based, life-changing, core truth. And they teach how to apply that truth to everyday living. Churches are distribution channels for the transformational power of Jesus Christ. Jesus brings light to darkness, healing to pain, and forgiveness for sin in loving response to repentance. For centuries churches have been beacons of His light, teaching what God says in His Word about today and eternity. However, today's churches must not focus exclusively on "right" truth and "right" living, although understanding core truths about life are as important as ever. Nor can churches major on preserving traditions of the past, although traditions may be valued. *The priority of the local church today must be to relationally model truth, upward, inward, and outward; and to develop loving and vibrant relationships with God, fellow believers, and unbelievers.* The church can lovingly flavor its community, like salt (Matthew 5:13), with the love of Jesus. When the church truly functions as God intends, people are drawn to the transformational power of Jesus, who promised, *"I will build my church, and the gates of Hades [hell] will not overcome it"* (Matthew 16:18).

Related Scriptures

Psalm 111:1; Malachi 3:8-10; Acts 2:42-47, 16:5; Romans 12:5; 1 Corinthians 16:2; 2 Corinthians 9:6-7; Hebrews 10:24-25

For Further Reading

Bach, R. A. Bach & Schmidt, D. M., eds. *We Believe: Principles in Christian Living*. Des Moines, IA: Open Bible Publishers, 1992.

Erickson, Millard J. *Introducing Christian Doctrine, 2nd ed*. Grand Rapids, MI: Baker Academic, 2001.

Ferguson, David. *Kingdom Calling: Transformed by God's Love*. Cedar Park, TX: Relationship Press, 2004.

Time to Interact

Take some time to interact with the following questions. Consider writing your answers in a journal and/or discussing them with a fellow believer for deeper reflection and insight.

1. Despite seasons of both persecution and corruption, the Church (the body of Christ, not just the local church) has not only persisted since the time of Christ, but flourished. Why do you think that is? What is God's purpose in increasing His Church worldwide?

2. What has been your experience in churches you have attended in your life so far? How does that relate to the description and purposes described in this chapter? What are your hopes for the Church as we step into the future? What is your role in helping the Church become all it is meant to be?

3. How do you understand the difference between unity and uniformity? How can we, as the Church, pursue unity with one another without entering into the pitfalls of uniformity?

4. How is your connection to a local body of believers helping to fulfill the mission of the Church? How has God called you to serve? How does your involvement and role in your local church connect you to the power and presence of the Holy Spirit?

Time to Integrate

The local church is not meant to be a corporation comprised of an administrative hierarchy and passive members. Rather, it is a family of believers walking out demonstrations of love for God and for one another in mutual accountability. Consider the following steps as you embrace the truths of this chapter.

1. What is your relationship to your local church body? Occasional visitor? Faithful attender? Active participant? What might God want to accomplish in you by bringing you into a place of deeper relationship with other local believers? Ask the Holy Spirit to increase your passion for the localized body of Christ. Look for a way to contribute to the Lord's work through your church by your determined involvement and service.

2. Just like any family, people experience heartache as well as joy in the midst of relationship. Sometimes people carry hurts from disappointments and misunderstandings in past church situations. What does God want to heal in you? How can you contribute to a healing, restorative climate in your local church? Confess any areas of bitterness and apprehension about the church to the Lord and ask Jesus to bring you cleansing. Purpose to embrace others in your church as works of art, still in progress, and decide how to best honor both God and them!

CHAPTER 7

Relating to Each Other:
Community Life

CHAPTER 7
Relating to Each Other:
Community Life

CHURCH RELATIONSHIP

> We believe Christians should assemble regularly for edification, worship, fellowship, and proclamation of the gospel. All believers should do the work of the ministry according to their spiritual gifts and should tithe and otherwise contribute financially to their church."

CIVIL GOVERNMENT

> "We believe civil government is ordained of God, and all people should be subject to the laws of the land, except those contrary to Scripture. In times of war, the individual's participation in actual combat and taking of human life shall be governed by one's own conscience.

THE CHURCH'S ORIGIN

The full expression of being a Christ follower is meant to be grounded in the midst of a loving community of believers. Psalm 68:6 says that *God sets the lonely in families.* No individual is meant to travel this journey of faith alone. Throughout Scripture, as God calls people to Himself, He does so in the larger context of raising up a people group among whom He will dwell and be the center.

When people receive Jesus as the Lord of their lives, they enter into the deepest bonds of love that can be found. With God as Father, believers are adopted into His family. We are born again as His children and become brothers and sisters in Christ with one another. This becomes true regardless of gender, ethnicity, age, education, or economic status. We become family! God's great desire is to see His original intention for relationships restored in us. It's the reason Jesus affirms that the greatest command in all of Scripture is to *"Love the Lord your God with all your heart and with all your soul and with all your mind."* He continues, *"And the second is like it: Love your neighbor as yourself. All the Law and the Prophets hang on these two commandments"* (Matthew 22:37-40). Loving God and the people around us with all we are is the central component of the Christian life. Discovering and expressing this love is what we call "community."

All believers in Jesus are on a similar journey to discover the fullness of who He is and to embrace the purpose and destiny He has for each one of us. He has created each of us to know Him intimately and for our lives to be an "offering" of worship unto Him. The Apostle Paul sums up this purpose by writing, **Therefore, I urge you, brothers, in view of God's mercy, to offer your bodies as living sacrifices, holy and pleasing to God – this is your spiritual act of worship** (Romans 12:1). Paul is writing to the Church collectively. We are meant to live out a shared experience of community life and an offering of ourselves in joint worship and mission. There can be no greater sense of fulfillment than embracing the totality of this destiny.

COMMUNITY LIFE IN THE OLD TESTAMENT

Consider the account of creation found in the first two chapters of Genesis. On the day that God established the sky and separated it from the water, creating the land and seas, He stood back and saw that *it was good* (Genesis 1:6-10). The next day, He created vegetation, including seed-bearing plants and fruit-bearing trees, and again saw that it was good. This pattern continued through the remaining days of the creation, each one ending with this same declaration of goodness. In chapter 2, however, we get a more detailed picture of how God made man. There, He formed man from the dust of the earth, breathed life into him, and gave him charge over the creation. However, God then determined, *"It is not good for the man to be alone. I will make a helper suitable for him"* (Genesis 2:18).

For the first time in recorded history, something was declared "not good." This was before sin had come into the world. And it was before the influence of Satan brought destruction and separation from God. Aloneness has never been the intention or plan of God. From the very beginning, He has pointed to the importance of being connected to others. Since then God has been working to establish people in deep relationships: husbands and wives; parents and children, extended families and relatives, friends and neighbors, communities and towns, geographical regions and nations. Each is an opportunity to demonstrate the love and goodness that is found in Him. People are meant to be connected…to one another and ultimately to Him.

After the fall of humankind into sin, God began to affirm His intention to restore humanity into right relationship with Him and with one another. He did this by calling to a man named Abram, instructing him to go to a new and spacious land that He would give to him and his descendants. Along the way, Abram grew in relationship with God, eventually undergoing a transformation during which God changed his name to Abraham. Abraham, the servant of God, became the father of a new race of people, the Israelites. God marked the Jewish people as a unique nation, one belonging to Him. He would be their God, and they would be His people. Through His special relationship with them, He would once again reveal Himself to the world.

The Old Testament gives apt detail of the successes and failures, and the joys and heartache this group experienced over many centuries. This includes great accounts of miraculous deliverance and care, and the establishment of the Law of God to define and empower right relationship with Him and others. It culminates in the creation of the Temple in Jerusalem as a focal point of sacrifice, cleansing, and worship before God. Through it all, the Israelites learned the importance of what it meant to be "the people who belong to the Lord." All of life came to be centered around Him.

None of this, however, was God's ultimate hope for mankind. It merely helped pave the way for something greater. The writer of Hebrews says of Abraham, when he finally reached the land promised to him by God:

> *By faith he made his home in the promised land like a stranger in a foreign country; he lived in tents, as did Isaac and Jacob, who were heirs with him of the same promise. For he was looking forward to the city with foundations, whose architect and builder is God* (Hebrews 11:9-10).

In other words, Abraham's eyes were fixed on a greater reality yet to come. The writer then speaks of numerous other biblical heroes. ***These were all commended for their faith, yet none of them received what had been promised. God had planned something better for us so that only together with us would they be made perfect*** (Hebrews 11:39-40). This "something better" would be revealed in the New Testament.

COMMUNITY LIFE IN THE NEW TESTAMENT

Through the death and resurrection of Jesus, God didn't just restore right relationship between Himself and the Jewish people, but also between Himself and all who would put their trust in Him regardless of who they were or what they had done. Jesus is the Savior of the entire world! The Apostle John records Jesus' words: *"For God so loved the world that he gave his one and only Son, that whoever believes in him shall not perish but have eternal life. For God did not send his Son into the world to condemn the world, but to save the world through him"* (John 3:16-17).

The Apostle Paul also demonstrates God's heart for the entire world when He writes that *through the gospel the Gentiles are heirs together with Israel, members together of one body, and sharers together in the promise in Christ Jesus* (Ephesians 3:6). Because Christ dwells in the hearts of all believers, each one is part of the bigger whole, regardless of background. We are a new community, a connected people, a family. The Apostle Peter confirmed this, writing to all believers everywhere, when he declared,

> *But you are a chosen people, a royal priesthood, a holy nation, a people belonging to God, that you may declare the praises of him who called you out of darkness into his wonderful light. Once you were not a people, but now you are the people of God* (1 Peter 2:9-10).

Jesus referred to this new sense of commonality and belonging as His "Church." When Peter came to the ultimate realization that Jesus is the Messiah and the Son of God, Jesus responded,

> *"Blessed are you, Simon son of Jonah, for this was not revealed to you by man, but by my Father in heaven. And I tell you that you are Peter, and on this rock I will build my church, and the gates of Hades will not overcome it"* (Matthew 16:17-18).

The Lord is establishing a new community of believers that incorporates all who have come before and all who will come later.

This Church came suddenly into formation on the day of Pentecost as described in Acts 2. Having been filled with the Holy Spirit, Peter gave his first sermon to the crowd, calling on them to repent and be baptized in the name of Jesus. Suddenly, the early group of 120 believers who had gathered in an upper room awaiting the outpouring of the Spirit expanded to include three thousand more! Throughout the rest of the book of Acts, and the corresponding letters to the numerous local gatherings of believers that emerged over time, we can see how the people began to function and relate to one another as a community. Soon after the church's birth it was rapidly expanding across the known world.

FOUNDATIONS FOR COMMUNITY LIFE

As people came to know Christ for themselves, they soon began to gather together on a regular basis. Acts 2:42 indicates that, *They devoted themselves to the apostles' teaching and to fellowship, to the breaking of bread and to prayer.* This illustrates the importance of at least four foundations in embracing the fullness of community life as the Church.

Teaching

First listed is the necessity of being devoted to the apostles' teaching. Our understanding of God, His ways, and our ongoing transformation into the likeness of Christ must come from the truths of Scripture. As believers heard the messages being presented by the church leaders, they worked at applying them to their lives. This is more than just an individual attempt; it is a communal endeavor. We see this emphasis confirmed in the Apostle Paul's letter to the local church in Colosse:

> *Let the message of Christ dwell in you richly as you teach and admonish one another with all wisdom, and as you sing psalms, hymns, and spiritual songs with gratitude in your hearts to God* (Colossians 3:16).

The teaching of the apostles provided not only for correct thinking about God, but also for transformational encounters with Him as that teaching was applied to everyday living. The writer of Hebrews reminds us that the *word of God is living and active. Sharper than any double-edged sword, it penetrates even to dividing soul and spirit, joints and marrow; it judges the thoughts and attitudes of the heart* (Hebrews 4:12). In his second letter to Timothy, Paul also focuses on the importance of continual study and the transformational power of the Word of God, writing:

> But as for you, continue in what you have learned and have become convinced of, because you know those from whom you learned it, and how from infancy you have known the Holy Scriptures, which are able to make you wise for salvation through faith in Christ Jesus. All Scripture is God-breathed and is useful for teaching, rebuking, correcting and training in righteousness, so that the man of God may be thoroughly equipped for every good work (2 Timothy 3:14-17).

Community life as the Church of Jesus Christ includes ongoing growth and transformation stemming from the teachings of the Word of God. The local church gathers to hear the Word presented by teachers, and then is meant to discuss, work through, and apply this teaching to daily life. In the sharing and doing of God's Word, the whole church finds strength and maturity.

Fellowship

The second foundation of community life in the early Church was their devotion to fellowship. The original Greek text calls it "the fellowship." This illustrates the importance of a localized identity and of deep life connections with the others who are gathered. By joining themselves to Christ through faith and repentance, the believers have not just entered into a superficial connection with other Christ followers, but rather have also embraced relationships that are practical and authentic. They come together regularly with the same people, again and again, for mutual edification, strengthening, accountability, ministry, and growth.

This sense of fellowship demonstrates a decision to open one's life and thought processes to others. It involves the sharing of hopes, dreams, and strengths as well as frustrations, fears, and weaknesses. It includes the determination to reveal one's heart in order to be fully known and to fully know others. The Apostle Paul provides a picture of this kind of relational living when he writes,

> Therefore, as God's chosen people, holy and dearly loved, clothe yourselves with compassion, kindness, humility, gentleness and patience. Bear with each other and forgive whatever grievances

> *you may have against one another. Forgive as the Lord forgave you. And over all these virtues put on love, which binds them all together in perfect unity* (Colossians 3:12-14).

True fellowship is marked by a commitment to compassion and unity, being one with the Lord and His intentions for this new way of living. Paul continues in his corresponding letter to the Ephesian church:

> *As a prisoner for the Lord, then, I urge you to live a life worthy of the calling you have received. Be completely humble and gentle; be patient, bearing with one another in love. Make every effort to keep the unity of the Spirit through the bond of peace. There is one body and one Spirit – just as you were called to one hope when you were called – one Lord, one faith, one baptism; one God and Father of all, who is over all and through all and in all* (Ephesians 4:1-6).

Implicit in the definition of New Testament community life is the underlying principle that we must value and esteem our relationships with one another. There must be a commitment to biblical fellowship. There is no other way to experience this than through regular, mutual, life-giving connections with other local believers.

Breaking of Bread

With a very common understanding, breaking bread certainly includes the idea of sharing a meal together. When the Acts passage declares that the community life of the early Church included the breaking of bread, there is no question that it points to the importance of eating together. In a shared meal, there is opportunity to serve and provide for one another. We learn what it is to put others first and serve them. By eating together people grow in relationship, discussion, and friendship. Fellowship grows and deepens.

Because of the sacrifice of Christ, however, the phrase also signifies something more. Since the time of Jesus' last supper with the disciples, the phrase *breaking bread* has forever become connected to the death and resurrection of Jesus, taking on new significance (which we will discuss in greater detail in chapter 10). When believers join in this "communion" together, we recognize that we are connected to one another and to God by the sufferings of Jesus and the victory He has won over the grave. The importance of this connection and its implications should not be underestimated.

Prayer

The fourth foundation of community life described in Acts 2:42 was their resolved commitment to combined prayer. By its simplest definition, prayer is simply communication with God. Regular moments set aside for the purpose of lifting our thoughts, desires, needs, weaknesses, hopes, praises, thanks, and devotion to the Lord, as well as learning to be still before Him and hear from Him, are essential to the development of any relationship with God. Intentional conversation with God is a core discipline for every Christ follower. In addition, as we shall see in the following examples from the book of Acts, there is powerful effect when God's people come together in joint intercession.

Let's consider the impact of joint intercession as recorded in the book of Acts alone:

- Through prayer, God revealed His choice for an additional apostle (Acts 1:24).
- During prayer, the Holy Spirit came suddenly, filling all who were gathered together (Acts 1:14; 2:1-4).
- A man who had been lame his entire life was instantly healed as Peter and John were on their way to a prayer gathering (Acts 3:1).
- As the church had come together to pray, power from God was poured out, enabling them to be bold in their sharing of the Gospel message (Acts 4:31).
- Through prayer, additional leaders were appointed and commissioned to serve the church, and the kingdom of God increased (Acts 6:5-7).
- Through the prayers of the church, Peter was supernaturally released from prison (Acts 12:1-17).
- As the church sought the Lord in prayer, the Holy Spirit set apart Paul and Barnabas for missionary service (Acts 13:1-3).
- Through prayer, elders and leaders were appointed in the newly formed churches (Acts 14:23).

Countless other examples can be found in Scripture. God works through the prayers of His people to accomplish His Kingdom purposes. In prayer, our hearts become aligned with His. Our will becomes submitted to the Father. Supernatural empowerment is released to meet needs and either alter circumstances, or to apprehend the grace to rise above them. Paul writes to the Philippian church,

> *Do not be anxious about anything, but in everything, by prayer and petition, with thanksgiving, present your requests to God. And the peace of God, which transcends all understanding, will guard your hearts and your minds in Christ Jesus* (Philippians 4:6-7).

John also confirms the effectiveness and necessity of praying together in his first letter:

> *This is the confidence we have in approaching God: that if we ask anything according to his will, he hears us. And if we know that he hears us – whatever we ask – we know that we have what we asked of him* (1 John 5:14-15).

These four foundations of community were not meant simply for the establishment of the church long ago. They are meant to be hallmarks of the gathering of believers in every generation. When we come together as the Church, these priorities of devotion to the apostles' teaching, to heartfelt fellowship, to the sharing of meals and communion with the Lord, and to fervent intercession should all still be cornerstone pieces that define who we are as the people of God.

EXPRESSIONS OF COMMUNITY LIFE

The Bible uses many different metaphors to illustrate and describe the nature of who we are as the Church of Jesus. Chief among them is the understanding that believers, together, comprise the Body of Christ. Additionally, it is also worth noting that the Scripture refers to the Church as the Temple of God.

The Church is the Body of Christ

As followers of Christ, we are connected. This walk with God we have embraced is not meant to be only a private, individual relationship with Him. Of course we are meant to know Him personally, but we are also called to function as part of something bigger. The Apostle Paul writes to the Roman church:

> *Just as each of us has one body with many members, and these members do not all have the same function, so in Christ we who are many form one body, and each member belongs to all the others* (Romans 12:4-5).

He confirms this thought in his first letter to the Corinthians:

> *The body is a unit, though it is made up of many parts; and though all its parts are many, they form one body. So it is with Christ. For we were all baptized by one Spirit into one body – whether Jews or Greeks, slave or free – and we were all given the one Spirit to drink. Now the body is not made up of one part but of many* (1 Corinthians 12:12-14).

With that in mind, each of us must recognize that other believers have an integral part in the healthy spiritual development of our lives, and we hold the same role in theirs. As with our human bodies, each individual part is highly important and contributes greatly to the health and prosperity of the whole. Though each member has a different function, all are needed and must be highly valued.

The implications of this thought are many. First, no part is supposed to feel useless or out of place. Second, no individual part should make unjust comparisons to another. All of us have different gifts, talents, strengths, weaknesses. However, no part is to be seen as unnecessary. Paul continues:

> *If the foot should say, "Because I am not a hand, I do not belong to the body," it would not for that reason cease to be part of the body. And if the ear should say, "Because I am not an eye, I do not belong to the body," it would not for that reason cease to be part of the body. If the whole body were an eye, where would the sense of hearing be? If the whole body were an ear, where would the sense of smell be? But in fact God has arranged the parts in the body, every one of them, just as he wanted them to be. If they were all one part, where would the body be? As it is, there are many parts, but one body.*
>
> *The eye cannot say to the hand, "I don't need you!" And the head cannot say to the feet, "I don't need you!"* (1 Corinthians 12:15-21).

Every part of the Body is important. Every part of the Body has a part to play. Every part of the Body has something to offer. Each member has been redeemed by God and filled with His Holy Spirit. From the Holy Spirit comes the operation of spiritual gifts that are given for the common good to strengthen the entire Body (as discussed in chapters 6 and 11). Rather than feeling small or insignificant, we must recognize that our active involvement and participation are intricately connected to the growth of the Kingdom of God where we live. Each individual church is a localized expression of the larger Body of Christ, and as we lovingly serve through our church setting, we personify the love and compassion of Jesus.

This is why many local churches emphasize a call to official membership. Having been born into the Kingdom of God through the saving work of Jesus, Christ followers are encouraged to intentionally pledge themselves to local bodies of believers for purposes of accountability, relationship, service, and mutual edification. Being part of the Body is not just a clever use of words in a spiritual metaphor, but especially points to our need for practical, deliberate, and continual relationship with real people!

As the Body of Christ, we become a visible image of the love and ministry of Jesus. That love is demonstrated as each member of the Body serves and does its part. When we begin to think more highly of ourselves than we ought, when we begin to think that we can get along in this journey of faith through our own private knowledge and encounters with God, we typically lose our way. Paul says, **Such a person… has lost connection with the Head, from whom the whole body, supported and held together by its ligaments and sinews, grows as God causes it to grow** (Colossians 2:18, 19). Jesus is our head, and as we choose to value, strengthen, serve, and support one another in mutual submission to Christ, the Body grows and matures.

The truth of this principle is reiterated in Ephesians 4:16, **From him the whole body, joined and held together by every supporting ligament, grows and builds itself up in love, as each part does its work.** In other words, the contribution of each part of the Body is essential for the overall growth and maturity of the community. Consider the New Living Translation:

> He makes the whole body fit together perfectly. As each part does its own special work, it helps the other parts grow, so that the whole body is healthy and growing and full of love (Ephesians 4:16, NLT).

Each believer has an essential place in the Body of Christ. The joy of community life is fully discovered as each part of the Body embraces its identity and serves others in the spirit of love and compassion.

The Church is the Temple of the Lord

A second expression of community life is the understanding that God dwells among us when we gather as His people. We know that individually, when we surrender to the lordship of Jesus and become believers, the Spirit of God takes residence on the inside of us. In one sense, we personally become temples of the Holy Spirit. In an expanded sense, this is also true collectively as we recognize who we are together.

In the Old Testament, it was King David's dream to build a permanent temple for the Lord in which to dwell and to be worshipped. Before then, it was the Tabernacle (a moveable tent established during the time of Moses) that served as the place reserved for encountering and giving honor to God. The innermost chamber of this tent was called the "Holy of Holies" and was recognized as a physical location that literally housed the glory of God. David's son, King Solomon, brought this dream to fruition, and the temple of God became the center of Jewish society.

Writing to the Corinthian community of believers, Paul says, **Don't you know that you yourselves are God's temple and that God's Spirit dwells in you?** (1 Corinthians 3:16). This is meant to be understood both joyously and reverently. It is joyous in the sense that the Living God, the One who loves us and gave Himself for us, is present in our midst as we gather to worship and celebrate Him. Even Jesus said, "**For where two or three come together in my name, there am I with them**" (Matthew 18:20). At the same time, this is also meant to be a very sobering concept as we recognize the serious implications of having God in our midst.

If the awesome, powerful, and holy God dwells among us, then the pursuit of righteous living and honoring Him become a paramount focus of the Church. The Bible calls us to live a set-apart life, marked by a conscious consecration unto the Lord. Paul again writes to the Corinthians:

> *Do not be yoked together with unbelievers. For what do righteousness and wickedness have in common? Or what fellowship can light have*

> with darkness? What harmony is there between Christ and Belial? What does a believer have in common with an unbeliever? What agreement is there between the temple of God and idols? For we are the temple of the living God. As God has said: "I will live with them and walk among them, and I will be their God, and they will be my people" (2 Corinthians 6:14-16).

How we live, whom we influence, and who we are influenced by all matter. Choices we make and sins we tolerate matter. The world is meant to understand that God is alive and active in His Church, and the church community should reflect that. This doesn't mean we are to hold ourselves to an unrealistic standard of perfection, but it does mean we must make the most of the opportunity He has given us to be a repentant people, committed to His gracious process of inner transformation, and conform our lives to the truths of Scripture and the presence of the Spirit. The community life of the Church should convey the truth that the holy, righteous, loving, awesome God is very much present among us, making an impact on our interactions and life choices.

RESPONSIBILITIES OF COMMUNITY LIFE

As we value the understanding of who we are as the Body of Christ and the Temple of God, it is important to embrace the responsibilities that naturally emerge. These responsibilities affect at least four aspects of our walk with God: how we honor God, how we demonstrate His love to one another, how we respect authority, and how we minister to the world.

Honoring God

How we live and the choices we make together are meant to honor God in ever increasing measure. In his letter to the Thessalonians, Paul tells the church, **brothers, we instructed you how to live in order to please God, as in fact you are living. Now we ask you and urge you in the Lord Jesus to do this more and more** (1 Thessalonians 4:1). Part of our responsibility in the community life of the church is to give our all to honor Him.

We honor God when we work at deepening our relationship with Him. When we first call on the name of the Lord, trusting in Him for our salvation, we become new creations in Christ with the assurance of spending eternity with Him in glory. We identify with the crucifixion of Christ, die to our old lives, and then are raised with Him into newness of life. Our lives now belong to Him. This is not the final objective of the Christian life, but rather the starting point. We now choose to grow, develop, and mature in Christ as we come to reflect Him more and more. Peter exhorts us:

> *For this very reason, make every effort to add to your faith goodness; and to goodness, knowledge; and to knowledge, self-control; and to self-control, perseverance; and to perseverance, godliness; and to godliness, brotherly kindness; and to brotherly kindness, love. For if you possess these qualities in increasing measure, they will keep you from being ineffective and unproductive in your knowledge of our Lord Jesus Christ. But if anyone does not have them, he is nearsighted and blind, and has forgotten that he has been cleansed from his past sins. Therefore, my brothers, be all the more eager to make your calling and election sure. For if you do these things, you will never fall, and you will receive a rich welcome into the eternal kingdom of our Lord and Savior Jesus Christ* (2 Peter 1:5-11).

We honor God when we embrace ministry and service, pursuing His calling and purpose for our lives. Paul writes, *For we are God's workmanship, created in Christ Jesus to do good works, which God prepared in advance for us to do* (Ephesians 2:10). The work of ministry is not just for appointed leaders. In fact, the Scripture declares that their responsibility is *to prepare God's people for works of service, so that the body of Christ may be built up* (Ephesians 4:12). Peter confirms this when he writes:

> *Each one should use whatever gift he has received to serve others, faithfully administrating God's grace in its various forms. If anyone speaks, he should do it as one speaking the very words of God. If anyone serves, he should do it with the strength God provides, so that in all things God may be praised through Jesus Christ. To him be the glory and the power for ever and ever. Amen* (1 Peter 4:10-11).

We honor God when we financially support the work of the ministry. In the Old Testament, the people of God were asked to devote ten percent (a tithe) of their increase (income) to the Lord as part of the law (Leviticus 27:30). Even before this, both Abraham and his grandson, Jacob, separately offered a tithe to God as a natural act of devotion and thanks (Genesis

14:20; 28:20-22). The seriousness and importance of bringing the tithe to God was proclaimed by the prophet Malachi:

> *"Will a mere mortal rob God? Yet you rob me. But you ask, 'How do we rob you?'*
>
> *"In tithes and offerings. You are under a curse – the whole nation of you – because you are robbing me. Bring the whole tithe into the storehouse, that there may be food in my house. Test me in this," says the LORD Almighty, "and see if I will not throw open the floodgates of heaven and pour out so much blessing that you will not have room enough for it"* (Malachi 3:8-10).

In the New Testament, financial giving was no longer limited to the tenth. During times of great financial need, many churches gathered funds to send to others to help advance God's Kingdom work and to meet needs. About this, Paul declared:

> *Remember this: Whoever sows sparingly will also reap sparingly, and whoever sows generously will also reap generously. Each man should give what he has decided in his heart to give, not reluctantly or under compulsion, for God loves a cheerful giver. And God is able to make all grace abound to you, so that in all things at all times, having all that you need, you will abound in every good work* (2 Corinthians 9:6-8).

This principle of generosity was one of the signs of community life evident from the very early days of the Church. Acts 2:44-45 records that all the believers were together and had everything in common. Selling their possessions and goods, they gave to anyone as he or she had need.

Two chapters later, we are told:

> *All the believers were one in heart and mind. No one claimed that any of his possessions was his own, but they shared everything they had. With great power the apostles continued to testify to the resurrection of the Lord Jesus, and much grace was upon them all. There were no needy persons among them. For from time to time those who owned land or houses sold them, brought the money from the sales and put it at the apostles' feet, and it was distributed to anyone as he had need* (Acts 4:32-25).

Today, the Kingdom of God is advanced, lives are changed, and God is honored when His people embrace the spirit of generosity and cheerfully take on the responsibility of giving tithes and offerings.

We honor God when we commit to regularly gather in His name.
It's hard to experience the blessings of community life unless the believers are regularly and intentionally coming together. We've already mentioned how the early Church gathered in homes to study, fellowship, break bread, and pray. In addition, they also met in larger groups for joint worship and a greater corporate experience. Luke writes, *The apostles performed many signs and wonders among the people. And all the believers used to meet together in Solomon's Colonnade* (Acts 5:12). There are numerous other accounts of people coming together in synagogues, in houses, by riversides, and just about anywhere they could find in order to jointly honor and worship the Lord.

Remember, from the very beginning of creation, God declared that it was not good for man to be alone. One way the Lord continues to meet this need and remove our sense of aloneness is by calling us to come together often in His name. The writer of Hebrews makes this very clear:

> *Let us hold unswervingly to the hope we profess, for he who promised is faithful. And let us consider how we may spur one another on toward love and good deeds. Let us not give up meeting together, as some are in the habit of doing, but encouraging one another – and all the more as you see the Day approaching* (Hebrews 10:23-25).

Separated and alone, we can become easy targets for discouragement and weakness. Together, we can lift each other up, find encouragement and strength, and honor God by continuing to be steadfast in our love and devotion.

Demonstrating Love

Essential to the ongoing community life of the church is the flow of continual, relational love. Paul opens his second letter to the Thessalonians by saying, *We ought always to thank God for you, brothers, and rightly so, because your faith is growing more and more, and the love every one of you has for each other is increasing* (2 Thessalonians 1:3). The answer to the following question is a real indicator of the health of any church: Are we continually increasing in our love for one another?

The original twelve disciples were from a variety of backgrounds. Among them, Andrew, Peter, James, and John were uneducated fishermen. Simon was a political zealot and prepared to see the Roman government overthrown by force. Matthew had been a tax collector for Rome and represented everything Simon would have despised. Thomas became known for being a doubter. Nathaniel, at first, questioned the background of Jesus and was biased against Him. The point is that they were an otherwise unlikely bunch for the Lord to bring together. Nevertheless, He not only called them to be His disciples, He let them know that if they would walk out His new commandment to love one another, then all who saw them would know they belonged to Jesus (John 13:35). If a group like that could learn to love, it must be because of God!

This call to walk in authentic love is a directive meant not only for these first disciples, but also for all who would follow Christ. In fact, the New Testament is full of instruction on how to practically live out what it means to lovingly be the Church together. Here's a quick listing of 10 scriptural ways to express love (and many more could be included):

- *Be devoted to one another in brotherly love. Honor one another above yourselves* (Romans 12:10).

- *Live in harmony with one another. Do not be proud, but be willing to associate with people of low position. Do not be conceited* (Romans 12:16).

- *Let no debt remain outstanding, except the continuing debt to love one another, for he who loves his fellowman has fulfilled the law* (Romans 13:8).

- *Therefore let us stop passing judgment on one another. Instead, make up your mind not to put any stumbling block or obstacle in your brother's way* (Romans 14:13).

- *I appeal to you, brothers, in the name of our Lord Jesus Christ, that all of you agree with one another so that there be no divisions among you and that you may be perfectly united in mind and thought* (1 Corinthians 1:10).

- *Aim for perfection, listen to my appeal, be of one mind, live in peace. And the God of love and peace will be with you* (2 Corinthians 13:11).

- *Be completely humble and gentle; be patient, bearing with one another in love* (Ephesians 4:2).

- *Be kind and compassionate to one another, forgiving each other, just as in Christ God forgave you* (Ephesians 4:32).

- *Submit to one another out of reverence for Christ* (Ephesians 5:21).

- *Do nothing out of selfish ambition or vain conceit, but in humility consider others better than yourselves. Each of you should look not only to your own interests, but also to the interests of others. Your attitude should be the same as that of Christ Jesus: Who, being in very nature God, did not consider equality with God something to be grasped, but made himself nothing, taking the very nature of a servant, being made in human likeness* (Philippians 2:3-7).

Respecting Authority

The church does not live in isolation, but is embedded in culture. It will take on the flavor and customs of its local settings. Our role is not to hide from (or even fight) the world, but to influence it. Within all kinds of political systems, geographic regions, and the various nations of the world, God is raising up His people to be representatives of His light and goodness. As part of that Kingdom work, the Bible calls us to demonstrate the love of Christ by obeying the civil authorities that govern us.

This is not the same as always agreeing with authority. We are all going to have moments where we disagree regarding how laws should be implemented and enforced. Every political structure is comprised of imperfect people who are working to govern society, and they will make decisions that are at best honest mistakes and at worst agenda-driven and power-serving. Regardless, the Scripture calls us to be people who can demonstrate peace and love through respectful obedience. We honor earthly authorities because God is transforming us into an honor-giving people! Consider the instruction of Paul to the Roman church:

> *Everyone must submit himself to the governing authorities, for there is no authority except that which God has established. The authorities that exist have been established by God. Consequently, he who rebels against the authority is rebelling*

> *against what God has instituted, and those who do so will bring judgment on themselves. ...This is also why you pay taxes, for the authorities are God's servants, who give their full time to governing. Give everyone what you owe him: If you owe taxes, pay taxes; if revenue, then revenue; if respect, then respect; if honor, then honor* (Romans 13:1-2; 6-7).

The only exception to this admonition should be instances where compliance with governmental regulation (local, state, or national) is in direct confrontation with scriptural commands. As each of us works to apply the Word of God to our lives, we must first and foremost choose to obey God. If there are occasions in which this brings us into disagreement with civil authority, how we express and act on that disagreement should still be something that demonstrates the character and love of Christ with all respect and honor. Keep in mind that the Apostle Paul wrote four of his letters while being falsely imprisoned, but never once spoke ill of those over him. Honoring authority, even when we have valid reason to disagree, is part of reflecting God's light to all those around.

Ministering to the World

The final responsibility of the community life of the Church is to expand the community. This is done as we communicate the love and work of Jesus to the rest of the world. Just before He ascended into Heaven, Jesus told His followers: *"But you will receive power when the Holy Spirit comes on you; and you will be my witnesses in Jerusalem, and in all Judea and Samaria, and to the ends of the earth"* (Acts 1:8). He also declared, *"All authority in heaven and on earth has been given to me. Therefore go and make disciples of all nations, baptizing them in the name of the Father and of the Son and of the Holy Spirit, and teaching them to obey everything I have commanded you"* (Matthew 28:18-20).

The Church has been both empowered and commissioned to demonstrate the kingdom of God and bring people into it. There is an incredible joy that comes when we take part in the ministry of Christ as He brings transformation and life to a broken and hurting world. As we live out how to honor God and love people, under the guidance and grace of the Holy Spirit, we open up an opportunity for someone else to experience the hope of a new life. Aloneness gets removed and the sense of community expands!

Together, we both experience and demonstrate the overwhelming presence and power of the Holy Spirit and the reality that Jesus is alive and well. In the midst of our community, the fullness of God is experienced, and we are transformed into a people of deep relationship, responsibility, and maturity. Through the loving expression of this community life, we become shining beacons of hope to the world. Shine on, Church!

Related Scriptures

Church Relationship -
Psalm 111:1; Malachi: 3:8-10; Acts 2: 42-47, 16:5; Romans 12:5; 1 Corinthians 16:2; 2 Corinthians 9:6-7; Hebrews 10: 24-25

Civil Government -
Mark 12:17; Acts 5:29; Romans 13:1-7; 1 Timothy 2:1-2; Hebrews 12:14

Time to Interact

Take some time to interact with the following questions. Consider writing your answers in a journal and/or discussing them with a fellow believer for deeper reflection and insight.

1. What are your thoughts about the idea that humankind was created to be in divine relationship not only with God, but also with fellow human beings? How can your involvement in the community life of the church minister to someone's aloneness? How might it affect yours?

2. Which of the four foundations of community life (teaching, fellowship, breaking bread, and prayer) appeals to you the most? How can you grow in some of the other areas? Why do you think these areas matter to God?

3. How have you been changed through regular interaction and participation with your fellow believers? How is God using others to refine you? How is He equipping you to bless the community?

Time to Integrate

Let's explore some avenues to expand your church community experience and involvement.

1. Compare your current participation in community with the biblical instruction to honor God. How are you choosing to deepen your relationship with Him? How are you embracing your responsibilities for ministry, service, and generosity? Pinpoint areas where you need to grow and admit them to the Father, inviting His transforming grace. What will you purpose to do differently this week?

2. If we squeeze a particular fruit, it will release juice! What comes out of you when you are emotionally squeezed or stressed? Can the world recognize that you belong to Jesus simply from the love that comes oozing out of you? Who in your circle of influence could really use an expression of love? A spouse? A child? Your grumpy co-worker or boss? A neighbor? That difficult person at church? How can you embrace a commitment to community life and act on the love of God?

3. The Apostle Paul gives us a picture of healthy community life when he writes:

> *Therefore if you have any encouragement from being united with Christ, if any comfort from his love, if any common sharing in the Spirit, if any tenderness and compassion, then make my joy complete by being like-minded, having the same love, being one in spirit and of one mind. Do nothing out of selfish ambition or vain conceit. Rather, in humility value others above yourselves, not looking to your own interests but each of you to the interests of the others* (Philippians 2:1-4).

What practical steps will you take this week to fulfill this Scripture?

CHAPTER 8

His Future for Us:
Next Things

CHAPTER 8

His Future for Us: Next Things

SECOND COMING OF CHRIST

" We believe the second coming of Christ will be personal, visible, and triumphant."

FINAL JUDGMENT AND HELL

"We believe there will be a final judgment for all unbelievers. Hell is an actual place of great suffering, bitter sorrow, and remorse reserved forever for the devil and his angels and all whose names are not written in Christ's book of life."

HEAVEN

"We believe heaven is an actual place of happiness and security where believers will dwell forever with God and receive the reward of their deeds done while on earth. "

The three statements above in Open Bible's Statement of Faith are intended to convey one overarching truth: there is more to life than this world has to offer. Our lives as we know them in this world are not "one and done," to use a contemporary sports tournament analogy.

Rather, because of the promises the Bible makes concerning the return of Christ and a final judgment with its ultimate consequences of an eternal hell or heaven, it appears this life is a preparation for that which follows for all of us. An eternal existence of loneliness, pain, and suffering or an eternal existence of companionship, joy, and worship await us on the other side of this life.

This chapter will address the biblical nature of the Statement of Faith regarding Next Things. We will also look at some of the common scriptural teachings and errors that emanate from attempts to reconcile biblical prophecy with the "end times" and "next things." Finally we will address several issues related to why these three basic and important biblical truths are sometimes neglected or thought to be irrelevant in our modern twenty-first century where relativity, pluralism, and universalism dominate so much of our culture, philosophy and, yes, even our theology.

The Bible tells us that our lives on earth are only a brief moment on an infinite timeline. And although many people ignore or deny God's existence, all of history is moving toward the inevitable culmination of God's plan. We don't know all the details of that plan, but we do know that Jesus will return to earth one day, sin and death will be no more, and where each person will spend eternity depends on whether or not he or she chooses to accept God's free gift of grace during life.

THE RETURN OF CHRIST

The Return of Christ Will Be *Personal*

Approximately 500 years before the time of Christ, Zechariah prophesied concerning the return of Christ that *A day of the Lord is coming. ... On that day **his** feet will stand on the Mount of Olives, east of Jerusalem* (Zechariah 14:1-4). This is just one of the many Old Testament prophecies concerning the return of Christ, but this one is significant in helping us see that His return is personal. On that day "His feet," not another's feet will stand there.

As Jesus was preparing His disciples to ready themselves for His death, burial, resurrection, and ascension into heaven He shared these words with them:

> *"Do not let your hearts be troubled. Trust in God; trust also in me. In my Father's house are many rooms; if it were not so, I would have told you. I am going there to prepare a place for you. And if I go and prepare a place for you, I will come back and take you to be with me that you also may be where I am"* (John 14:1-3).

Jesus announced to His disciples and to all who follow Him that He would personally return for them and us. The repeated use of the personal pronoun "I" is significant here.

As Jesus ascended into heaven in the presence of the apostles He had chosen, Luke tells us that *he was taken up before their very eyes, and a cloud hid him from their sight. They were looking intently up into the sky as he was going,* when suddenly two men dressed in white stood beside them. "Men of Galilee," they said, "why do you stand here looking into the sky? This same Jesus, who has been taken from you into heaven, **will come back in the same way** you have seen him go into heaven" (Acts 1:9-11). Just as they saw Him go physically into the heavens, so "this same Jesus" will come back in the "same way."

The apostle writing to the early church at Thessalonica about the return of Christ continues this theme of Jesus' Second Coming being personal with these words: *For **the Lord himself** will come down from heaven, with a loud command, with the voice of the archangel and with the trumpet call of God* (1 Thessalonians 4:16).

This then is our hope, that Jesus Himself will personally come again. Not another, but this same Jesus will come back from heaven to earth and His feet will stand on the Mount of Olives on that day to take us to heaven where we will be with Him and the Father for all eternity.

The Return of Christ Will Be *Visible*

Jesus Christ will return to earth and His return will be **visible**. The Scriptures are consistent in this matter. The Apostle Paul addresses this on multiple occasions in his writings.

To the Thessalonians he wrote:

> *This will happen when the Lord Jesus is **revealed** from heaven in blazing fire with his powerful angels* (2 Thessalonians 1:7).

And this is what he wrote to the young pastor Titus in Crete:

> *For the grace of God that brings salvation has appeared to all men. It teaches us to say 'No' to ungodliness and worldly passions, and to live self-controlled, upright and godly lives in this present age, while we wait for the blessed hope – the glorious **appearing** of our great God and Savior, Jesus Christ* (Titus 2:11-13).

During the latter half of the first century A.D. the Apostle John wrote these words:

> *Dear friends, now we are the children of God, and what we will be has not yet been made known. But we know that **when he***

> ***appears**, we shall be like him, for we **shall see him as he is*** (1 John 3:2).

And in the introduction to the **Revelation** of Jesus Christ, John recorded for our instruction and inspiration:

> ***Look**, he is coming with clouds, and **every eye will see him**; even those who pierced him, and all the peoples of the earth will mourn because of him. So shall it be! Amen* (Revelation 1:7).

The return of Jesus, the second coming of the Lord, will be visible not just by His followers, but even by those who pierced him. Believer and unbeliever alike will witness the visible return of Jesus at His coming again.

The Return of Christ Will Be *Triumphant*

When Zechariah wrote *On that day his feet will stand on the Mount of Olives* (Zechariah 14:4), the prophet provided us with a picture of triumph and victory when Jesus Christ returns to earth. Capturing and maintaining the "high ground" is a strategic tactic in defeating the enemy in warfare. The return of Christ ushers in the final stages of the greatest war ever fought – the struggle between good and evil, righteousness and sin, Jesus and Satan – the struggle and warfare for the souls and eternal existence of all mankind. While Zechariah introduces us to that ultimate triumph with this picture, other biblical writers help us to understand clearly the triumphant nature of the return of Christ.

Matthew quotes the words of Jesus in this way:

> *"At that time the sign of the Son of Man will appear in the sky, and all the nations of the earth will mourn. They will see the Son of Man coming on the clouds of the sky, with **power and great glory**. And he will send his angels with a loud trumpet call, and they will gather his elect from the four winds, from one end of the heavens to the other* (Matthew 24:30-31).

Another triumphant passage relative to the return of Christ is found in Paul's Epistle to the Thessalonians:

> *For the Lord himself will come down from heaven, with a loud*

command, with the voice of the archangel and with the trumpet call of God, and the dead in Christ will rise first. After that we who are still alive and are left will be caught up together with them in the clouds to meet the Lord in the air. And so we will be with the Lord forever* (1 Thessalonians 4:16-18).

And again in his second letter to the Thessalonians, Paul continues this theme of victory and triumph with these words:

*This will happen when the Lord Jesus is revealed from heaven in **blazing fire with his powerful angels**. He will punish those who do not know God and do not obey the gospel of our Lord Jesus. They will be punished with everlasting destruction and shut out from the presence of the Lord and from the majesty of his power on the day he comes to be glorified in his holy people and to be marveled at among all those who have believed* (2 Thessalonians 1:7-10).

And of course, the Book of Revelation magnificently escorts us to a vision of Jesus and His followers celebrating that final victorious and triumphant battle over evil, sin, and the devil himself. There we see Jesus, who says, *"I am the Alpha and the Omega … who is, and who was, and who is to come, the Almighty"* (Revelation 1:8), gaining the final triumphant victory over the devil who is *thrown into the lake of burning sulfur* [where he] *will be tormented day and night forever and ever* (Revelation 20:10).

And there we join a great multitude in the grand finale song of triumph and victory shouting, *"Hallelujah! For our Lord God Almighty reigns. Let us rejoice and be glad and give him glory!"* (Revelation 19:6-7).

All these references provide us with powerful picture words that depict a grand triumphant return of our Lord Jesus Christ.

The Bible clearly teaches that the second coming of Christ will be personal, visible, and triumphant. All who have trusted Christ for forgiveness and salvation *wait for the blessed hope – the glorious appearing of our great God and Savior, Jesus Christ, who gave himself for us to redeem us from all wickedness and to purify for himself a people that are his very own, eager to do what is good* (Titus 2:13-14).

FINAL JUDGMENT, HEAVEN, AND HELL

The return of Christ will set in motion events that will lead up to and result in the consummation or the perfect completion of the kingdom of God. With Jesus' sacrificial death on the cross, through the grace of God, we received complete forgiveness for all our sins. When we accepted the price He paid for us we were adopted into the family and became citizens of the kingdom of God. Peter reminds us:

> *But you are a chosen people, a royal priesthood, a holy nation, a people belonging to God, that you may declare the praises of him who called you out of darkness into his wonderful light. Once you were not a people, but now you are the people of God; once you had not received mercy, but now you have received mercy. Dear friends, I urge you, as aliens and strangers in the world, to abstain from sinful desires, which war against your soul. Live such good lives among the pagans that, though they accuse you doing wrong, they may see your good deeds and glorify God on the day he visits us* (1 Peter 2:9-12).

The children of God live in two worlds or two kingdoms. As followers of Jesus, we have been redeemed and adopted into the family of God. Because we are members of God's family in Christ, we have all the rights and privileges as citizens of His Kingdom. But we also live (as citizens of that heavenly Kingdom) in a pagan and fallen world. Peter calls it a world of darkness and sin that wars against the soul. We are called to live in this world as aliens and strangers because of its contrary nature to the kingdom of God.

Evil and sin are vividly and transparently apparent in this fallen world and have been throughout history. In the twentieth century we saw the horrible manifestation of evil perpetrated by Hitler's Nazi Germany where we are told that six million Jews and several million non-Jews were slaughtered. Following Hitler, there were mass killings in Stalin's Soviet Union, in the People's Republic of China, and under the Khmer Rouge in Cambodia.

The twenty-first century began with the devastating terrorist attacks of 9/11. Organizations like Al Queda, Boko Haram, and ISIS, to name a few of which there are many, continue to perpetrate atrocious and ghastly acts of terrorism.

The abortion statistics are also staggering. Each year in the United States alone, the lives of over one million innocent infants are terminated while still in their mothers' wombs. And when we consider the effects of a fallen world, such as individuals who struggle with hatred and disrespect of their fellow human beings, crippling addictions, pestilences like the Ebola virus, cancer and AIDS, hurricanes, earthquakes, tsunamis and other natural disasters, it is plain to see the dark nature of this pagan world in which we live as citizens of the kingdom of God.

The United States alone has had five major wars since the conclusion of World War II. These include Korea (1950-1953), Vietnam (1961-1973), the Gulf War (1991), Afghanistan (2001-ongoing as of 2015) and Iraq (2003-2010). That means that we have been at war with other nations for approximately forty years since the close of WWII seventy years ago. And that doesn't even take into account other skirmishes in which we have sent troops to overthrow, stabilize or assist a nation with our military strength. Cuba, Dominican Republic, Lebanon, Grenada, Panama, Somalia, Haiti, Bosnia, and Kosovo all fall into this latter category.

It would be staggering, nearly impossible to wrap one's mind around the number of civil wars, internal coups, and other armed conflicts throughout the world.

In Luke 21, Jesus taught us to be aware of the coming end of this age when His disciples asked, *"Teacher ... when will these things happen? And what will be the sign that they are about to take place?"* (verse 7). He replied with these words:

> *"Watch out that you are not deceived. For many will come in my name, claiming, 'I am he,' and, 'The time is near.' Do not follow them. When you hear of wars and revolutions, do not be frightened. These things must happen first, but the end will not come right away. ...Nation will rise against nation, and kingdom against kingdom. There will be great earthquakes, famines and pestilences in various places, and fearful events and great signs from heaven"* (Luke 21:8-10).

Jesus clearly described the kinds of major traumatic events that will occur during the last days – events we now see every day on the news. Training as a rocket scientist is not necessary to discern the fallen nature of this pagan and corrupt world. Jesus was "spot on" with His description of what we could expect to see in our fallen world as the clock of civilization as we know it marches to its completion.

Speaking about the end of the age and the consummation of the kingdom of God, Jesus used one of His famous parables to communicate the truth that evil will be purged from the earth with His return. When His disciples asked Him to explain the parable of the weeds this is what He told them:

> "The one who sowed the good seed is the son of Man. The field is the world, and the good seed stands for the sons of the kingdom. The weeds are the sons of the evil one, and the enemy who sows them is the devil. The harvest is the end of the age, and the harvesters are angels. As the weeds are pulled up and burned in the fire, so it will be at the end of the age. The Son of Man will send out his angels, and they will weed out of his kingdom everything that causes sin and all who do evil. They will throw them into the fiery furnace, where there will be weeping and gnashing of teeth. Then the righteous will shine like the sun in the kingdom of their Father. He who has ears, let him hear" (Matthew 13:37-43).

On another occasion Jesus showed us what the judgment and the end of the age will look like when He returns to earth to establish the kingdom of God:

> "When the Son of Man comes in his glory, and all the angels with him, he will sit on his throne in heavenly glory. All the nations will be gathered before him, and he will separate the people one from another as a shepherd separates the sheep from the goats. He will put the sheep on his right and the goats on his left. The King will say to those on his right, 'Come, you who are blessed by my Father; take your inheritance, the kingdom prepared for you since the creation of the world.'... .Then he will say to those on his left, 'Depart from me, you who are cursed, into the eternal fire prepared for the devil and angels.' ... Then they will go away to eternal punishment, but the righteous to eternal life" (Matthew 25: 31-46).

The three statements in the Open Bible Churches Statement of Faith concerning the return of Christ, the final judgment, hell, and heaven are articulated in these teachings by Jesus explaining the parable of the weeds and the account of the sheep and goats.

1) There is a final judgment for all unbelievers.

2) Hell is an actual place of great suffering, bitter sorrow, and remorse reserved forever for the devil and his angels and all whose names are not written in the Book of Life.

3) Heaven is an actual place of happiness and security where believers will dwell forever with God and receive the reward of their deeds while on earth.

But for some the return of Christ, judgment, and heaven and hell are very difficult pills to swallow. In our contemporary culture, changing social values, globalization, and a lessening of the prominence of the Church in some areas have diminished the acceptance of these teachings of Scripture.

Religious pluralism, relativism, and theological universalism are just three of the popular views in our western social structures that have served as theories that "cloud" or "block" many from accepting the Bible as a divinely inspired authoritative word on the issues of the return of Christ, final judgment, and heaven and hell.

Religious pluralism is one of the fallouts of these societal changes in our time. The website www.gotquestions.org describes religious pluralism as "the belief in two or more religious world views as being equally valid or acceptable. More than mere tolerance, religious pluralism accepts multiple paths to God or gods as a possibility and is usually contrasted with 'exclusivism,' the idea that there is only one true religion or way to know God." A comparison of this concept with Jesus' words in John 14:6, *"I am the way and the truth and the life. No one comes to the Father except through me,"* makes it easy to see the conflict of these values.

The popularity of relativism is another stumbling block for many who struggle with the concepts of the return of Jesus, a final judgment, and the reality of heaven and hell. Relativism teaches that there is no absolute truth that holds universal validity for everyone. Individuals, cultures, environments, and societies all form their own truths. Hence even so-called "biblical truths" are not valid for everyone, but only for those who choose to validate them.

Likewise, theological universalism, the teaching that all people will eventually be saved as a result of God's divine love and mercy, leaves no room for a condemnation of non-believers to suffering in an eternal hell.

THE CONSUMMATION AND NEXT THINGS

The Book of Revelation opens with these words:

> *The revelation of Jesus Christ, which God gave him to show his servants what must soon take place. He made it known by sending his angel to his servant John, who testifies to everything he saw – that is, the word of God and the testimony of Jesus Christ* (Revelation 1:1-2).

In the final chapter of that same beautiful, mysterious book we read these words from the lips of Jesus, *"I am coming soon!"* (22:20). In response to those words of our Lord, John concludes the book by writing **Amen. Come, Lord Jesus. The grace of the Lord Jesus be with God's people. Amen** (22:20-21).

Since those words were recorded the followers of Jesus have been asking these questions, "When is soon?" and "How much longer, Lord Jesus, until we are delivered from this alien and strange land?" "When will you return and establish Your Kingdom and bring to an end all this corruption, sin, warfare, violence, pestilence, and natural disasters?"

In fact the followers of Jesus were asking similar questions prior to John penning those words. In Matthew 24:3 the disciples came to Jesus privately while He was on the Mount of Olives and asked Him, *"When will this happen, and what will be the sign of your coming and of the end of the age?"* Again following His resurrection and just prior to His ascension into heaven they asked, *"Lord, are you at this time going to restore the kingdom to Israel?"* (Acts 1:6).

In both instances Jesus gave them similar answers. On the Mount of Olives His response was, *"No one knows about that day or hour, not even the angels in heaven, nor the Son, but only the Father"* (Matthew 24: 36). Likewise to the pre-ascension question He replied, *"It is not for you to know the times or dates the Father has set by his own authority"* (Acts 1:7).

Today we continue to seek answers to the "when" question. That continual anticipation of the moment all evil is destroyed, the final judgment of all humanity occurs, Satan is obliterated, and the kingdom of God is eternally established and consummated has led biblical scholars, commentators, and a host of others to formulate theories, philosophies, and doctrines concerning "end times" and "next things" relative to the Lord's return.

We know some of these attempts to be illegitimate, unscriptural, and terribly off course. The "specific date setters" for the Lord's return have so far all been proven wrong. One of the earliest "correctives" addressing this issue came as early as twenty years after Christ's ascension, when the Apostle Paul wrote to the Thessalonians urging them *not to become easily unsettled or alarmed by some prophecy, report or letter supposed to have come from us, saying that the day of the Lord has already come. Don't let anyone deceive you in any way, for that day will not come until the rebellion occurs and the man of lawlessness is revealed, the man doomed to destruction* (2 Thessalonians 2:2-3).

This was the first of many attempts to identify when the Day of the Lord had already or would soon come. Since then, down through the centuries there have been an abundance of these false date setters. One of the latest of these was a radio preacher in the United States who placed billboards all over America and posted ads in major newspapers declaring that the Lord's Return and Judgment Day would be on May 21, 2011.

We know from what Jesus said that, *"No one knows about that day or hour, not even the angels in heaven, nor the Son, but only the Father"* (Matthew 24:36). Peter adds to that understanding with his divinely inspired words:

> *But do not forget this one thing, dear friends: With the Lord a day is like a thousand years, and a thousand years are like a day. The Lord is not slow in keeping his promise, as some understand slowness. He is patient with you, not wanting anyone to perish, but everyone to come to repentance* (2 Peter 3:8-9).

While attempting to calculate the exact day and hour of Christ's return is always wrong, the Scriptures do describe some of the world conditions and events which will lead up to His return. Luke 21 provides a litany of events that have always been a part of our world, but that are even more apparent to us in our world of today. This litany includes wars between nations and kingdoms; natural disasters like earthquakes, famines, and pestilences; persecution by the hands of kings and governors of those who follow Jesus; a time when the Gentiles will no longer hold sway in Jerusalem; signs in the heavens and tsunamis in the oceans; and men fainting because of terror.

The web site www.nydailynews.com lists the most devastating natural disasters of the twenty-first century. Included among these are the Indian earthquake of 2001 that killed over 150,000 people, the Indian Ocean earthquake and tsunamis in 2004 that left over 230,000 dead, Hurricane Katrina (2005) that struck the Mississippi Gulf coast and devastated New Orleans, leaving nearly 2,000 people dead, the Myanmar cyclone that killed over 138,000 people (2008), the 2010 earthquake that decimated Haiti, and the 8.9 magnitude earthquake and subsequent tsunami that struck Japan (2011).

When you add to this list of natural disasters the ever increasing persecution of Christians at the hands of fanatical religious and political leaders, it is evident that Jesus' words in Luke 21 are being fulfilled in the present. The website www.opendoors.org reports that 322 Christians are killed each month for believing in Jesus and that "according to the United States Department of State, Christians in more than 60 countries face persecution from their governments or surrounding neighbors because of their belief in Jesus Christ."

And there are multiple cases in the United States of attempts to silence the Christian voice, not just in the public square, but also in private settings. We see again and again the events and conditions described by Jesus as present among us in our day, from attempts to ban Christ from Christmas, to a federal judge threatening incarceration to a high school valedictorian unless she remove references to Jesus from her graduation speech, to discrimination charges filed against bakeries that refuse to make wedding cakes for "gay" weddings, to a government official seeking to censor a pastor's prayer during a Memorial day ceremony honoring veterans at a national cemetery.

Biblical scholars have studied the seemingly increasing prevalence of these events and attempted to combine them with the prophetic apocalyptic dreams and visions recorded in Daniel, Revelation, and other scriptural passages. The word "revelation" is the English translation of the Greek word "apokalupsis." The genre of apocalyptic literature is an ancient style of writing that uses dreams and visions to "uncover" or "reveal" otherwise hidden truths. The purpose of this literary genre was to give words of assurance that God was in charge regardless of how bad the situation might look.

Hence Daniel, writing during the Babylonian captivity and the early Medo-Persian times, uses the apocalyptic genre to assure his fellow countrymen that a day of release and freedom is coming in accordance with God's plan.

Likewise, John the Apostle used this same literary technique at the end of the first century A.D. when Christians were being persecuted by Rome. John himself was the victim of this Roman persecution, having been banished to *the island of Patmos because of the word of God and the testimony of Jesus* (Revelation 1:9).

These apocalyptic writings in Daniel and Revelation not only had meaning for those who lived during the sixth century B.C. (Daniel) and the first century A.D. (John) but they also "reveal" events and situations at the time of Christ's return and what believers can expect "next." It is to these writings that biblical scholars look, to match them with the teachings of Jesus and other passages concerning the return of Christ.

THE MILLENIUM, THE RAPTURE, AND THE TRIBULATION

There are three significant words that frequently appear from the attempts to synchronize details in the Book of Revelation with other biblical references concerning Christ's return. These are *millennium, tribulation,* and *rapture.*

A millennium is a thousand years. Revelation 20 addresses a one-thousand-year period that is connected with the return of Christ. The first section of this chapter (verses 1-3) records that Satan will be seized and bound for a thousand years. Then he will be thrown into the Abyss which will be locked and sealed. There confined he will be kept *from deceiving the nations anymore until the thousand years were ended. After that, he must be set free for a short time.*

The succeeding paragraph (verses 4-6) of this chapter tells about **those who had been beheaded because of their testimony for Jesus…who had** *not worshiped the beast or his image and had not received his mark on their foreheads or their hands. They came to life and reigned with Christ a thousand years.*

Then in verses 7-10 we read about the final demise of the devil when he is *thrown into the lake of burning sulfur, where the beast and the false prophet had been thrown. They will be tormented day and night forever and ever.* But this happens after *the thousand years are over* [when] *Satan will be released from his prison and will go out to deceive the nations in the four corners of the earth.*

The final paragraph of Revelation then concludes with an account of the final judgment when the dead are raised and *judged according to what they had done as recorded in the books. ... Then death and Hades were thrown into the lake of fire. ... If anyone's name was not found written in the book of life, he was thrown into the lake of fire* (Revelation 20:13, 15).

Christians continue to debate the issues of the millennium spoken of in Revelation 20 as they relate to Christ's return. Three primary teachings or understandings of these issues are what are referred to as the pre-millennial, post-millennial, and a-millennial views.

The pre-millennial view holds that the second coming of Christ precedes this thousand-year period while those who accept a post-millennial return of Christ teach that the millennium is a time when many people will be saved and righteousness will prevail on earth prior to His return. Finally, a-millennial means that there is no literal one-thousand year period, but that this, like much of apocalyptic literature, is figurative and symbolic language having to do with the time (however long) between the ascension and the return of Christ, or what we classically refer to as the *church age*.

The second key word mentioned here is *tribulation*. The reality of persecution, trial, and tribulation is what gave birth to apocalyptic literature with its focus on offering a vision for hope and restoration beyond the present situation. During the seventy-year period when Israel was captive in Babylonia and subsequently Media-Persia, Daniel presents a word of hope, release, and escape from those hard times. Speaking of the collapse of the conquering powers and the establishment of God's Kingdom he writes, *In the time of those kings, the God of heaven will set up a kingdom that will never be destroyed, nor will it be left to another people. It will crush all those kingdoms and bring them to an end, but it will itself endure forever* (Daniel 2:44).

It is into a strikingly similar scenario that John penned the Book of Revelation. By the close of the first century A.D., Rome was persecuting Christians for their refusal to acknowledge Caesar as Lord, claiming that their only Lord was Jesus Christ. And like Daniel, John's intention is to encourage the believers that a time is coming when Jesus will return as **"KING OF KINGS AND LORD OF LORDS"** (Revelation 19:16). At that time they will be delivered from their trials and tribulations.

Since the worldly kingdoms have not yet been destroyed and Jesus has not yet returned, these words from Daniel and John are as relevant for us today as they were for the Israelites in the sixth century B.C. and the Christians in the first century A.D.

Chapters six through sixteen of Revelation describe a horrible time of tribulation and suffering that precedes the return of Christ. We read about wars, famine, death, economic woes, persecution, earthquakes and other natural disasters, peculiar and changing weather patterns, fires, cosmic changes, pollution of the earth's water sources, an anti-Christ world government, and the ultimate collapse of the world's kingdoms and its economic, social, and political systems. It is to this time of tribulation and suffering that Jesus said, *"There will be great distress, unequalled from the beginning of the world until now – and never to be equaled again"* (Matthew 24:21).

Views of this time of tribulation have been developed into three categories by those who accept a pre-millennial return of Christ. These are pre-, mid-, and post-tribulation views, each meaning, just as they sound, that Christ comes to take the church out of the world either before, during, or at the close of the tribulation period. These positions are all based on the concept of the *Rapture*, our third key word.

The word Rapture has been used to describe the ascent of the believers who will be "caught up" with Jesus as described in 1 Thessalonians 4:16-17:

> *For the Lord himself will come down from heaven, with a loud command, with the voice of the archangel and with the trumpet*

call of God, and the dead in Christ will rise first. After that, we who are still alive and are left will be caught up together with them in the clouds to meet the Lord in the air. And so we will be with the Lord forever.

Of the three views of when the Rapture occurs the pre-tribulation one has been the most popular. Those who ascribe to this view are often referred to as *dispensational premillennialists*. They teach that the tribulation as described in Revelation is a distinct seven-year period following the *dispensation* of the church age. The church is *raptured* out of the world and a new dispensation (or a major time period or era) begins for the perfecting of the nation of Israel.

Therefore of necessity, the Rapture event of Thessalonians and the return of Christ to bring final judgment, destroy evil, confine Satan permanently and consummate the kingdom of God are separated by this seven-year period. Or in the case of those who hold to a mid-tribulation or a post-tribulation premillennial Rapture, the time line separating the two events would be three and one-half years or less.

Conversely, postmillennialists and amillennialists teach that the Rapture and the return of Christ to establish His Kingdom are simultaneous or near simultaneous events with no discernible time gap in between. When Jesus returns in accordance with the account in 1 Thessalonians to rapture the believers, it is then at that time that the events of Revelation regarding the demise of Satan, the final judgment, and the consummated Kingdom are employed and activated.

CONCLUSION

What all of these views hold in common is that Jesus is coming again and when He comes there will be a final judgment of all who have rejected God's plan of salvation in Christ. Satan and all evil will be destroyed. The kingdom of God will be consummated, all true believers will be rewarded by being in the presence of the Lord forever where **the dwelling of God is with men, and he will live with them. They will be his people, and God himself will be with them and be their God. He will wipe every tear from their eyes. There will be no more death or mourning or crying or pain, for the old order of things has passed away** (Revelation 21:3-4).

We have a great description of the return of Jesus in 1 Corinthians 15: 19-27:

> *If only for this life we have hope in Christ, we are to be pitied more than all men. But Christ has indeed been raised from the dead, the firstfruits of those who have fallen asleep. For since death came through a man, the resurrection of the dead comes also through a man. For as in Adam all die, so in Christ all will be made alive. But each in his own turn: Christ, the firstfruits; then, when he comes, those who belong to him. Then the end will come, when he hands over the kingdom to God the Father after he has destroyed all dominion, authority and power. For he must reign until he has put all his enemies under his feet. The last enemy to be destroyed is death. For he has put everything under his feet.*

Over and over the Bible is clear on this. Jesus is coming again and all who belong to Him will be raised with Him. Then the end will come (Matthew 24:14). He will destroy all dominion, authority, and power in opposition to Him and He will reign forever and ever in the new heaven and new earth that John wrote about in Revelation, chapters 21 and 22.

Amen. Come Lord Jesus.

For Further Reading

Grenz, Stanley J. *The Millennial Maze, Sorting Out Evangelical Options.* Downers Grove, IL: InterVarsity Press, 1992.

Jones, Timothy Paul, PhD; Gunderson, David, MDiv, ThM; Galan, Benjamin, MTS, ThM. Rose *Guide to End-Time Prophecy.* Torrance, CA: Rose Publishing, Inc., 2011.

Lucado, Max. *When Christ Comes.* Nashville, TN: Word Publishing, 1999.

Matsdorf, Gary. *What Must Soon Take Place.* Kaneohe, HI: Straight Street Publishing, 1996.

On-line Sources Cited:

http://newworldencyclopedia.com.: Article on the United Nations.

Got Questions Ministries. "What is Religious Pluralism? 2002-2015 www.gotQuestions.org

"Tsunami Hits Japan: The Most Devastating Natural Disasters of the 21st Century." March 14, 2011. www.nydailynews.com

Open Doors International. 2015. "About Christian Persecution." www.opendoors.org

Related Scriptures

Second Coming of Christ -
Zechariah 14:4; Matthew 24:36-44; Acts 1:11; 1 Thessalonians 4:16-18; 2 Thessalonians 1:7-10, 2:8; Titus 2:12-13; Revelation 1:7

Final Judgment and Hell -
Matthew 13:41-43, 25:41; Mark 9:43-44; Revelation 14:10-11, 20:10-15, 21:7-8

Heaven -
John 14:2; 1 Corinthians 2:9, 3:10-15; Revelation 7:15-17, 21:4, 22:5

Time to Interact

Take some time to interact with the following questions. Consider writing your answers in a journal and/or discussing them with a fellow believer for deeper reflection and insight.

1. Jesus proclaims, *"If I go and prepare a place for you, I will come back and take you to be with me that you also may be where I am"* (John 14:3). How do these words make you feel? Is there a difference between the general understanding that Jesus will return and the idea that He is returning for you? How so?

2. What is your understanding of current global events and conditions? How would you compare the nature of world violence, sin, and natural disasters today with the experience of past generations? What does this suggest to you about the timing of Christ's return?

3. Which of the various biblical understandings of the return of Christ make the most sense to you as you study the Scripture? Who in your church could possibly help you with a deeper understanding and exploration of these concepts?

4. What might you say to someone who believes that this life is all

there is, that there is no heaven or hell? What is the impact of such a belief on how people live? How could the compassion of Christ flow through you to minister to those who are unprepared for the realities of the life to come?

Time to Integrate

The return of Christ is a biblical certainty that is meant to fill the heart of every believer with great expectation. Ask the Holy Spirit to overwhelm your heart with this joyous hope as you work through the following steps.

1. Read through the book of Revelation this week. What stands out to you from the seven letters of Jesus to the seven churches in the first three chapters? What might He be saying to you in this current season of life? As you contemplate the imagery and actions of the later chapters, what do you suppose the emotions were in the Apostle John's heart as he experienced this revelation? How does this book expand your view of Christ and the triumph of the kingdom of God?

2. If the return of Christ and the possible end of the age are truly drawing close, are there changes you would like to make in your life? What values do you want to be sure to embrace? What Kingdom goals do you want to be sure to pursue? What relational impact do you hope to have on the people around you? How can you better move toward those intentions now?

3. Who in your life seems least prepared for the life to come? Ask the Holy Spirit to fill your heart with His compassion for that person and choose to regularly lift him or her before the Lord in prayer. How can you possibly come alongside that person to help make the realities of the next life known?

CHAPTER 9

New Life in Christ:
Salvation and Sanctification

CHAPTER 9

New Life in Christ:
Salvation and Sanctification

SALVATION

> We believe, because of our total inability to save ourselves, salvation is by God's grace alone. It is received by faith with repentance and acceptance of Jesus Christ as personal Savior."

THE PLAN OF REDEMPTION

> "We believe Jesus Christ was the sacrifice God planned from the foundation of the world for the sin of the human race. By shedding His blood and dying on the cross, Jesus made provision for the salvation of all people.

SALVATION

It is not hard for us to look around today in our fallen world and see the results of war, crime, greed, and family strife – all of which have left this planet in a perilous state. Much of what we see is because of humankind's sin, our rebellion against God and His principles. It is not difficult to see our own human condition – our anger, our addictions, our self-centeredness – and to realize that we are sinners often unable to change our condition when left to our own resources. So, it is wonderful to know that God has provided a gracious solution to humankind's dilemma. We call that solution "salvation." This "good news" lies at the heart of the gospel and gives every Christian a reason to live and a reason to share with others.

The Meaning of Salvation

Simply stated, salvation is deliverance from sin and its consequences. But more than that, salvation is a glorious hope of a future of abundant and eternal life. Let's look a little more closely at this great truth.

The word *salvation* is the translation of the Greek word *soteria*, derived from the word *soter* meaning "savior." (This is the origin of the word soteriology, which is the formal theological term for the doctrine of salvation).

The word *salvation* communicates the thought of deliverance, safety, preservation, soundness, restoration, and healing. The angel said to Joseph, *"You shall call His name Jesus, because He will save His people from their sins"* (Matthew 1:21, NKJV).

Salvation Past, Present, and Future

Who [God] **delivered** *us from so great a death, and* **does deliver** *us; in whom we trust that He* **will still deliver** *us* (2 Corinthians 1:10, NKJV).

The wonderful truth is that when we receive Christ as Savior, He saves us once and for all. Your salvation is a finished work. *But when the kindness and love of God our Savior appeared, he saved us, not because of righteous things we had done, but because of his mercy* (Titus 3:4-5). In short, we have been saved from the *penalty* of sin.

Not only has God saved us, the Scripture makes it clear that we are presently and continually being saved. *For the message of the cross is foolishness to those who are perishing, but to us who are being saved it is the power of God* (1 Corinthians 1:18). While the finished work of salvation is a work of the cross, our ongoing salvation is a work of the Holy Spirit in a process we call sanctification. We will discuss that in more detail later in this chapter. In short, we are continually being saved from the *power* of sin.

Finally, the "blessed hope" is that we will be saved. Jesus said, *"All men will hate you because of me, but he who stands firm to the end will be saved"* (Matthew 10:22). What does this mean? It does not mean that we must continue to do works in order to be saved, but that we must stand firm in our faith to the end. Please note: Some would lead you to believe that once you have been saved (past tense) it is impossible for you to lose your salvation (future tense). This passage and many others make it clear that a believer must continue to stand firm in their faith in Christ. Revelation 3:5 reads, *"He who overcomes will, like them, be dressed in white. I will never blot out his name from the book of life, but will acknowledge his name before my Father and his angels."* So let us purpose to receive the future salvation God has in store for us, into His presence forever.

The Motivation for Salvation

When we look at how rebellious and sinful man has been over the course of centuries, we might ask ourselves, "Why should God even bother to save us?" And, even more important, we might ask, "Why would God sacrifice the life of His only Son, allow Him to suffer as He did, and turn His back on Him on the cross as He carried our sins?" Here are the amazing reasons:

1. **God saved us because of His love.** God spanned the gulf between sinful man and a holy God by giving His only Son on the cross. No act of love could be greater than that. Jesus said, *"For God so loved the world that he gave his one and only Son, that whoever believes in him shall not perish but have eternal life"* (John 3:16).

2. **God saved us because of His grace,** the unmerited favor of God. *That in the ages to come He might show the exceeding riches of His grace in His kindness toward us in Christ Jesus. For by grace you have been saved through faith, and that not of yourselves; it is the gift of God* (Ephesians 2:7-8, NKJV). Only our Christian faith offers to mankind a deliverance that is in no way based on our own efforts, but simply on the undeserved favor or grace of God.

3. **God saved us because of His holiness.** Because He is a holy God and cannot look upon sin, He sought for a way to restore fellowship with mankind whom He had created for that purpose. The Scripture says, *For all have sinned and fall short of the glory of God* (Romans 3:23). The solution to the relationship dilemma was found in the person of Jesus Christ. In His sinless sacrifice, both the holiness of God and the love of God are satisfied. His holiness is satisfied in that Christ took our sins on Himself. And God's love is satisfied in that mankind could be restored to relationship with God.

The Necessity of Salvation

Salvation is necessary for several reasons:

1. **Because mankind is separated from a holy God.** It is comfortable for us to think of God as a God of love, which He is, but the Bible actually has more to say about God's holiness and His disdain for sin. Isaiah 57:15 declares that His "name is holy."

When one's name is holy, it is a reference to the very character of the one bearing that name. In Isaiah 6:3, the seraphim are pictured as continuously worshipping a God who is holy. After seeing this vision, Isaiah cried out, *"Woe to me! … I am ruined! For I am a man of unclean lips, and I live among a people of unclean lips, and my eyes have seen the King, the Lord Almighty"* (Isaiah 6:5).

These and many other passages point to a God who is perfectly holy and to the fact that God cannot and will not act in a manner contrary to His holy nature. If He is completely just and completely righteous in everything He does, how can He have a relationship with sinful man who is completely unjust and unrighteous in who he is and in what he does?

2. **Because every person is born with a sinful nature.** The Scripture says, *Therefore, just as sin entered the world through one man, and in this way death came to all men, because all sinned* (Romans 5:12). This verse teaches that Adam's spiritual death has been passed down to all of humanity. This means we are all born spiritually dead. This is the fatal ailment that infests the soul of every person. The Bible says, *There is no one righteous, not even one … for all have sinned and fall short of the glory of God* (Romans 3:10, 23).

3. **Because the penalty of sin is death.** Because God is holy and humans are sinful, God's perfect justice declares that humans are guilty as charged and must receive the penalty of their sin, which is to spend eternity separated from God. The Bible indicates that the Old Testament law serves as the basis for the indictment. When we violate that law, we are clearly guilty and under the penalty of sin. Romans 6:23 reads, *For the wages of sin is death, but the gift of God is eternal life in Christ Jesus our Lord.* Apart from salvation, every person will die in their sin eternally separated from God. The Bible concludes that *in Adam all die* (1 Corinthians 15:22). Humanity's position in Adam brings spiritual death, eventually physical death, and ultimately eternal death – eternal separation from God. Because humankind inherited Adam's sinful nature, they will experience spiritual death,

eventually physical death, and ultimately eternal death - forever separated from God. Death is the terrible consequence of sin (Genesis 2:17; Ephesians 2:1, 5).

This means that people in themselves have no spiritual life or spiritual capacity to attain eternal life. No matter what kind of effort they make, they continue to fall short of God's holy nature. We simply cannot save ourselves, no matter how hard we try or how sincere we are. This is the reason Jesus told Nicodemus, who was very religious, *"You must be born again"* (John 3:7). This was Christ's way of teaching Nicodemus, and all of us for that matter, that he needed a new spirit, a rebirth by the Holy Spirit of God in order to see, understand, and be a part of the kingdom of God.

Please note: Some today teach that all of humankind will eventually be saved. This is called Universalism. But the Scripture is clear when Jesus said, *"Then they (the wicked) will go away to eternal punishment, but the righteous to eternal life"* (Matthew 25:46). These words were spoken by Jesus in the Parable of the Ten Virgins. The parable describes a group of people who were invited to a marriage feast. Five of them were ready to go, and five were not. The parable makes it plain that the five that were not ready would be eternally punished. In fact, no one in Scripture talked more about hell as an eternal reality than Jesus Himself (Matthew 5:22-30; 10:28; 18:9; 23:33; Mark 9:43-47; Luke 12:5).

The Nature of Salvation

1. **It is initiated by God.** Salvation is an act initiated by God on behalf of humankind and is in no sense a work people could initiate on behalf of themselves. The prophet Jonah wrote, *Salvation comes from the Lord* (Jonah 2:9). In Ephesians 1:4-5, the Apostle Paul writes, *In love he predestined us to be adopted as his sons through Jesus Christ, in accordance with his pleasure and will.* What a wonderful truth! Even before we were born, God had in mind that we would be His children.

2. **It is offered to us because of His grace.** *In him we have redemption through his blood, the forgiveness of sins, in*

accordance with the riches of God's grace (Ephesians 1:7). We do not deserve God's salvation, but, simply because of God's grace – His unmerited favor – we have received forgiveness for our sins.

3. **It is a free gift.** Most things in life are not free. They come with a price tag. But the greatest gift of all, the gift of salvation, is absolutely free. There is nothing we can pay; there is nothing we can do to earn it. *For the wages of sin is death, but the gift of God is eternal life in Christ Jesus our Lord* (Romans 6:23).

4. **It does not come to us through our good works or sincere effort.** Many people believe they can get into heaven by keeping the Ten Commandments, or by living according to the Golden Rule, or by helping those less fortunate than they are, or by being good in other ways. But the Scripture makes it clear that nothing we could ever do is good enough to satisfy the requirements of a righteous, holy God. *He saved us, not because of righteous things we had done, but because of his mercy* (Titus 3:5).

5. **It is a finished work.** The last words uttered by the Savior just before He died on the cross were, *"It is finished"* (John 19:30). He was not referring to the end of His life and ministry, but rather He was declaring that He had finished the special work of salvation which the Father had given Him to accomplish. We speak of "the finished work of Christ" because there is nothing left to be done to provide man's salvation. God has done it all in the person and work of His Son and He raised Him from the dead as the proof of that very fact.

6. **It is a complete work.** There is not one thing we can add to the work of salvation. It is complete and fully sufficient for the believer. We are not partially saved, needing to work our way through steps to complete our salvation. We are completely saved. The transaction is signed, sealed, and delivered.

The Conditions for Receiving Salvation

1. **Repentance**. Repentance can be defined as recognizing our sin is offensive to God and turning away from it in heart, mind, and actions. In Peter's first sermon, he said, *"Repent and be baptized, every one of you, in the name of Jesus Christ for the forgiveness of*

your sins" (Acts 2:38). Until we recognize that we are sinners and have a willingness to fully surrender our lives to God, we are not ready to receive God's salvation.

2. **Faith**. Faith is truly the key to receiving God's free gift of salvation. The Bible says, *For it is by grace you have been saved, through faith* (Ephesians 2:8.) What is faith? It is not mere intellectual assent that Jesus Christ is God's Son and that He gave His life for our sins. The Bible says, *You believe that there is one God. Good! Even the demons believe that – and shudder* (James 2:19). We need a faith that trusts in Christ alone for our salvation. It means resting upon Christ alone and what He has done and not trusting in any way upon our own efforts.

3. **Confession**. The Scripture reads, *If you confess with your mouth, "Jesus is Lord," and believe in your heart that God raised him from the dead, you will be saved* (Romans 10:9). Our verbal expression of faith seals the work of salvation in our heart and starts us on the journey of abundant and eternal living.

Some Scriptural Terms for Salvation

1. **Reconciliation**. Before salvation, we were separated and alienated from God because of our sin. After salvation, we are no longer separated from God; we are in perfect fellowship with Him. *Not only is this so, but we also rejoice in God through our Lord Jesus Christ, through whom we have now received reconciliation* (Romans 5:11).

2. **Propitiation**. Propitiation is the scriptural truth that the person and death of Jesus Christ turned away God's wrath, satisfied His holiness, and so met God's righteous demands so that the sinner can be reconciled into God's holy presence. *And He Himself is the propitiation for our sins, and not for ours only but also for the whole world* (1 John 2:2, NKJV).

3. **Redemption**. This word comes from the Greek word *agora*, which means "marketplace." It literally means "to purchase, buy from the marketplace." In ancient times slaves were brought to the marketplace, put on the slave block, and then traded or sold

to the highest bidder. Some passages of Scripture that use this word are 1 Corinthians 6:20; 7:23; and 2 Peter 2:1. Christ saw us on the slave block of sin and death, purchased us with His own blood and gave us our freedom. *In him we have redemption through his blood, the forgiveness of sins, in accordance with the riches of God's grace* (Ephesians 1:7).

4. **Expiation**. Expiation means to remove the penalty officially imposed by law which indicts and proves the sinner guilty. *Having canceled the charge of our legal indebtedness, which stood against us and condemned us; He has taken it away, nailing it to the cross* (Colossians 2:14). Even as in our day an offender may have a crime he has committed expunged from his record as if it never happened, so at the moment of salvation God erases from our heavenly record the sentence of death, giving us a fresh new beginning and a new lease on life. This is expiation.

5. **Substitution**. Substitution means to take the place of another. Jesus Christ did that for us on the cross, when as the innocent Lamb of God, He died and suffered the penalty of death in our place. He voluntarily took on Himself the penalty of God's judgment which we rightly deserve. *But He was pierced for our transgressions; He was crushed for our iniquities; the punishment that brought us peace was upon him, and by his wounds we are healed* (Isaiah 53:5).

6. **Regeneration**. Regeneration is the supernatural work of God's Holy Spirit whereby the spiritual and eternal life of the Son, the Lord Jesus Christ, is imparted to us through faith in Jesus Christ. He saved us, not because of righteous things we had done, but because of his mercy. *He saved us through the washing of rebirth and renewal by the Holy Spirit* (Titus 3:5). We often hear the phrase "born again." In a sense, that is what regeneration is. Through our physical birth, we are given life and breath. When we are born again, we are given spiritual life, both abundant and eternal. *Who were born, not of blood, nor of the will of the flesh, nor of the will of man, but of God* (John 1:13, NKJV).

7. **Justification**. The word *justify* means "to place in right standing" or "to make right." It means "to pronounce not guilty, to acquit, or to vindicate." When we are saved, God never again holds our sin against us. As some say, "Just as if we have not sinned." Galatians 2:16 reads, *Know that a man is not justified observing the law, but by faith in Jesus Christ. So we, too, have put our faith in Christ Jesus that we may be justified by faith in Christ and not by the works of observing the law, because by the works of observing the law no one will be justified.*

8. **Imputation**. Imputation is the "charging to the account" of one what properly belongs on the account of another. Because of the person and work of Christ, God imputes or credits our sin to the person of Jesus Christ and imputes His righteousness to our account through faith in Him. As the old song says, "I owed a debt I could not pay; He paid a debt He did not owe." What does Scripture say? *"Abraham believed God, and it was credited to him as righteousness." Now when a man works, his wages are not credited to him as a gift, but as an obligation. However, to the man who does not work but trusts God who justifies the wicked, his faith is credited as righteousness* (Romans 4:3-5).

An Invitation

In the preceding sections, we have seen the work that God has done through His Son Jesus Christ to provide salvation for us. You may receive this free gift, right now. Although God has done this great work, it is not ours until we receive it by faith, until we trust Christ alone for our salvation. There is only one thing that can keep a person separated from God and lost in sin, and that is not receiving by faith the gift of eternal life that God freely offers and which He provided at the price of the death of His only Son, Jesus Christ, on the cross. If you will receive this gift by faith, God will give to you abundant and eternal life and set you free from debt of sin. If you would like to receive this great gift, pray a prayer like this:

> *"Lord Jesus, I ask You to come in and take over my life right now. I am a sinner, separated from God. But now I place my trust in You. I accept You as my Savior. I believe that You died for me. I receive You as Lord and Master of my life. Help me to turn from my sins*

and to follow You. I accept the free gift of eternal life. Thank You for hearing my prayer. Amen."

If you prayed this prayer and put your trust in Christ, we want you to know that you are now a child of God and beginning on a wonderful journey of faith. We encourage you to read your Bible, talk to the Lord through prayer, and find a good church where you can be encouraged to grow in your faith.

SANCTIFICATION

When we put our trust in Christ, at that very moment, **we are a new creation; the old has gone, the new has come!** (2 Corinthians 5:17). From God's perspective, the work of salvation is complete. The work of the cross is finished. Nothing can be added to it. Nothing can be taken from it. At judgment day our testimony will be, "I have trusted in Christ and have received eternal life." But practically speaking, we are in the infant stage of our new life and we need to grow spiritually so that we mature and become more and more like Christ. This process of spiritual growth is called *sanctification*.

At first glance sanctification seems like an irrelevant word, but it is actually very significant. It's like the hundreds of technical medical terms unknown to the average person. Nobody but doctors use them, but your life depends on the reality they stand for. You may never have heard of the word *myopia*, but you won't be able to see well unless you get glasses to correct it. You may never use the word *sanctification*, but you can be assured that it is something that will affect your life every day in a real way. Let's take a closer look at it.

The Meaning of Sanctification

Separated to God

The word sanctification or *sanctify* is used in both the Old and New Testaments of the Bible. In the Old Testament, its meaning is "to set apart for special use." This term was often applied to the priests who were expected to be set apart for the Lord's service. Leviticus 21:6 and 8 (NKJV) describes the priests in this way, **They shall be holy to their God and not profane the name of their God, for they offer the offerings of the LORD made by fire, and the bread of their God; therefore they shall be holy. ...Therefore you shall consecrate him, for he offers the bread of your God. He shall be holy to you, for I the LORD, who sanctify you, am holy.** Just as the priests in the Old Testament were set apart for God's service, we too, when we come in faith to Christ, are given a higher purpose, that is a purpose of pleasing God and living our lives for Him.

In the New Testament, the word *sanctify* is from the same Greek word as *holy*. To be sanctified means "to be made holy, set apart for God's use." The Scripture says, **For it is written: "Be holy, because I am holy"** (1 Peter 1:16). Therefore, our Christian growth or sanctification is a response to the love and call of a holy God who saved us for a purpose and who calls us to a higher level of Christian living.

Purity in Living

Dictionary.com defines purity as "freedom from anything that debases, contaminates or pollutes," such as drinking water. It is interesting how the word *pure* is a positive, wonderful word when it comes to drinking water to sustain our bodies. But somehow, many people who wouldn't think of drinking contaminated water will often ridicule people who desire to remain pure in their lives and relationships. The Scripture speaks often of this truth, **Don't let anyone look down on you because you are young, but set an example for the believers in speech, in conduct, in love, in faith and in purity** (1 Timothy 4:12).

Having said that, often times when we think of the word purity, we think of our actions, especially those that are sexual in nature. But Jesus made it clear in His teachings that purity begins with and is primarily a matter of the heart. *"Blessed are the pure in heart, for they will see God"* (Matthew 5:8). It is not enough to clean up our act on the outside and leave the inside unclean. Jesus Himself said, *"Woe to you, teachers of the law and Pharisees, you hypocrites! You clean the outside of the cup and dish, but inside they are full of greed and self-indulgence. Blind Pharisee! First clean the inside of the cup and dish, and then the outside also will be clean"* (Matthew 23:25). The religious people of Jesus' time prided themselves on living pure lives, but Jesus made it clear that purity begins with the heart. As we are on this journey of sanctification, let us pray the prayer that David prayed, **Create in me a pure heart, O God, and renew a steadfast spirit within me** (Psalms 51:10).

Dedication for Service

Dedication means "given up to," or "devoted to." It is used to describe those things which were devoted to the service of God. The word was often used in the Old Testament to describe possessions that were given to God. For instance, when the Temple was built, the people gave their gold, silver, and skills as a dedication to God for the construction of the Temple. These possessions were no longer their own. They belonged to God. So too we are challenged to dedicate not only our possessions, but, more important, our lives, including our bodies, as a dedication to God, no longer belonging to us but belonging to God. *Therefore, I urge you, brothers, in view of God's mercy, to offer your bodies as living sacrifices, holy and pleasing to God – this is your spiritual act of worship* (Romans 12:1).

Three Aspects of Sanctification

A Completed Work

To better understand sanctification, it is helpful to look at it in a past, present, and future tense. The Bible makes it clear that when we are saved, we are instantly transformed into the image of Christ. From the perspective of God's justice and mercy, the work is complete. Nothing can be added to it. We are positionally sanctified, set apart for God. A*nd that is what some of you were. But you were washed, you were sanctified, you were justified in the name of the Lord Jesus Christ and by the Spirit of our God* (1 Corinthians 6:11). Because Christ, by His death, has paid the penalty of the law, and, by His blood, has washed away all our guilt (1 Corinthians 6:11; Galatians 3:13; Revelation 1:5; 7:14), we have been legally sanctified. Our sinful, guilty soul has been transformed into His image! This work is completed; it is in the past; it is done.

An Ongoing Work

Nevertheless, when we come to Christ, the practical reality is that there are many attitudes, thoughts, and actions that need to change if we are going to walk in a manner pleasing to the Lord. Watchman Nee, in his classic book *Sit, Walk, Stand* describes the Christian life as featured in the book of Ephesians, using these three words of posture: sit, walk, and stand. When we are saved, we are immediately **seated with Christ in heavenly places** (Ephesians 2:6). Paul, in the first three chapters of Ephesians, describes this royal position in many ways. For instance, he writes, *Praise be to the God and Father of our Lord Jesus Christ, who has blessed us in the heavenly realms with every spiritual blessing in Christ. For He chose us in him before the creation of the world to be holy and blameless in his sight. In love he predestined us to be adopted as his sons* *through Jesus Christ, in accordance with his pleasure and will* (Ephesians 1:3-5).

Having received this wonderful position, the Apostle Paul, beginning in the fourth chapter of Ephesians, tells us how we ought to *walk* as a result of the position we have received. While sitting describes a prone position, walking implies movement or progression toward a goal. This movement we call *progressive sanctification*. In other words, for the rest of our years it should be our desire to walk out, in ever greater measures, the realities of the Christian life. Paul describes that life in Ephesians 4:1-6:10 in terms of our attitudes, our thoughts, our words, and our actions toward other believers, toward our families, in our work, and in society in general. This walk will go on throughout our entire life and will never be fully completed. **Since we have these promises, dear friends, let us purify ourselves from everything that contaminates body and spirit, perfecting holiness out of reverence for God** (2 Corinthians 7:1).

In addition, every believer must be reminded that the process of sanctification, or spiritual maturity, is marked by conflict and spiritual warfare. The reality is that new life in Christ is on a collision course with the world, is opposed by Satan, and fought by the sinful nature within us. Therefore, Paul tells us in Ephesians 6 that we need to *stand* strong, using the armor that God has given us so that we can be effective in our growth in Christ. **Stand firm then, with the belt of truth buckled around your waist, with the breastplate of righteousness in place, and with your feet fitted with the readiness that comes from the gospel of peace. In addition to all this, take up the shield of faith, with which you can extinguish all the flaming arrows of the evil one. Take the helmet of salvation and the sword of the Spirit, which is the word of God. And pray in the Spirit on all occasions with all kinds of prayers and requests** (Ephesians 6:14-18).

An Ultimate Work

The third aspect of our sanctification is the final perfection that will be ours when we are in heaven with God. This ultimate perfection will happen at the time of the resurrection of our bodies when we who believe are transformed into the likeness of Christ and presented to the Lord as holy. The indwelling of the Holy Spirit in the life of a believer on earth is the promise of this future glorification in heaven, which includes 1) the resurrection of the body, 2) an eternal and pure inheritance, and 3) deliverance from the future wrath of God. **In Him you also trusted, after you heard the word of truth, the gospel of your salvation; in whom also, having believed, you were sealed with the**

Holy Spirit of promise, who is the guarantee of our inheritance until the redemption of the purchased possession, to the praise of His glory (Ephesians 1:13-14, NKJV).

Sanctification: God's Initiation and Man's Obedience

It is clear from Scripture that sanctification is both a work of God and an obedient response of man. This two-part work of sanctification is well illustrated in Philippians 2:12-13: *Therefore, my dear friends, as you have always obeyed – not only in my presence, but now much more in my absence – continue to work out your salvation with fear and trembling, for it is God who works in you to will and to act according to his good purpose.* Working out our own salvation is the very obedience that is required of us to grow in Christ. But this Scripture also clearly tells us that God is working in us to have the *will* (desire, motivation, power) to be obedient in our lives.

God's Work in Sanctification

In Romans we read about two forces or laws that are at work in the world. One is called the law of sin. Paul describes it in this way, *So I find this law at work: Although I want to do good, evil is right there with me. For in my inner being I delight in God's law; but I see another law at work in the members of my body, waging war against the law of my mind and making me a prisoner of the law of sin at work within my members* (Romans 7:21-23). When we come to Christ, our soul is transformed into His image, but our body and mind are still subject to this law of sin. Let us compare this law to the law of gravity. Gravity holds your feet down to the ground because the mass of the planet exerts a gravitational pull on the mass of your body. That's how sin is. It tries to pull us down, to keep us down, and ultimately destroy us.

But, thank God, there is an even more powerful force at work in us. Romans 8:1 describes it as the law of the Spirit: *Therefore, there is now no condemnation for those who are in Christ Jesus, because through Christ Jesus the law of the Spirit of life set me free from the law of sin and death.* While the law of sin tries to pull us down, the law of the Spirit is at work to lift us up and to make us overcomers in this life. When we look up to the sky, we see huge airplanes flying gracefully through the air. These amazing machines are actually hundreds of tons of steel and other materials that naturally should be sitting on the ground. The law of gravity would never allow them to fly.

But there is another law at work, the law of aerodynamics. This law, or force, uses fuel that empowers the jet engine to create a thrust that is greater than the downward force of gravity. When the huge jet engines begin their thrust of power, the huge mass of steel that is an airplane is able to ascend into the sky and soar toward its destination. Such is the work of the Holy Spirit in our lives. When we are born again, a new spirit comes to dwell in us, the Holy Spirit. The Holy Spirit is a spirit of life, of lift, of power, of strength. As we learn to yield to the Spirit's power, our lives are transformed – our attitudes begin to change, our thoughts are cleansed, and our actions please the Lord. We are lifted from a life of sin to a life of victory over sin. *Those who live according to the flesh have their minds set on what the flesh desires; but those who live in accordance with the Spirit have their minds set on what the Spirit desires. The mind governed by the flesh is death, but the mind governed by the Spirit is life and peace* (Romans 8:5-6).

Man's Work in Sanctification: Obedience

While God initiates the work of sanctification within us, His work must be accompanied by our response if we are to grow in grace. This response can best be described by the word *obedience*. Salvation is not about following a set of rules or religious regulations. Rather, it is about following Jesus Christ as our Savior and Lord. When a person is lord, he is in charge. He is in a position of leadership. As the Lord, Jesus calls us to follow Him. He is our leader. He is in charge. This "followership" is a life of obedience. Here are a few ways we follow Jesus in obedience to His Lordship:

1. **Obedience to the Holy Spirit's promptings**. When Jesus ascended into heaven, He told His disciples that He would give them the Holy Spirit, who would guide them, empower them and, in general, represent the will of Jesus to them (Acts 1:8). Thus, when you gave your life to Christ, the Holy Spirit came to live within you. He is a living, breathing person and desires to lead you in a life of sanctification. Coming to recognize and respond to the Holy Spirit's promptings is one of the most important areas in which we can grow as Christians. Learning to recognize His voice is a lifetime learning opportunity and one that will save us from much heartache, even when we might not understand. We can think of the Spirit's prompting

as a "green light." When we are driving in our car, a green light tells us that we can proceed on the road that we are traveling. When the light is yellow, we are to proceed with caution. When the light is red, we are to come to a stop. So it is with the Holy Spirit's promptings. As we grow in this obedience, we learn to make decisions, speak words, and engage in activities when we have the "green" light of the Holy Spirit's promptings. These promptings are always accompanied by peace. *May the God of hope fill you with all joy and peace as you trust in him, so that you may overflow with hope by the power of the Holy Spirit* (Romans 15:13). Likewise, when we are headed into danger or toward something that is not pleasing to God, the Holy Spirit will prompt us with a "yellow" light or even a "red" light. The more obedient we are to these promptings, the more God's sanctifying work can continue in us.

2. **Obedience to the Word of God.** Relying on the promptings of the Holy Spirit without our lives being anchored by truth can result in much uncertainty. For as much as we may want to obey God, we must know the truth if we are going to be fully obedient. That is why God has given His Word, the Bible, to us.

> *But as for you, continue in what you have learned and have become convinced of, because you know those from whom you learned it, and how from infancy you have known the Holy Scriptures, which are able to make you wise for salvation through faith in Christ Jesus. All Scripture is God-breathed and is useful for teaching, rebuking, correcting and training in righteousness, so that the servant of God may be thoroughly equipped for every good work* (2 Timothy 3:14-16).

There are many things in life that Scripture is very clear about, such as we are always to tell the truth, we are to be faithful to our spouses, we are to work hard and never to steal. We don't need the Holy Spirit's promptings in these areas. We simply need to walk out our lives in obedience to His Word. The more we read, study and mediate upon the Word of God, the more equipped we will be to live a life of sanctification.

3. **Obedience in trials.** While difficulties, testings, and trials are

something that none of us look forward to, they are and always will be a reality. Jesus said, *"In this world you will have trouble. But take heart! I have overcome the world"* (John 16:33). The truth of the matter is that God uses testings and trials to help us grow in obedience and in patience. *Consider it pure joy, my brothers, whenever you face trials of many kinds, because you know that the testing of your faith develops perseverance. Perseverance must finish its work so that you may be mature and complete, not lacking anything* (James 1:2-4). While the Scriptures make it clear that God does not tempt us with evil (James 1:13), nevertheless, He does work through our testings to cause us to grow strong in our faith. The children of Israel had to wander around in the desert for 40 years, but in the process they were being made strong for the battles which lay ahead.

The Fruit of the Holy Spirit

As this sanctifying work continues in our life through a blending of the Holy Spirit's work and our obedient response, the fruit of the Spirit begins to grow and develop within us. This fruit is described in Galatians 5:22-23: *But the fruit of the Spirit is love, joy, peace, patience, kindness, goodness, faithfulness, gentleness and self-control. Against such things there is no law.* We become more and more like Christ and are sanctified for His service and witness.

God's wonderful work of salvation in Christ has been provided for us simply by His grace as we put our trust completely in Him. He continues the work in our lives, initiating a process of sanctification whereby we grow in grace and maturity as we respond in obedience. Let us live our lives, thankful for this *unspeakable gift* and purposing to walk worthy of Him until our life's journey is complete.

Related Scriptures

Salvation -
John 3:3, 3:16-17; 2 Corinthians 5:17; Ephesians 2:8-10; 1 Peter 2:24

The Plan of Redemption -
Isaiah 53:5; Titus 2:14; Hebrews 7:25; 1 Peter 1:18-20

For Further Reading

Grudem, Wayne. *Systematic Theology*. Downer's Grove, IL: Inter-Varsity Press, 1994.

Keathly, J. Hampton III, *Soteriology – The Doctrine of Salvation*, Bible.org, 2004.

Kennedy, D. James. *Evangelism Explosion*. Carol Stream, IL: Tyndale House Publishers, 1970, 1977.

Nee, Watchman. *Sit, Walk, Stand,* American Edition. Carol Stream, IL: Tyndale House Publishers, 1977.

Pearlman, Myer. *Knowing the Doctrines of the Bible*. Springfield, MO: Gospel Publishing House, 1937.

Piper, John. *Desiring God*. Colorado Springs, CO: Multnomah Books, 2003.

Time to Interact

Take some time to interact with the following questions. Consider writing your answers in a journal and/or discussing them with a fellow believer for deeper reflection and insight.

1. When did you first hear the Good News of the Gospel? How did you first respond? What is the impact of the Good News on you today? In what ways have you experienced the Lord's deliverance, safety, preservation, soundness, restoration, and healing?

2. What does it mean to you to "stand firm in our faith to the end?" How are you able to do that? What would you say to someone who feels like they are struggling and unsure about being able to stand firm?

3. What is the role of repentance in the work of salvation? What did this look like in your life? How does repentance continue to work in the process of sanctification? In what ways are you experiencing life change in this process? In what areas do you recognize you are still in need of transformation?

Time to Integrate

Our understanding of God's heart for our salvation and sanctification is meant to be the basis for an experiential faith that remakes our life. Step into that process anew as you engage with the following conversations.

1. Have you taken up the invitation yet to embrace Christ as Lord? If so, who would benefit from hearing your story? If not, what is hindering you? What fears or doubts yet stand in your way? Be honest with God about them and ask the Lord to undeniably show Himself to you.

2. Think about what the condition of your life would be if it were not for the loving, gracious, saving power of Christ. Spend some time acknowledging the debt of sin that you owed before God and the penalty you deserved. Offer prayers of thanksgiving for the Father's incredible love and faithfulness expressed in His provision for salvation. Tell somebody what God has done for you! Allow a grateful heart to spur you forward in your service and devotion to the Lord.

3. As part of the process of sanctification, God works in us to bring about both the inward transformation of our desires and an outward obedience with our actions. What areas of inward and/or outward struggle are you currently experiencing? How is the Father yet stretching you and helping you to grow in Christ? Discuss these areas with a fellow believer with whom you feel close. Pray together, thanking the Lord for equipping you and perfecting you in each area. What practical lifestyle changes will you make in cooperation with your prayer?

CHAPTER 10

Celebrating God's Grace:
Water Baptism and the Lord's Supper

CHAPTER 10
Celebrating God's Grace:
Water Baptism and the Lord's Supper

WATER BAPTISM

> "We believe water baptism by immersion in the name of the Father, Son, and Holy Spirit is an outward sign of an inward work and is commanded by God following conversion."

COMMUNION

> "We believe in partaking of the bread and the cup of communion in remembrance of the Lord's death, burial, and resurrection. We celebrate an open communion for all believers regardless of church affiliation."

Water baptism and the Lord's Supper are the only ordinances observed in Open Bible Churches because they are the two explicitly commanded in Scripture. (Although marriage is understood to be holy and God-ordained, it is not considered an ordinance because the Lord did not command that believers marry.) Other churches observe marriage and other rites such as Confirmation as sacraments, defined by St. Augustine as "an outward and visible sign of an inward and spiritual grace" (*New Dictionary of Theology*, by Ferguson, Wright and Packer). Open Bible Churches believes that water baptism and the Lord's Supper have particular biblical importance for believers, and so we encourage our churches and members to faithfully observe these practices.

It is important to examine these traditions (water baptism and the Lord's Supper) from a biblical/theological perspective so as to be able to establish their validity as important and meaningful expressions of faith and worship in the Christian church and also to compare our practice of these ordinances with the manner in which they are observed in other churches so as to be confident that what we believe and practice is in fact faithful to the teachings of the Scripture.

WATER BAPTISM
Pre-Christian Baptisms

The word *baptism* appears for the first time in the New Testament in Matthew 3:6, where it is associated with the ministry of John who is called "the Baptist." Matthew tells us that the Pharisees and the Sadducees were coming to John to be baptized (verse 7). This of course is a remarkable phenomenon, since the Jews never practiced baptism as a formal rite of initiation as members of the Jewish community, nor was it a requirement of the law of Moses. Further, the Jews did not regard baptism as necessary since all their **forefathers were all under the cloud and ... they all passed through the sea. They were all baptized into Moses in the cloud and in the sea** (1 Corinthians 10:1-2).

There has been much discussion and debate regarding the origin of the baptisms conducted by John the Baptist. It has been suggested that John's baptism originated in the baptism of proselytes (Gentiles initiated into Judaism). Theologian G.E Ladd acknowledges several points of similarity between John's baptism and proselyte baptism:

In both rites, John's and proselyte baptism, the candidates completely immersed themselves or were immersed in water. Both baptisms involved an ethical element in that the persons baptized made a complete break with their former manner of conduct and dedicated themselves to a new life. In both instances, the rite was initiatory, introducing the baptized person into a new fellowship: the one into the fellowship of the Jewish people, the other into the circle of those who were prepared to share in the salvation of the coming messianic Kingdom. Both rites were performed once for all (*A Theology of the New Testament*, by George Eldon Ladd).

Ladd notes, however, that there were three notable differences between the two baptisms. The first was that John's baptism prepared men for the coming Kingdom. Second, John's baptism was unrepeatable. Finally and perhaps most significantly, while proselyte baptism was administered to the Gentiles, John's baptism was applied to Jews.

If the baptism of Jews by John the Baptist was an unusual phenomenon, that Jesus would submit himself to John's baptism was even more astonishing. John's baptism was a baptism unto repentance (a sign of repentance). There was no reason why Jesus needed to be baptized. He had no sin of which to repent (John 8:46). John himself was surprised by Jesus' request and protested, saying, *"I need to be baptized by you, and do you come to me?"* (Matthew 3:14).

Why then did Jesus submit to John's baptism? R.B. Graffin Jr., in an interesting article on the baptism of Christ, states that "the baptism of Jesus was not merely a personal or private matter, … the baptism of Jesus was his 'coronation,' the occasion of his official, public installation as Messiah." Jeannine K. Brown is of the view that Jesus pursued John's eschatological baptism as a way of signaling the fulfillment of God's restoration (of His people) in Jesus himself. Additionally, she sees Jesus' baptism as an occasion for "God's affirmation of pleasure and love in the obedient son who has come to fulfill all righteousness" (*The Baker Illustrated Bible Commentary*, by Gary M. Burge and Andrew E. Hill).

It is also reasonable to assume that by His baptism Jesus was publicly declaring the purpose and intention of His mission, identifying with the sinners He had come to save. The Apostle Paul writes, **God made him who had no sin to be sin for us, so that in him we might become the righteousness of God** (2 Corinthians 5:21).

The baptism of Jesus was also an important aspect of His preparation for public ministry. The Holy Spirit descending in the form of a dove (a sign of God's anointing) and the voice of the Father (an affirmation of His pleasure) in the presence of witnesses would have made clear the authority that was key to the effectiveness and success of Jesus' ministry.

Finally, Jesus submitted Himself to John's baptism to provide us with an example to follow. If He who knew no sin submitted Himself to the rite of baptism, how much more then should His followers do the same? Further, Jesus endorsed the baptizing activities of His disciples during His earthly ministry (John 4:2), and toward the end of that ministry He commanded His disciples to *"make disciples of all nations, baptizing them in the name of the Father and of the Son and of the Holy Spirit"* (Matthew 28:19).

Christian Baptism

The origin of Christian baptism is generally associated with the birth of the Church on the Day of Pentecost. After hearing the Apostle Peter's sermon, the multitude, which included Jews from all over the then-known world, having been convinced of their sin, asked a very pertinent question: *"Brothers, what shall we do?"* Peter's response was, *"Repent and be baptized, every one of you, in the name of Jesus Christ for the forgiveness of your sins. And you will receive the gift of the Holy Spirit"* (Acts 2:37-38). Later in the same chapter we are told that *those who accepted his message were baptized, and about three thousand were added to their number that day* (Acts 2:41).

Several important inferences can be made from the passages cited above. First, in the early church, hearing the Word and genuine repentance was a prerequisite for baptism. Second, the rite of baptism was administered shortly after the profession of faith. Third, water baptism was a common preparatory step before a person received the fullness of the Holy Spirit. Fourth, the rite of baptism preceded membership into the church community. Finally, believers were all baptized in the name of Jesus.

Commenting on the significance of water baptism in the life of the early faith community, G.E. Ladd writes, "The practice of water baptism was carried over from the days of Jesus, but given a new significance. John had baptized in anticipation of the coming of the Kingdom, and the Fourth Gospel tells us that Jesus' disciples continued this practice (John 3:22; 4:1-2). Now that Jesus is recognized as the resurrected and exalted Lord, baptism becomes an outward sign of admission to the Christian fellowship, and believers are baptized 'in the name of Jesus' " (*A Theology of the New Testament*, by George Eldon Ladd).

Robert Webber, in *Ancient Future Evangelism*, sees a unity between conversion and water baptism. "Conversion and baptism are bound together. Certainly Paul saw the unity between the two. The teaching on justification in Romans 5 is immediately connected to Paul's great exposition on baptism in Romans 6." Citing Romans 6: 4 he adds, "Baptism is a sign of our identity with the death and resurrection of Jesus Christ."

Webber is also of the view that while the biblical record suggests baptism was administered shortly after conversion (the Philippian jailer, the Ethiopian eunuch, and Paul himself), there is also clear evidence to support the practice of delayed baptism in the early church. Citing the early church fathers, he states "in the early church, and as early as the *Didache*, a non-canonical document that describes early Christian practices of ministry… there was a delay in baptism. The delay was probably established because some converts fell away from the faith due to having no foundation enabling them to understand the meaning of their commitment of believing, behaving, and belonging."

In describing worship in daily life during the first years of the church Justo Gonzalez, author of *Church History: An Essential Guide*, concurs with Webber regarding the delay in the baptism of new believers. He writes, "Baptism, the rite of initiation and grafting into the Christian community, was the other central act of worship. It usually took place on Easter Sunday, after a long period of preparation for those who were to be baptized. During the last week before the great event on Easter, those who were already baptized also prepared themselves for the renewal of their own baptismal vows. This is the origin of Lent."

The Scriptures provide us with little detailed information regarding the mode of early Christian baptism. It may be reasonable to conclude, however, that baptism involved the immersion of the candidate in water. Two examples from Scripture support this view. The first is the baptizing activity of John the Baptist. We are told that the people who confessed their sins were baptized *in the Jordan River* (Matthew 3:6). Further, at the baptism of Jesus, **As soon as Jesus was baptized, he went up out of the water** (Matthew 3:16). The prepositions "in," "up," and "out" used in both passages suggest that in each instance the baptismal candidates were immersed in the water. Additionally, we are told that while Jesus and His disciples were baptizing out in the Judean countryside, **John also was baptizing at Aenon near Salim, because there was plenty of water, and people were constantly coming to be being baptized** (John 3:22-23).

The second example of baptism by immersion is the baptism of the Ethiopian eunuch. Luke the Evangelist records that when Philip and the eunuch came to a place where there was water, the eunuch gave orders to stop the chariot. **Then both Philip and the eunuch went down into the water and Philip baptized him. When they came up out of the water, the Spirit of the Lord suddenly took Philip away** (Acts 8:36-39).

There is no evidence in Scripture to support baptism by the sprinkling of water. In any case, the word for baptize used in the Greek New Testament is the word *baptizo*. For speakers of the Greek language the term meant "to put or go under water" as it is used for a ship that sinks, for a flooded city, or metaphorically for people immersed in debt. It should also be noted that when the Apostle wrote concerning the believer being *baptized* into the death of Christ Jesus (Romans 6:3) he used the same word *baptizo*. To argue in support of the view that baptism is by sprinkling, therefore, is to ignore the clear teaching of the Scriptures cited above and to embrace a practice based solely on tradition.

Regarding the baptismal formula, there is hardly any dispute among the Christian churches on this issue. The vast majority of Pentecostal/Evangelical faith communities adhere to the command by Jesus to baptize *"in the name of the Father and of the Son and of the Holy Spirit"* (Matthew 28:19). In recent times some Pentecostal groups have contended that the baptismal formula was altered on the Day of Pentecost. They argue that Peter commanded those who repented to be baptized in the "name of Jesus" and not in the "name of the Father and of the Son and of the Holy Spirit." The fact that Peter did not mention the Father and the Holy Spirit in no way suggests a change in the baptismal formula. Peter's audience believed in the Father and the Holy Spirit. They did not accept Jesus as the Son of God. In holding up Jesus as the one in whose name they should be baptized, Peter was simply affirming the deity of Jesus. In any case, in Jesus dwells the fullness of the Godhead. So to be baptized in the name of Jesus, is to be baptized in the name of the Father, the Son, and the Holy Spirit.

Before concluding our discussion on Christian baptism it might be helpful to comment briefly on the practice of infant baptism. This practice emerged in the fourth century primarily through the teaching and influence of St. Augustine. Augustine justified infant baptism based on his doctrine of original sin. He believed the seed of salvation was sown in baptism, and that while infants had no faith of their own, the faith of the church was of benefit to them.

There is no clear evidence in Scripture that supports the practice of infant baptism. Those who subscribe to this practice often appeal to those passages that refer to the baptism of households (Acts 10:48-11:14; 16:15, 33; 18:8). But as Ladd admits, while these "households" may have included infants, the expression could equally well designate only those of mature age who confessed their faith in Christ. The baptism of infants represented a significant departure from the early tradition of adult baptism. It also signaled a change in the process of spiritual formation. "Prior to Constantine [in the fourth century] the process was conversion, rigorous training in discipleship and Christian formation, followed by baptism and full admittance into the life of the church. After Constantine, however, the rise of infant baptism challenged the process and resulted in the breakdown of the process itself" (*Ancient Future Evangelism,* by Robert Webber).

One of the strongest arguments against infant baptism in modern times is expressed in the writings of twentieth century theologian Karl Barth, as cited by Alister E. McGrath. "Karl Barth directs three major lines of criticism against the practice, as follows.

1. It is without biblical foundation. All the evidence points to infant baptism having become the norm in the post-apostolic period, not the period of the New Testament itself.

2. The practice of infant baptism has led to the disastrous assumption that the individuals are Christians as a result of their birth. Barth argues, in terms which remind many of Bonhoeffer's idea of 'cheap grace,' that infant baptism devalues the grace of God and reduces Christianity to a purely social phenomenon.

3. The practice of infant baptism weakens the central link between baptism and discipleship. Baptism is a witness to the grace of God, and marks the beginning of the human response to this grace. In that infants cannot meaningfully make this response, the theological meaning of baptism is obscured" (*Christian Theology: An Introduction*, by Alister E. McGrath).

We may summarize Open Bible beliefs about water baptism as follows:

- Water baptism has its origin in the baptism of John the Baptist.
- Water baptism follows repentance and conversion.
- Initially baptism followed shortly after conversion, but in later times baptism was often delayed to facilitate instruction and spiritual formation.
- Water baptism is a rite of initiation into the community of faith.
- Water baptism is a sign of obedience to the life expected to be lived in the kingdom of God.

- Water baptism is a sign of identification with the death and resurrection of Jesus Christ.

- In the apostolic tradition water baptism was by immersion.

- In the apostolic tradition conversion and water baptism belonged together.

- In the apostolic tradition water baptism was reserved for believers, not infants.

- Water baptism is administered in the name of the Father, Son and Holy Spirit as well as in the name of Jesus.

Open Bible Churches embraces and practices water baptism of men and women, along with boys and girls who have reached an age of accountability. These people, who have responded to the Gospel and experienced conversion, are baptized in water by immersion, in the name of the Father, and of the Son, and of the Holy Spirit (Matthew 28:19-20, Acts 2:38, Romans 6:4). This public baptism is an outward sign of the inward work of conversion and regeneration that the Lord has done in the believer's life, and is a response of obedience to the command of Scripture.

THE LORD'S SUPPER

The institution of the Lord's Supper, sometimes referred to as Communion, the breaking of bread, the Lord's Table, or the Eucharist, is recorded in all four gospels (Matthew 26:20-30; Mark 14:17-26; Luke 22: 14-20; John 13:21-30) and by the Apostle Paul (1 Corinthians 11:23-30). That our Lord chose the Passover meal as the context for instituting the Supper suggests there was some connection between the two events. The Passover was one of five major festivals Jewish people were commanded to observe. The others were Pentecost, the Feast of Trumpets, the Day of Atonement, and the Feast of Tabernacles. The feast of Passover celebrated Israel's deliverance from Egyptian bondage. The significance of the Passover festival to the Hebrew people is highlighted by John D. Carr. He writes:

> *The miraculous events of the Passover season were of such magnitude that Israel was commanded to remember God's deliverance throughout all their generations. All the Israelites were*

> to remember that they were there, enduring the slavery, fearfully offering the paschal Lamb, faithfully applying the blood to the door, triumphantly departing from Egypt, standing in trepidation at the Red Sea, marching through the divided waters, watching in awe the destruction of Egypt's armies and singing the songs of triumph (*Passover: The Festival of Redemption*, by John D. Carr).

An essential feature of the Passover celebration is the Passover meal. The Passover meal consists of certain designated elements and a prescribed order, or *seder*, to ensure the meal is properly observed. Hillel, an eminent Rabbi one generation before Jesus' time, explained that only three elements were necessary for the proper observance of the Passover: the lamb, unleavened bread, and bitter herbs. Later, other sages added elements to the *Haggadah* (narrative) in its proper order.

Paul's description of the Lord's Supper recorded in 1 Corinthians 11 is perhaps the most definitive statement on the meaning of the Lord's Supper in the New Testament. Paul wrote:

> *For I received from the Lord what I also passed on to you: The Lord Jesus, on the night he was betrayed, took bread, and when he had given thanks, he broke it and said, "This is my body, which is for you; do this in remembrance of me." In the same way, after supper he took the cup, saying, "This cup is the new covenant in my blood; do this, whenever you drink it, in remembrance of me." For whenever you eat this bread and drink this cup, you proclaim the Lord's death until he comes* (1 Corinthians 11:23-26).

F. F Bruce suggests that this might even be the earliest written record of the institution of the ordinance, predating the account recorded in Mark's Gospel (*Paul: Apostle of the Free Spirit*). It should be noted that Paul claims to have received his information, not from one of the original apostles, but from the Lord Himself. This immediately suggests the importance of the Supper as well as its authenticity as an ordinance to be observed by the Church.

It was stated earlier that there seemed to be some connection between the Lord's Supper and the Passover meal. Four connecting points can be identified. First, both meals are memorials, or times of remembrance.

Passover commemorates deliverance from Egyptian bondage while the Lord's Supper commemorates our Lord's death on the cross. Second, both meals were ordinances in the sense that they were specifically commanded. Third, bread and wine were key elements in both meals. Finally, in both meals there is the element of praise and thanksgiving. Actually, the term *Eucharist*, another term used for the Lord's Supper, is derived from the Greek word *eucharisto*, meaning "to give thanks."

In the New Testament it appears that the Lord's Supper was part of a common meal regarded as a "love feast" in which the more fortunate members shared their meal with the less fortunate ones. At Corinth the feast was thrown into disrepute, being characterized by divisions, selfishness, pride, drunkenness and other forms of abuse (1 Corinthians 11: 17-22). This then, is the context in which Paul's teaching on the Lord's Supper is to be understood. The Lord's Supper was intended to be a communal activity, a coming together of the body of Christ (table fellowship) for the mutual benefit of all members.

To fully appreciate the meaning of the Lord's Supper, it is important to pay particular attention to what Jesus did and what He said. The Scriptures tell us that **Jesus …took bread, and when he had given thanks, he broke it and said "This is my body, which is for you; do this in remembrance of me." In the same way, after supper he took the cup, saying, "This cup is the new covenant in my blood; do this, whenever you drink it, in remembrance of me"** (1 Corinthians 11:23-25).

What is the teaching here? In the Lord's Supper the elements, the bread and the cup (wine), represent the body and the blood of the Lord. Additionally, Jesus says that the cup represents the new covenant in His blood. By His sacrifice, Jesus has inaugurated the new covenant promised in Jeremiah 31:31-34. The Lord's Supper, therefore, was a sign that a new age had dawned. Further, our Lord admonished His friends to remember Him whenever they came together to eat of the bread and drink of the cup. When Christians, as a believing community, gather together to "eat the bread" and "drink of the cup," therefore, it is an occasion to remember and celebrate the life and death of our Lord. (To prevent the spread of illness, most churches avoid use of a common chalice, opting to provide partakers with individual, disposable cups.)

For the Apostle Paul the Lord's Supper was also an occasion for proclaiming the gospel. He said, **"For whenever you eat this bread and drink this cup, you** *proclaim the Lord's death until he comes"* (1 Corinthians 11:26). Moreover this activity, which was to continue until the Lord returned, was also an occasion of communion (fellowship) with Christ and members of His body. Based on the passage cited above we may regard the Lord's Supper as having three dimensions: looking back (remembering the sacrifice of the Christ), looking around (proclaiming His death), and looking ahead (anticipating His return).

In Paul's view the significance of the Lord's Supper was to be found not only in the action and words of Jesus, but also in the elements and what they represented – so much so that it was possible for one to partake of the elements in an unworthy manner. James Davis, commenting on Paul's interpretation of the elements in the Lord's Supper, writes, "Because of the significance invested in these elements, anyone who consumes them in a manner that is not in keeping with their purpose of uniting believers with each other and with their Lord 'will be guilty of the body and blood of the Lord' (1 Corinthians 11:27). He will have failed to distinguish the consumption of these elements from ordinary food and drink" (*The Baker Illustrated Bible,* "First Corinthians," by James Davis).

It is for this reason that members of the faith community are admonished to examine themselves before partaking of the elements. This is reminiscent of the commandment given to the Israelites to remove all leaven from every house prior to the Passover (Exodus 12:15).

The Apostle Paul may have had the Passover in mind when he wrote, **Don't you know that a little yeast works through the whole batch of dough? Get rid of the old yeast that you may be a new batch without yeast – as you really are. For Christ, our Passover lamb, has been sacrificed. Therefore let us keep the Festival, not with the old yeast, the yeast of malice and wickedness, but with bread without yeast, the bread of sincerity and truth** (1Corinthians 5:6-8).

The apostle Paul further warned that anyone who eats the bread and drinks of the cup in an unworthy manner will be guilty of sinning against the body and blood of the Lord. The offense here is not the desecration or disrespect of the elements per se, but disregard for the other members of the body of Christ – "not recognizing the body of the Lord." It is to be noted that there are serious personal consequences to those who eat and drink in an unworthy manner: **many are weak and sick, and a number of you have fallen asleep** (died) (1 Corinthians11:30).

When our Lord instituted the Supper, He took bread, gave thanks and broke it, and gave it to his disciples, saying, *"Take and eat; this is my body."* Then he took the cup, gave thanks and offered it to them, saying, *"Drink from it, all of you. This is my blood of the covenant"* (Matthew 26:26-28). In the apostolic era, the elements – bread and wine – were most likely regarded as symbolic; that is, they represented the *body* and *blood* of the Lord. This is how the disciples would have understood it, given the fact that Jesus was physically present with them when He gave them the bread and the wine. Accordingly, Open Bible also views the elements of communion as representative symbols of the body and blood of Christ, not as literal bodily substances.

Another way to more deeply appreciate the Lord's Supper is to consider what is actually happening as we gather together for this event. The general idea is that at the Supper Christ is present – not in the elements, but among His people who are gathered to celebrate His death and its benefit to those who have placed their trust in Him. The manifest presence of Christ at the Supper provides an opportunity for a divine encounter between the Lord and His people. Robert Webber puts it this way, "the Lord's Supper… is an extremely important part of our Christian life. We need to be present at the celebration of the Lord's Table as frequently as possible, because it is there that divine action is taking place. Through the Lord's Supper, divine healing and comfort and sustenance occur" (*Practical Christianity*, by LaVonne Neff).

As Open Bible people, we believe that the Lord's Supper is a memorial, a time to remember the Lord's death and all that it means to us. We also believe Jesus' own words, *"where two or three come together in my name, there am I with them"* (Matthew 18:20), and in the presence of the Lord all things are possible. Moreover we believe that enlightenment, encouragement, and faith can be experienced in the "breaking of bread" as the disciples discovered at Emmaus (Luke 24:30-35). On the basis of these truths, we regard the Lord's Supper as a very important ordinance and one that should be taken seriously by all members of our churches.

Related Scriptures

Water Baptism -
Matthew 28:19; Acts 2:38; Romans 6:4;

Communion -
Luke 22:7-20; 1 Corinthians 11:23-28

For Further Reading

Bach, R. A. Bach & Schmidt, D. M., eds. *We Believe: Principles in Christian Living*. Des Moines, IA: Open Bible Publishers, 1992.

Bruce, F. F. *Paul: Apostle of the Heart Set Free*. Grand Rapids, MI: Wm. B. Eerdmans Publishing Company, 1977.

Burge, G. M., & Hill, A. E., eds. *The Baker Illustrated Bible Commentary*. Grand Rapids, MI: Baker Publishing Group, 2012.

Carr, John D. *Passover: The Festival of Redemption*. Atlanta, GA: Golden Key Press, 2012.

Ferguson, .S. B., Packer, J. I., & Wright, D. F., eds. *New Dictionary of Theology*. Downers Grove, IL: Inter Varsity Press, 1988.

Gonzales, Justo. *Church History: An Essential Guide*. Nashville, TN: Abingdon Press, 1996.

Ladd, George Eldon. *A Theology of the New Testament*. Grand Rapids, MI: Wm. B. Eerdmans Publishing Company, 1974.

Webber, Robert E. *Ancient Future Evangelism*. Grand Rapids, MI: Baker Books, 2003.

Time to Interact

Take some time to interact with the following questions. Consider writing your answers in a journal and/or discussing them with a fellow believer for deeper reflection and insight.

1. How have you witnessed and/or experienced water baptism? What is the connection between water baptism and repentance? Based on this chapter, what significance does water baptism have in the life of a Christ follower? How has that been reflected in you?

2. What is your reaction to this chapter's discussion of infant baptism? In what ways does infant baptism differ from descriptions of baptism in the Scripture? In light of your

deeper understanding of the meaning of baptism, you might even consider celebrating a renewal of your baptismal vows.

3. What connections do you see between the New Testament ordinance of the Lord's Supper and the Old Testament Passover meal? How are they aligned? Why is it important to remember and honor the body and blood of Jesus?

4. What does it mean to take of the communion elements in an "unworthy manner?" Why does the apostle Paul instruct us to discern the health of our relationships as we are participating in the Lord's Supper? What does this tell you about God's hope and intention for relationships between those in the Body of Christ?

Time to Integrate

Let's take a fresh opportunity to experience the benefits of both water baptism and the Lord's Supper.

1. How does your church practice water baptism? Do you need to be baptized in water in accordance with the Scripture? Who can you talk to about this? What steps can you take? Also, is there a believer in your church that needs encouragement regarding water baptism? What role can you play in experiencing or assisting in the ordinance of water baptism?

2. In addition to taking part in the Lord's Supper in the midst of a church service, are there other gatherings and occasions where this ordinance would be appropriate? Perhaps a small group? What about observing the ordinance as a family? What could this look like with a friend? Is there a way to share with a shut-in or a person in pain? Consider what other avenues and opportunities you have to partake in the Lord's Supper. How could you act on that yet this week?

CHAPTER 11

Experiencing Renewal:
Baptism in the Spirit and Spiritual Gifts

CHAPTER 11

Experiencing Renewal:
Baptism in the Spirit and Spiritual Gifts

BAPTISM IN THE HOLY SPIRIT

" We believe the Holy Spirit comes to dwell in every believer at the moment of salvation. The baptism in the Holy Spirit is distinct from salvation, releasing the power of the Holy Spirit through faith. Consistent with biblical accounts, believers should anticipate Spirit-baptism to be accompanied by speaking in tongues and other biblical manifestations. The baptism in the Holy Spirit is given to endue the believer with power from God, to offer an inspired witness for Christ, to lead the believer in a life of holiness, and to equip for a Spirit-filled life of service."

SPIRIT-FILLED LIFE

"We believe every Christian should walk and abide in daily fellowship with the Holy Spirit and experience continual renewing of God's power to live a Spirit-filled life in attitudes, thoughts, speech, and conduct. In order to build up and equip both individual believers and the Church of Jesus Christ, the Holy Spirit gives spiritual gifts that are to be earnestly desired and exercised in the spirit of love. The fruit of the Spirit to be cultivated in the life of every believer is love, joy, peace, patience, kindness, goodness, faithfulness, gentleness, and self-control."

DIVINE HEALING

"We believe the power of God to heal the sick and afflicted is provided for in Christ's death on the cross. God is willing to and does heal today. "

One of the hallmarks of Open Bible Churches across North America and around the globe has been our commitment to a life-changing, dynamic relationship with the third person of the Trinity, the Holy Spirit. In earlier chapters we discussed the relationship between the Father, Son, and Holy Spirit. We discussed the role of the Spirit in the life and ministry of

Jesus, and we anticipated the promised sending of the Holy Spirit by Jesus after His death, resurrection, and ascension to heaven. In this chapter we want to highlight two specific aspects of the work of the Holy Spirit in the life of the believer: the baptism in the Holy Spirit, and the manifestation and operation of gifts of the Holy Spirit through believers in the context of the Christian community.

When John the Baptist prepared the way for Jesus' earthly ministry, he declared that the coming Messiah *"will baptize you with the Holy Spirit and fire"* (Matthew 3:11). During His three years of ministry Jesus preached the kingdom of God, taught with authority, healed those who were sick, and delivered those who were oppressed with demons. His ministry culminated with the events of Passion Week when Jesus rode into Jerusalem on a donkey, cleansed the Temple, shared the Last Supper with His disciples, washed the disciples' feet, and then submitted to the rejection and brutality that led to His crucifixion on Calvary. He died for the sins of the world, and then demonstrated His victory over hell and death by rising from the dead.

After His resurrection Jesus appeared to His followers on many occasions before ascending to heaven in clouds of glory. Many times Jesus encouraged His listeners by explaining that it was actually better for them if He went away, because upon leaving them and returning to the Father, He would send the Comforter, the Holy Spirit. Jesus then instructed the disciples to wait in Jerusalem for the promised One. And so they did. In Acts 2 we find that while they were all together in one place, on what we now call the Day of Pentecost, the Holy Spirit came upon them like a mighty rushing wind. What looked like flaming tongues of fire fell on each of the 120 persons gathered, and they all began to speak in unknown tongues (a language they did not know) and prophesy (spoke messages from God as prompted by the Holy Spirit).

This outpouring of the Spirit amazed thousands of pilgrims who had gathered in Jerusalem from every corner of the world to celebrate the annual Feast of Pentecost. These simple men and women from Israel were speaking languages and praising God in languages they had never learned, yet their speech was entirely understandable to the visitors to Jerusalem. These visitors were actually hearing amazing truths spoken in their own dialects. In the midst of their awe and wonder, the Apostle Peter stood and preached the gospel to them. Thousands were brought to faith in Christ that day. Thus this miraculous Day of Pentecost is often regarded as the day the Church was born.

The rest of the book of Acts tells the story of the first decades of the early Church. In these exciting chapters we see that the first generation of Christians were learning to live together in community as they spread the good news of Jesus Christ to Jews and Gentiles alike. In their evangelistic and missionary efforts, the Word of God was preached with boldness and was often accompanied by miracles and other manifestations of the Spirit. The powerful work of the Holy Spirit was evident in the variety of miracles that occurred, including healings, deliverance from demons, amazing escapes from imprisonment, and multiple examples of the accompanying manifestations of persons speaking in other tongues and prophesying.

This empowering presence of the Holy Spirit is also confirmed throughout Paul's letters to the churches. Paul reminded the believers in Rome, **God has poured out his love into our hearts by the Holy Spirit, whom he has given us** (Romans 5:5). He admonished the Ephesians, **Do not get drunk on wine, which leads to debauchery. Instead, be filled with the Spirit** (Ephesians 5:18). He told the church in Thessalonica, **Our gospel came to you not simply with words, but also with power, with the Holy Spirit and with deep conviction** (1 Thessalonians 1:5), and that God **gives you his Holy Spirit** (4:8). He warned them, **Do not put out the Spirit's fire** (5:19). Nonetheless, Paul's strongest teaching concerning the activity of the Holy Spirit in the early Church is found in his first letter to the Corinthians. Paul's instructions (and corrections) to the believers gathered in Corinth offer a substantive foundation for our understanding of the reception and operation of spiritual gifts. We'll discuss gifts of the Holy Spirit, but first we'll consider the importance of the doctrine and experience of the baptism in the Holy Spirit.

BAPTISM IN THE HOLY SPIRIT

After Jesus' death and resurrection He appeared to His disciples many times. On one such occasion He instructed them that *"repentance and forgiveness of sins will be preached in his name to all nations, beginning at Jerusalem. You are witnesses of these things. I am going to send you what my Father has promised; but stay in the city until you have been clothed with power from on high"* (Luke 24:47-49). This beautiful passage shows clearly that the Holy Spirit was promised to Jesus' followers and that they should expect and wait for that promise to be fulfilled. It also gives a hint of the character of the coming of the Spirit – namely, that when the Spirit comes there is an accompaniment of God's power. And third, the purpose of such power is spelled out. Believers need the power of the Holy Spirit in order to be most effective as witnesses because they are being sent into the nations of the world, preaching the good news of salvation through Christ. Immediately before His ascension to heaven, Jesus told His followers, *"You will receive power when the Holy Spirit comes on you; and you will be my witnesses in Jerusalem, and in all Judea and Samaria, and to the ends of the earth"* (Acts 1:8).

On five occasions in the book of Acts, the coming of the Holy Spirit upon believers of the early Church is described in colorful detail. Each time specific accompaniments and outcomes are mentioned. Luke, who carefully recorded these events, believed it was important for us to see clearly what was happening to these pioneer Christians. As we note these particulars we get a glimpse of what we can anticipate in our own experience of the Spirit. Let's summarize each of these passages:

First Occasion (Acts 2). After Jesus ascended to heaven, about 120 believers were gathered in an upstairs room praying (Acts 1:13, 15). The Holy Spirit came upon them in this way: *Suddenly a sound like the blowing of a violent wind came from heaven and filled the whole house where they were sitting.… All of them were filled with the Holy Spirit and began to speak in other tongues as the Spirit enabled them.* Since there was a feast taking place in Jerusalem at that time, men and women from nearly every country in that part of the world were present, and they were amazed and perplexed, saying, *"We hear them declaring the wonders of God in our own tongues!"* (Acts 2:2-12).

Second Occasion (Acts 8). A leader in the early church, Philip was preaching in Samaria. Many signs accompanied his preaching, including people being healed of sickness and delivered from demons. As the Samaritan people responded in faith to the preaching of the gospel and became believers, Peter and John came from Jerusalem and *prayed for them that they might receive the Holy Spirit,* placing their hands on them as they prayed (Acts 8:14-17). Specific manifestations such as speaking in tongues and prophecy are not mentioned here, but the power of God was so evident that a misguided man named Simon offered to pay money to the apostles so he could lay hands on people wherever he went and see them receive the Holy Spirit. He was rebuked by Peter for attempting to purchase the experience of the Spirit; nevertheless, this episode is further testimony of the tangible signs of the Spirit's presence.

Third Occasion (Acts 10). Peter had a vision that prepared him to go to the house of a Gentile (non-Jewish) family in order to preach the gospel. He then went to the house of a military officer named Cornelius, in the town of Caesarea. After Peter preached the good news of Jesus Christ, Cornelius and his entire household became believers in Christ. Luke (author of the book of Acts) tells us, *While Peter was still speaking these words, the Holy Spirit came on all who heard the message* (Acts 10:44). The Jewish believers who were with Peter *were astonished that the gift of the Holy Spirit had been poured out even on the Gentiles. For they heard them speaking in tongues and praising God* (Acts 10:45-46). Peter baptized them in water and acknowledged that *they have received the Holy Spirit just as we have* (Acts 10:47).

Fourth Occasion (Acts 11). Peter went back to Jerusalem to explain to the other apostles and church leaders what had happened with Cornelius's household. As he recounted the story of preaching the good news of Christ, he stated, *"As I began to speak, the Holy Spirit came on them as he had come on us at the beginning. Then I remembered what the Lord had said: 'John baptized with water, but you will be baptized with the Holy Spirit.' So if God gave them the same gift as he gave us, who believed in the Lord Jesus Christ, who was I to think that I could oppose God?"* (Acts 11:15-17). This passage refers back to the manifestations (speaking in tongues and praising God) that occurred in Cornelius's house (chapter 10) and also on the Day of Pentecost (chapter 2), accompanying the baptism in the Holy Spirit each of these groups experienced.

Fifth Occasion (Acts 19). On the Apostle Paul's third missionary journey, he came to the town of Ephesus in what is now modern-day Turkey. He found some followers of Christ there who had matured as believers under the teaching of Priscilla, Aquila, and Apollos (Acts 18). Paul asked them, *"Did you receive the Holy Spirit when you believed?"* These young Christians explained that they had not received teaching on the Holy Spirit, after which Paul prayed for them to *be baptized into the name of the Lord Jesus* (Acts 19:1-5). Luke continued, *When Paul placed his hands on them, the Holy Spirit came on them, and they spoke in tongues and prophesied* (Acts 19:6).

A review of these five chapters in the book of Acts shows that this fullness of the experience of the Holy Spirit, or baptism in the Holy Spirit, was a powerful experience that the leaders of the early Church thought to be essential for believers everywhere. The baptism in the Holy Spirit was emphasized in the ministries of many leaders (Peter, John, Philip, Paul), and in many places (Jerusalem, Samaria, Ephesus). In all these occurrences there were powerful manifestations that accompanied the presence of the Spirit – speaking in other tongues, prophesying, praising God, joy, boldness, and evangelistic fervor. Jesus promised that when the Holy Spirit filled believers, they would receive power to be His witnesses in the world (Acts 1:8). The gospel was preached in these locations with many people becoming believers in Christ and with accompanying miraculous signs and wonders.

With these biblical precedents in view, Open Bible Churches holds firmly to the belief that every believer is encouraged to enter into a deeper relationship with God through the baptism in the Holy Spirit, which will enable them to be more effective witnesses in the world for Christ and to grow in their capacity to exercise gifts of the Holy Spirit for the building up of the Church.

What Baptism in the Holy Spirit Is and Is Not

First, baptism in the Holy Spirit is *not* salvation. We receive Christ by faith, and our sins are forgiven – we are justified before God and born again of the Spirit (John 3:5-8). The Spirit indwells us from that time on. And yet Scripture promises that we can enter into the fullness of the Holy Spirit and receive and exercise spiritual gifts. The gateway into this life of fullness of the Spirit is the experience described in the passages above, called baptism in the Holy Spirit. Through this experience there is a release of the grace and power of God as the Spirit flows through us (John 7:37-39; Acts 1:8). So this experience is distinct from salvation and often is received and released sometime after a person comes to faith in Christ. Baptism in the Holy Spirit is the fulfillment of Jesus' promise that His disciples would be *"clothed with power from on high"* (Luke 24:49), or *"baptized with the Holy Spirit"* (Acts 1:5). He said to His followers, *"But you will receive power when the Holy Spirit comes on you"* (Acts 1:8). Jesus immediately makes clear why this incredible gift of God's power is to be bestowed on us – *"and you will be my witnesses in Jerusalem, and in all Judea and Samaria, and to the ends of the earth."* Baptism in the Holy Spirit is empowerment for witness. If we wish to fully participate in fulfilling the Great Commission (Matthew 28:19-20) and reaching the world for Jesus Christ, we will accept the Lord's invitation to us and will allow Him to baptize us, to overwhelm us with the presence and power of the Holy Spirit.

How to Receive the Baptism in the Holy Spirit

There is no set formula for receiving this wonderful experience. People enter into the fullness of the Spirit in a variety of ways. For some, Spirit-baptism takes place in the context of a corporate worship service or prayer meeting; for others, it occurs in the quiet moments of their daily devotional lives. A few general principles can be stated:

- Baptism in the Spirit is received by faith. It's that simple, and no special additional steps are necessary.

- Baptism in the Spirit often is released in the context of spoken worship and praise. Since we have seen in Scripture (Acts 2, 8-11, 19) that believers regularly prayed in a language unknown to the speaker (spoke in other tongues) and spoke words of prophecy as an accompaniment of Spirit-baptism, and since these signs of Spirit-baptism are spoken with the mouth, believers can expect that their baptism in the Holy Spirit experience will include such manifestations and can be encouraged to speak openly in worship and praise as they enter into the fullness of the Holy Spirit.

- Sometimes baptism in the Spirit occurs when a seeker is prayed for by other Christians. A biblical practice in this regard is the "laying on of hands" while such prayer takes place (Acts 8:17; Acts 19:6; 2 Timothy 1:6).

- Our focus should remain exclusively on God, not on ourselves. Immature and misguided attempts to exercise spiritual gifts are those which focus on self rather than God. Receiving the baptism in the Holy Spirit and operating with the Spirit's gifts have little in common with emotionalism and attempts to draw attention to ourselves. We warn against such excesses in our expression of the Spirit's work in us, and yet we refuse to allow the fear of them to rob us of the full experience of the Spirit He has available to us.

Someone might reasonably ask, "Do I have to speak in tongues in order to receive the baptism in the Holy Spirit?" Some churches are adamant, maintaining that if you don't pray in a prayer language, you have not received the baptism in the Holy Spirit. Others would not be so insistent. A balanced answer might be, "Even if you don't have to speak in tongues, you *get* to." While God in His sovereignty uses people to make a difference in the world in wonderful ways whether or not they have allowed the language of the Spirit to become part of their devotional lives, our belief is that the experience of the fullness of the Spirit is available to all, and speaking in other tongues (or releasing a prayer language) is a wonderful aspect of that experience. Through the exercise of a prayer language a person can grow in intercession and prayer, and this experience can be a gateway, a catalyst for the exercise of the gifts of the Spirit. So while it may be possible for a person to experience baptism in the Holy Spirit without enjoying a spiritual language of prayer and praise, since God so freely offers it to us for our benefit, we encourage all believers to expect and enter into this wonderful dimension of life in the Spirit.

A Prayer to Receive the Fullness of (or baptism in) the Holy Spirit (from Jack Hayford, *The Beauty of Spiritual Language*)

Dear Lord Jesus,

I thank you and praise you for your great love and faithfulness to me. My heart is filled with joy whenever I think of the great gift of salvation you have freely given to me, and I humbly glorify you, Lord Jesus, for you have forgiven me all my sins and brought me to the Father. Now I come in obedience to your call. I want to receive the fullness of the Holy Spirit. I do not come because I am worthy myself, but because you have invited me to come. Because you have washed me from my sins, I thank you that you have made the vessel of my life a worthy one to be filled with the Holy Spirit of God. I want to be overflowed with your life, your love and your power, Lord Jesus. I want to show forth your grace, your words, your goodness, and your gifts to everyone I can. And so with simple, childlike faith, I ask you, Lord, fill me with the Holy Spirit. I open all of myself to you, to receive all of yourself in me. I love you, Lord, and I lift my voice in praise to you. I welcome your might and your miracles to be manifested in me for your glory and unto your praise.

Rather than simply saying Amen and concluding the prayer, Jack Hayford encourages believers to enter into a time of worship and praise, and to expect that the biblical manifestations that occurred in the early Church will take place once again – a new language of prayer and praise, prophetic words, and waves of God's love, power and grace. Countless believers can testify that this is precisely what has taken place in their own worship lives.

GIFTS OF THE HOLY SPIRIT

Jesus promised us that if we asked the Father, He would give us good gifts (Matthew 7:11). These good gifts come from the Holy Spirit, who Himself is the greatest gift we can receive (Luke 11:13). Scripture abounds with descriptions of God's gracious outpouring of gifts to His people. In the Old Testament, Isaiah 11:2 is part of a Messianic prophecy that describes the character of the Spirit of the Lord, which will rest on Jesus Christ, referred to in Isaiah as the Righteous Branch. *The Spirit of the Lord will rest on him – the Spirit of wisdom and of understanding, the Spirit of counsel and of power, the Spirit of knowledge and of the fear of the Lord.* These aspects of the Spirit's role in the life of the coming Messiah also give us glimpses of the variety of spiritual gifts that are graciously offered to the early Church after the Spirit is poured out beginning on the Day of Pentecost.

Several New Testament books discuss gifts of the Holy Spirit. The Apostle Paul goes into great detail in his first letter to the church in Corinth, not only outlining many spiritual gifts that are available to Christians, but also providing important instruction regarding the purpose of these gifts and their most appropriate and effective use as believers receive them and share them with others. In 1 Corinthians 12:4-6, Paul points to a variety of ways the Holy Spirit offers Himself to us: *There are different kinds of gifts (but the same Spirit), different kinds of service (but the same Lord), and different kinds of working (but the same God works all of them in all men).* The different terms Paul uses in this chapter underscore the beautiful array of ways the Holy Spirit comes and does His work in and through us. At various times he uses forms of the Greek words *charismata* (gifts of grace, 1 Corinthians 12:4); *diakonia* (service or ministry, verse 5), *phanerosis* (manifestations, verse 7); and *pneumatikoi* (spiritual things, verse 1). Let's look at some categories of spiritual gifts, in specific groupings:

Manifestation Gifts

*To one there is given through the Spirit the **message of wisdom**, to another the **message of knowledge** by means of the same Spirit, to another faith* by the same Spirit, to another **gifts of healing** by that one Spirit, to another **miraculous powers**, to another **prophecy**, to another **distinguishing between spirits**, to another speaking in different kinds of **tongues**, and to still another the **interpretation of tongues** (1 Corinthians 12:8-10).

These gifts are often described as manifestation gifts and are often expressed within the context of corporate worship services or in public ministry situations. There seem to be three subsets of three gifts each in this list: discernment gifts (message of wisdom, message of knowledge, and distinguishing between spirits), power gifts (faith, gifts of healing, and miraculous powers), and word gifts (prophecy, tongues, and the interpretation of tongues).

Motivational Gifts

Another list provided by the apostle Paul is found in Romans 12: 6-8, a grouping which is often described as motivational gifts: *We have different gifts, according to the grace given us. If a man's gift is **prophesying**, let him use it in proportion to his faith. If it is **serving**, let him serve; if it is **teaching**, let him teach; if it is **encouraging**, let him encourage; if it is **contributing to the needs of others**, let him give generously; if it is **leadership**, let him govern diligently; if it is showing **mercy**, let him do it cheerfully.*

Ministry Offices/Gifts

There are other places in the New Testament where gifts of the Spirit may be in evidence as well. What we call the "five-fold ministry offices" mentioned by Paul in Ephesians 4:11 carry a sense of Holy Spirit gifting: *It was he who gave some to be **apostles**, some to be **prophets**, some to be **evangelists**, and some to be **pastors** and **teachers**.*

Additional Expressions of God's Grace

Similarly, while the following are not universally accepted as gifts of the Holy Spirit, we can acknowledge that Scripture indicates that the Lord is at work in the lives of men and women in unique ways as He gives them grace to accomplish his work: **celibacy** (1 Corinthians 7:7), **hospitality** (1 Peter 4:9), **helping** (1 Corinthians 12:28), **voluntary poverty** (1 Corinthians 13:3), **intercession** (Ephesians 6:18; Romans 12:12; 1 Thessalonians 5:17; James 5:15-16), and **administration** (1 Corinthians. 12:28). Also, Bible scholars look at the amazing testimony of Stephen in Acts 6 and 7 and wonder whether the Holy Spirit sometimes give special grace to those called to **martyrdom**.

We do not believe the Holy Spirit is limited to this listing. But in summary, we can mention each of these gifts (and other expressions of God's grace) that have clear biblical support, including a brief description of their usage (some of these descriptions were taken or adapted from the *We Believe* manual, 1992):

Manifestation Gifts (1 Corinthians 12:8-10):

Message of wisdom – the ability to have some of God's wisdom as a direct result of the revelation of the Spirit and not through experience or gradual understanding

Message of knowledge – knowledge revealed supernaturally by God about a person or a situation

Faith – not saving faith, but a manifestation of supernatural faith related to a particular need

Gifts of healing – the impartation of restoration for various types of physical ailments and afflictions

Miraculous powers – the operation of the power of God beyond human ability

Prophecy – the ability to speak forth a message from God

Distinguishing between spirits – the supernatural ability to understand what kind of spirit is controlling or motivating an individual or situation

Speaking in tongues – the manifestation of an unknown and unlearned language as a message to be interpreted for the edification (or the building up) of the Body of Christ

Interpretation of tongues – the ability to interpret to a gathering of believers the sense of the meaning conveyed by a message in tongues

Motivational Gifts (Romans 12:6-8):

Prophesying – speaking forth the truth, in a message from God in one's own language to a gathering of believers

Serving – meeting practical needs

Teaching – clarifying, validating, and presenting foundational truth

Encouraging – stimulating the faith of others by giving direction or steps of action

Giving – making one's assets available to the kingdom of God

Leadership – coordinating the efforts of others to accomplish a common goal

Mercy – an attraction to, understanding of, and ministry to people who are in distress

Ministry Gifts/Offices (Ephesians 4:11):

Apostle – one sent by God for a certain time and to a certain place to establish and oversee the work of God

Prophet – one called of God and empowered by the Holy Spirit to speak forth revelations of divine truth

Evangelist – one gifted to preach the gospel to unbelievers

Pastor – one gifted to exercise leadership and care over a local body of believers

Teacher – one gifted to instruct believers in all righteousness

Additional Expressions of God's Grace (1 Corinthians 7:7; 1 Corinthians 12:28; 1 Corinthians 13:3; Acts 6-7)

Celibacy – grace from God to live a life of purity before the Lord as a single person

Hospitality – the ability to provide a godly welcoming presence and care for strangers and guests on behalf of the Church

Helping – grace to assist those suffering, in weakness and in need on behalf of the Church

Voluntary poverty – grace from God to live a life of extreme simplicity for the sake of the Kingdom

Intercession – grace to pray with great fervor, often in the context of spiritual warfare and sometimes exercised alongside a gift of faith

Administration – giftedness to guide and govern in various settings on behalf of the Church

Martyrdom – special grace by God to follow Christ fully, even unto death

Common Questions About Gifts of the Spirit

1) Do I receive only one gift? Some Bible instructors have taught that each believer is given a particular gift to possess, to the exclusion of other gifts. Once that particular gift is discovered, there is no need to consider the possibility that another gift might also be bestowed. But the teaching of Paul in Corinthians appears to offer another view. In his discussion of spiritual gifts Paul teaches that *Now to each one the manifestation of the Spirit is given for the common good* (1 Corinthians 12:7). This description of the gifts of the Spirit as manifestations supports the way Paul outlines the use of these gifts. They occur at various times as the Spirit *gives them to each one, just as he determines* (1 Corinthians 12:11). Believers should remain open to the Holy Spirit using them to exercise spiritual gifts whenever they are needed "for the common good." Each of us will discover particular gifts through which God will enable us to serve more often than others, but we can also expect that from time to time He will move through us in surprising and unexpected ways – for the common good, just as He determines.

2) Are my spiritual gifts merely my talents and skills? God certainly wires each of us with talents and inclinations with which we are born, and over time we can develop great capacities and skills through training and education. But a gift of the Holy Spirit is something that comes to us because God extends His grace in a particular way, at a particular time, for a particular purpose. That purpose will be to build up others in the faith and point them to Christ. If a person has the skill to be a teacher or is a talented administrator, the Holy Spirit may provide a supernatural grace at times that enables a person to go even beyond his or her already considerable capabilities.

3) How do I discover what spiritual gifts the Lord may want me to receive and exercise? The Lord will be faithful to distribute His gifts to those who "eagerly desire" them, so they can use them to minister to others. Pray and ask the Lord to use you to serve and be a blessing to others and to grace you with gifts from His Spirit. He'll do it! Ask trusted spiritual mentors in your life whether they see gifts of the Holy Spirit present in your life. Pastors, youth leaders, family, and friends may see glimpses of gifts already at work in your life, possibly in a rough or raw form. Begin to practice those gifts and receive feedback from those trusted mentors. Don't be discouraged if you don't immediately feel comfortable with the gifts the Holy Spirit has distributed to you, or if you make a few mistakes in your initial attempts to exercise them. God will teach you, and He'll enable you to develop the capacity to share your spiritual gifts more and more effectively over time. And if you're a bit timid about being used by God in gifts of the Holy Spirit, you're in good company. Timothy had to be encouraged by the Apostle Paul to *fan into flame the gift of God, which is in you through the laying on of my hands. For God did not give us a spirit of timidity, but a spirit of power, of love and of self-discipline* (2 Timothy 1:6-7).

4) Is there a difference between praying in tongues in my devotional life on the one hand, and exercising the gift of tongues in corporate worship on the other? One of the ongoing benefits of the baptism in the Holy Spirit is the delightful and powerful privilege of praying in the Spirit, or speaking in other tongues. This experience is available to all who enter into the Spirit's fullness, and praying in the language of the Spirit can become a daily element of a person's devotional life. Indeed, Paul seems to hint at the ongoing benefit of praying in the Spirit in 1 Corinthians 14:18, when he says *I thank God that I speak in tongues more than all of you.* And in verse 15 he states that *I will pray with my spirit, but I will also pray with my mind; I will sing with my spirit, but I will also sing with my mind.* Praying in the Spirit is a wonderful way to communicate with God, and, just as Paul says, there is great benefit to us as we do. So Paul tells the believers in Corinth, *I would like every one of you to speak in tongues* (14:5).

And yet, in that same chapter Paul discusses order and priority for the sake of the encouragement of the gathered community. His priority in the church (14:19), or in the context of corporate worship, is that people be able to understand what is being said so they can be encouraged in the Lord. So if someone speaks in tongues in a public worship service, Paul knows they are personally not speaking to people but to God and *utter mysteries by the Spirit* (14:2); they are being built up in their own spiritual lives. *He who speaks in tongues edifies himself* (14:4).

So this is of great value to the individual speaking in tongues. But Paul wants believers to earnestly desire and to excel in spiritual gifts that edify and strengthen their fellow brothers and sisters in Christ. So he insists that in these public gatherings, people are not to offer a message in tongues unless there is also someone who can offer an interpretation of that message (14:27-28). On the other hand, the entire gathering would be encouraged by a word of prophecy (14:5). In any case, Paul is clear that the Church should not forbid speaking in tongues, but should love one another enough to seek to exercise spiritual gifts that help others grow in their faith (14:39).

Open Bible Churches encourages every believer to enter into the experience of the baptism in the Holy Spirit. We invite every believer to speak in tongues and use the language of the Spirit in their daily devotional, worship, and prayer lives. We encourage every believer to "eagerly desire gifts of the Spirit," especially those that build up and encourage their fellow believers such as prophecy (14:1). And we encourage every believer to take heed to Paul's *more excellent way*, the way of love (1 Corinthians 12:31; 13:1; 14:1).

SPECIAL FOCUS: DIVINE HEALING

We have outlined among the gifts of the Holy Spirit those gifts which are often associated with supernatural healing, including gifts of healing, faith, and miraculous powers. God often enables one or more of these gifts to be manifest through believers, resulting in healings of the body, mind or emotions. But, in a more general sense, we can see that throughout the Bible provision is made for healing and that men and women everywhere are encouraged to pray in faith, believing that God will provide for the healing promised in his Word. Among the many passages that support Open Bible Churches' strong commitment to the biblical doctrine of divine healing are the following:

- Exodus 15:26: *He said, "If you listen carefully to the Lord your God and do what is right in his eyes, if you pay attention to his commands and keep all his decrees, I will not bring on you any of the diseases I brought on the Egyptians, for I am the Lord, who heals you."*

- Isaiah 53:4-5: *Surely he took up our infirmities and carried our sorrows, yet we considered him stricken by God, smitten by him, and afflicted. But he was pierced for our transgressions, he was crushed for our iniquities; the punishment that brought us peace was upon him, and by his wounds we are healed.*

- Matthew 8:16-17: *When evening came, many who were demon-possessed were brought to him, and he drove out the spirits with a word and healed all the sick. This was to fulfill what was spoken through the prophet Isaiah: "He took up our infirmities and carried our diseases."*

- Matthew 10:7-8: *"As you go, proclaim this message: 'The kingdom of heaven has come near.' Heal the sick, raise the dead, cleanse those who have leprosy, drive out demons. Freely you have received; freely give."*

- Acts 3:16: *"By faith in the name of Jesus, this man whom you see and know was made strong. It is Jesus' name and the faith that comes through him that has completely healed him, as you can all see."*

- James 5:14-16: *Is any one of you sick? He should call the elders of the church to pray over him and anoint him with oil in the name of the Lord. And the prayer offered in faith will make the sick person well; the Lord will raise him up. If he has sinned, he will be forgiven. Therefore confess your sins to each other and pray for each other so that you may be healed. The prayer of a righteous man is powerful and effective.*

Open Bible Churches embraces the doctrine and practice of divine healing because the Bible clearly and repeatedly affirms these truths: that God is our Healer and loves to heal people; that Jesus' ministry on earth was filled with demonstrations of God's desire to touch people with His healing power; and that each of us, as followers of Jesus Christ, are invited to both trust God for healing and to pray in faith that God would release His power to heal others.

A common question about healing: Why doesn't healing always occur when I pray? This is an important question, and Christians have sometimes struggled to find a meaningful and balanced response. Because it takes courage to pray and ask God for healing, we sometimes want to find a quick and easy explanation when a person does not immediately experience healing. (As a matter of fact, sometimes after we pray for people they get more ill or even die.) Simplistic answers are sometimes offered, such as that there must be sin for which the person has not repented, either in that person or the person praying; or possibly that the person praying didn't have "enough faith" in God. These answers are not helpful and not biblical. The truth is that we don't fully understand why some people are healed and others are not; it is a mystery. And so, because of our lack of understanding we can be tempted to avoid praying for healing altogether because we don't want to be disappointed in the result. But the Bible is clear – God desires to heal, and He invites us to ask Him for good gifts such as healing, as this passage makes clear:

> "Ask and it will be given to you; seek and you will find; knock and the door will be opened to you. For everyone who asks receives; he who seeks finds; and to him who knocks, the door will be opened. Which of you, if your son asks for bread, will give him a stone? Or if he asks for a fish, will give him a snake? If you, then, though you are evil, know how to give good gifts to your children, how much more will your Father in heaven give good gifts to those who ask him!" (Matthew 7:7-11).

We live in a fallen, sinful world that is not perfect, and sickness is a part of that world. God does wonderful things in our lives as we trust in Him. He forgives us, He saves us, and sometimes He heals us. Our challenge as followers of Christ is to keep looking to Him and trusting in Him for the good gifts He wants to give us, including healing for ourselves and others. God is good and will give us strength to endure illness and difficulty. At times we will see His miraculous healing power at work to shorten the length of that illness; at other times He will give us the grace to endure suffering as a faithful son or daughter. But in all cases we can look to our loving, caring, powerful Heavenly Father with gratitude in our hearts.

Related Scriptures

Baptism in the Holy Spirit -
John 7:37-39, 14:16; Acts 1:8, 2:4, 2:38-39, 8:14-17, 10:44-46, 19:6;
1 Corinthians 3:16

Spirit-Filled Life -
John: 15:4, 15:8; Acts 4:31; Romans 8:1, 8:5, 12:1-2, 12:6-8; 1 Corinthians 3:16, 12:7-11, 12:31; 2 Corinthians 7:1; Galatians 5:16-25; Ephesians 4:11, 4:30-32, 5:18; 1 Thessalonians 5:19-22; 1 Peter 1:15, 4:10-11; 1 John 2:6

Divine Healing -
Isaiah 53:4-5; Matthew 8:16-17; Mark 16:18; Acts3:16, 10:38; James 5:14-16; 1 Peter 2:24

For Further Reading

Arrington, French. *Christian Doctrine: A Pentecostal Perspective*. Cleveland, TN: Pathway Press, 1994.

Bach, R. A. Bach & Schmidt, D. M., eds. *We Believe: Principles in Christian Living*. Des Moines, IA: Open Bible Publishers, 1992.

Hayford, Jack. *The Beauty of Spiritual Language: Unveiling the Mystery of Speaking in Tongues*. Nashville, TN: Thomas Nelson Publishers, 1996.

Morris, Robert. *The God I Never Knew: How Real Friendship with the Holy Spirit Can Change Your Life*. Colorado Springs, CO: WaterBrook Press, 2013.

Time to Interact

Take some time to interact with the following questions. Consider writing your answers in a journal and/or discussing them with a fellow believer for deeper reflection and insight.

1. What stands out to you about the presence and power of the Holy Spirit from the five occasions discussed in the book of Acts? What hopes, dreams, apprehensions, and possibilities are stirred in you after reading these accounts?

2. Why is the baptism in the Holy Spirit understood to be a work distinct from the salvation experience? What is the difference between the indwelling presence of the Spirit and the baptism in the Holy Spirit?

3. Why do you think there is such a scriptural emphasis on speaking in tongues (or praying devotionally in a prayer language) in connection with the baptism in the Holy Spirit? What role does

that gift play in your life? What is your attitude and expectation regarding speaking in tongues? Why do you think God wants to equip and empower believers in this fashion?

4. In what possible ways could the Holy Spirit want to display spiritual gifts through your life? How can you work to embrace the spiritual admonition to **Follow the way of love and eagerly desire gifts of the Spirit"** (1 Corinthians 14:1)?

5. What are the Holy Spirit's intentions for the ministry of healing through your life? How might He want to work through you in greater ways to carry hope and healing to others?

Time to Integrate

Let's make some space for a fresh encounter in the presence of the Holy Spirit.

1. Have you acted on the invitation to receive the baptism in the Holy Spirit? If so, how has your life changed? How are you growing and developing in the utilization of your spiritual gifts? Sometimes people have fears about the baptism in the Holy Spirit or have actually been taught against it. How does this chapter help answer questions and provide clarity? Revisit the section entitled "How to Receive the Baptism in the Holy Spirit" and embrace the model prayer as your own. Expect to be filled and empowered. In Luke 11:13 Jesus says, *"If you then, though you are evil, know how to give good gifts to your children, how much more will your Father in heaven give the Holy Spirit to those who ask Him!"* Are you asking? He is giving!

2. Do you know what your spiritual gifts are? Apparently we have some say in what they can be because the Apostle Paul tells us to eagerly desire them, and especially to prophesy. Consider the influence of your life. What difference do you want to make in the lives of others? What situations and needs stir your heart? What specific spiritual gifts could bring significant breakthrough and help the people around you to encounter the kingdom of God in a life-changing way? Ask God to manifest those gifts through you and be alert for opportunities and possibilities for Holy Spirit empowered ministry.

3. How did you relate to the closing discussion concerning why healing doesn't always occur? Have you ever been reluctant or timid to pray for healing out of fear of being disappointed? Invite the Holy Spirit to do a fresh work in you. Confess your apprehension to the Father and ask Him to replace it with a sanctified boldness. Look for opportunities to lovingly pursue the ministry of healing. Who do you know that could benefit from the in-person prayers of a caring friend right now?

CHAPTER 12

Our Great Commission:
Evangelism and Missions

CHAPTER 12
Our Great Commission:
Evangelism and Missions

> " We believe the Great Commission of our Lord Jesus Christ commands us to carry the gospel message to the entire world – to every nation, ethnicity, culture, and language. The growth and strength of the Church depend on its wholehearted sacrifice and support for world evangelization. "

Within the heart of every healthy person lies an innate desire to be significant and make an impact. God hardwired that desire into each man and woman when He created Adam and Eve and commissioned them with the task of tending the Garden. *"Be fruitful and increase in number; fill the earth and subdue it,"* God instructed them (Genesis 1:28).

At the beginning of Jesus' ministry, He wasted no time calling disciples to Himself and to a significant life task. *"Come, follow me," Jesus said, "and I will make you fishers of men."* At once they left their nets and followed him (Mark 1:17).

Right after His resurrection, Jesus appeared to His disciples, a group of men and women before whom He had modeled His message, His motives, and His methods. While they were still trembling with both joy and awe, stunned that their crucified Master now stood before them fully alive, Jesus looked into their eyes and said, *"Peace be with you! As the Father has sent me, I am sending you."* And with that he breathed on them and said, *"Receive the Holy Spirit"* (John 20:21-22).

Some time later, just prior to His ascension, Jesus reiterated this charge in fuller form: *"Go and make disciples of all nations, baptizing them in the name of the Father and of the Son and of the Holy Spirit, and teaching them to obey everything I have commanded you"* (Matthew 28:19-20). The fact that these were Jesus' final words while He was physically present with the disciples dramatically emphasizes their importance.

Jesus called those disciples to a life of significance. He invited them to continue through the power and anointing of the Holy Spirit the work that He had begun by that same power and anointing. The charge to "be fruitful and multiply" took on a new meaning.

Two thousand years later, followers of Jesus continue to take seriously this *Great Commission*. Men and women find their greatest sense of significance develops when they participate with God's Holy Spirit in changing the world with the Gospel of Jesus Christ.

Before plunging into this exciting subject, defining a few key terms would be helpful.

Gospel simply means "good news."

Evangelism is a broad term that denotes the process of sharing the gospel message with others, inviting them to receive God's invitation to salvation and discipleship.

Missions generally refers to the same task (of evangelism) being undertaken in cross-cultural settings.

People who participate in evangelism and missions embrace Jesus' disciple-making mandate given in His Great Commission. They engage in activities that promote the gospel message. They call others to join them in their journey as followers of Jesus.

Living with the knowledge that their lives can make a difference, they co-labor with Jesus to transform the world with the gospel of Jesus Christ. Participants in evangelism and missions enjoy the satisfaction of knowing their lives are profoundly significant and that they were born **for such a time as this** (Esther 4:14). Rather than pursuing everything this world has to offer, they live as though heaven is their home and this life is one big short-term mission trip.

The evangelistic mandate given by Jesus to His followers is also given to present-day believers, who can participate in spreading the gospel.

THE DIVINE MANDATE IN JESUS' OWN WORDS

After His death and resurrection, just prior to His ascension, Jesus gave final instructions to His disciples. Matthew, Mark, and Luke each recount those instructions somewhat differently, illuminating important elements of the commission.

Matthew quotes Jesus saying, *"Go and make disciples of all nations, baptizing them in the name of the Father and of the Son and of the Holy Spirit, and teaching them to obey everything I have commanded you"* (Matthew 28:19-20).

Mark's Gospel records the commission this way: *"Go into all the world and preach the good news to all creation. Whoever believes and is baptized will be saved, but whoever does not believe will be condemned. And these signs will accompany those who believe: In my name they will drive out demons; they will speak in new tongues; they will pick up snakes with their hands; and when they drink deadly poison, it will not hurt them at all; they will place their hands on sick people, and they will get well"* (Mark 16:15-18).

Luke writes, *"This is what is written: The Christ will suffer and rise from the dead on the third day, and repentance and forgiveness of sins will be preached in his name to all nations, beginning at Jerusalem. You are witnesses of these things. I am going to send you what my Father has promised; but stay in the city until you have been clothed with power from on high" (Luke 24:46-49)*. *"You will receive power when the Holy Spirit comes on you; and you will be my witnesses in Jerusalem, and in all Judea and Samaria, and to the ends of the earth"* (Acts 1:8).

Examining the Great Commission requires giving attention to several key truths. First, what exactly is this good news Jesus' followers are commissioned to proclaim?

THE CONTENT OF THE GOSPEL MESSAGE
The Gospel of Salvation or the Gospel of the Kingdom?

When teaching about signs of the end times, Jesus notes, *"And this gospel of the kingdom will be preached in the whole world as a testimony to all nations, and then the end will come"* (Matthew 24:14). Throughout His earthly ministry, Jesus seeks to educate His disciples about the "kingdom of God," also called "the kingdom of heaven." Both John the Baptist and Jesus proclaim that the kingdom of God is "near" and "at hand" (Matthew 3:2; 4:17). He begins many parables with the words, *"The kingdom of God is like…."*

Interestingly, Jesus' *Good News* is far more expansive than salvation alone. While the disciples and the crowds hope Jesus plans to overthrow the Roman Empire and reestablish the throne of David in Jerusalem, in reality His Good News heralds the coming of a spiritual kingdom. In this kingdom Jesus will be Savior, Lord, and King. In this kingdom sin, sickness, death, and demons will all be under His feet. Through this kingdom, all the forces of darkness will be defeated. At the end of His earthly ministry, Jesus firmly secured the victory and supremacy of that kingdom through His own death, resurrection, and ascension to the right hand of the Father.

Why does this matter? Invitations to follow Jesus are invitations to become part of this spiritual kingdom in which Jesus reigns as King of kings. He invites disciples to receive Him not just as Savior, but also as Lord. After all, how can a kingdom be established without a king? Yes, the Good News of the gospel does promise salvation and the forgiveness of sins on the one hand. On the other hand, the Good News also calls would-be followers to make a change of allegiance from the kingdom of darkness from which they have been rescued to the kingdom of God.

To many, the thought of having their sins forgiven and escaping the consequence of eternity in hell sounds appealing. However, all too many people find the call to make a change of allegiance from the kingdom of darkness to the kingdom of God far less attractive. They want salvation without lordship, desiring heaven on their own terms.

Jesus preached this gospel to literally thousands of men and women, yet only a comparative handful decided to follow Him. In fact, He turned many eager would-be followers away because their commitment was half-hearted.

Yes, the gospel of the kingdom is Good News, but it is Good News that comes with expectations. Thus, calling it "the gospel of salvation" falls short of completely representing the message of the gospel. By identifying the Good News as "the gospel of the kingdom," those proclaiming its message rightly demonstrate that salvation and lordship go hand in hand. The call to salvation necessarily includes the call to lordship, not as an upgrade or an add-on, but as part of the basic package.

Lordship holds first place as a core component of the gospel of the kingdom.

Repentance Precedes Forgiveness and Salvation

Allegiance to this new kingdom and its King naturally requires a change of behavior. For this to occur, would-be disciples need to *repent* of (turn from) their sins and turn towards God.

In fact, the gospel of the kingdom as spoken by both John the Baptist and Jesus begins with these words: *"Repent, for the kingdom of heaven is at hand"* (Matthew 3:2; 4:17). Emphasizing the importance of these words, Matthew's account records this as the very first sentence spoken by both John the Baptist and Jesus in their public ministries. As if to "bookend" His ministry by reiterating the first key principle of the kingdom, Jesus declares that *"repentance and forgiveness of sins"* will be preached *"in his name to all nations"* (Luke 24:47).

Neither Jesus nor the apostles ever downplayed sin or repentance in their presentations of the gospel message to make the message more palatable. They spoke forthrightly about sin, sin's eternal consequences, and the call to repentance. The following passages illustrate this point:

- *Then Jesus began to denounce the cities in which most of his miracles had been performed, because they did not repent. "Woe to you, Korazin! Woe to you, Bethsaida! If the miracles that were performed in you had been performed in Tyre and Sidon, they would have repented long ago in sackcloth and ashes. But I tell you, it will be more bearable for Tyre and Sidon on the day of judgment than for you. And you, Capernaum, will you be lifted up to the skies? No, you will go down to the depths. If the miracles that were performed in you had been performed in Sodom, it would have remained to this day. But I tell you that it will be more bearable for Sodom on the day of judgment than for you"* (Matthew 11:20-24).

- *The men of Nineveh will stand up at the judgment with this generation and condemn it; for they repented at the preaching of Jonah, and now one greater than Jonah is here* (Matthew 12:41).

- *Jesus said to them, "I tell you the truth, the tax collectors and the prostitutes are entering the kingdom of God ahead of you. For John came to you to show you the way of righteousness, and you* did not believe him, but the tax collectors and the prostitutes did. And even after you saw this, you did not repent and believe him" (Matthew 21:31-32).

- *They went out and preached that people should repent* (Mark 6:12).

- *Jesus answered them, "It is not the healthy who need a doctor, but the sick. I have not come to call the righteous, but sinners to repentance"* (Luke 5:31-31).

- *Jesus answered, "Do you think that these Galileans were worse sinners than all the other Galileans because they suffered this way? I tell you, no! But unless you repent, you too will all perish. Or those eighteen who died when the tower in Siloam fell on them – do you think they were more guilty than all the others living in Jerusalem? I tell you, no! But unless you repent, you too will all perish"* (Luke 13:2-5).

- *"In the same way, I tell you, there is rejoicing in the presence of the angels of God over one sinner who repents"* (Luke 15:10).

- *Peter replied, "Repent and be baptized, every one of you, in the name of Jesus Christ for the forgiveness of your sins"* (Acts 2:38).

- *"Repent, then, and turn to God, so that your sins may be wiped out, that times of refreshing may come from the Lord"* (Acts 3:19).

- *"God exalted him to his own right hand as Prince and Savior that he might give repentance and forgiveness of sins to Israel"* (Acts 5:31).

- *When they heard this, they had no further objections and praised God, saying, "So then, God has granted even the Gentiles repentance unto life"* (Acts 11:18).

- *"In the past God overlooked such ignorance, but now he commands all people everywhere to repent"* (Acts 17:30).

- *"I have declared to both Jews and Greeks that they must turn to God in repentance and have faith in our Lord Jesus"* (Acts 20:21).

- *Therefore let us leave the elementary teachings about Christ and go on to maturity, not laying again the foundation of repentance from acts that lead to death, and of faith in God* (Hebrews 6:1).

- *The Lord is not slow in keeping his promise, as some understand *slowness. Instead he is patient with you, not wanting anyone to perish, but everyone to come to repentance* (2 Peter 3:9).

Becoming a true disciple requires authentic, heartfelt repentance from sin. Repentance means much more than just a simple "I'm sorry for my sins." Children and adults say those words often because they are sorry they got caught and hope to avoid the consequences of their actions.

Repentance reflects a person's true desire to turn from sin and turn towards God. According to Jesus, one does not just say "I'm sorry" to receive forgiveness of sin; an individual repents for *"the forgiveness of sins"* (Luke 24:47). *Repentance* is a critical part of the message. Repentance precedes forgiveness and salvation. Any "sinner's prayer" that does not include heartfelt repentance falls short of the whole gospel message.

The Gospel of the Kingdom Includes a Call to Radical Discipleship

The Great Commission calls Jesus' followers to "make disciples," not just gather "decisions for Christ." Too often the activities of evangelism and missions focus primarily on getting individuals to pray the so-called "sinner's prayer." In this way Christians can live with the illusion that disciples are being made, but a decision does not necessarily make a disciple.

Who is a disciple? Again, a disciple is one who has chosen to repent of sin, turn from sin, and make Jesus Lord. A disciple is one who determines that he or she wants to live and walk in the way of the Master. A disciple is one who has chosen to change the trajectory of his or her life by following after Jesus. If no change occurs, no real decision has been made. John the Baptist tells the religious leaders to *"produce fruit in keeping with repentance"* (Matthew 3:8). James emphatically states that, *faith without deeds is dead* (James 2:26).

To be clear, no one receives salvation because of his or her works. Salvation is a free gift from God, freely given by His grace and appropriated by faith (Ephesians 2:8-9). However, people's actions speak more loudly about that in which they put their faith than do their words. Works can never result in salvation, but they do demonstrate the reality of whether one has truly put his or her faith in Jesus Christ. When people choose to repent and turn from their sin in order to follow Christ, they confirm through actions what they profess verbally.

Each time Jesus called another disciple, the gospel writers noted what the would-be disciples did or did not leave behind. Peter, Andrew, James, and John left their boats, their nets, and their fathers to follow Jesus. By contrast, the rich young ruler just could not bring himself to leave his riches to follow Jesus. Though he lived a moral, upright life, his material possessions were of greater importance to him than following Jesus.

In short, actions reflect what lies deep within people's hearts. The gospel of the kingdom calls people to change their allegiances to the kingdom of darkness at the heart level, leave it behind, and turn to the kingdom of God. Repentance represents the part of the "Good News" that describes what people must leave behind in order to embrace the kingdom of God and receive the grace that comes with it.

While it is true that "in evangelism one does not clean the fish before catching it," believers give an incomplete presentation of the gospel message if the *expectation for repentance and change* is not mentioned. Yes, Jesus meets people where they are, but at the same time He calls them to leave where they are.

Minimizing the discipleship expectations of the gospel in order to get people to pray "the sinner's prayer" reduces evangelism to marketing Jesus. Such an approach amounts to little more than a form of "bait and switch." The books of Matthew, Mark, Luke, and John depict a Jesus who, as He calls people, never hides from them the kind of devotion He expects from those who follow Him.

Christians who follow Jesus' model do not "sell" the Gospel message by attaching minimal expectations to it to get a prospect to pray the "prayer." That is dishonest! In His ministry, Jesus never modeled minimizing the expectations for following Him. Continually, He "raised the bar." These words from Jesus illustrate just how much:

> • *Large crowds were traveling with Jesus, and turning to them he said: "If anyone comes to me and does not hate his father and mother, his wife and children, his brothers and sisters – yes, even his own life – he cannot be my disciple. And anyone who does not carry his cross and follow me cannot be my disciple. Suppose one of you wants to build a tower. Will he not first sit down and estimate the cost to see if he has enough money to complete it? For*

if he lays the foundation and is not able to finish it, everyone who sees it will ridicule him, saying, 'This fellow began to build and was not able to finish'" (Luke 14:25-30).

- As they were walking along the road, a man said to him, *"I will follow you wherever you go." Jesus replied, "Foxes have holes and birds of the air have nests, but the Son of Man has no place to lay his head." He said to another man, "Follow me." But the man replied, "Lord, first let me go and bury my father." Jesus said to him, "Let the dead bury their own dead, but you go and proclaim the kingdom of God." Still another said, "I will follow you, Lord; but first let me go back and say good-by to my family." Jesus replied, "No one who puts his hand to the plow and looks back is fit for service in the kingdom of God"* (Luke 9:57-62).

The dichotomy of the gospel message is that while salvation is free, it is not cheap. Those who want to follow Jesus will inevitably find themselves leaving much behind. At times, that repentance will involve a dramatic turning of one's back on sin and selfishness. At other times, repentance may require a person to leave behind what appears to be good in favor of God's best.

Why? The message is the "gospel of the kingdom," not just "the gospel of salvation." Individuals can no longer maintain their long-held allegiance to sin, self, materialism, Satan, or anything else if they want to follow Jesus. They choose instead to *repent* and declare their new allegiance to Jesus, the King of kings.

Water Baptism Figures Prominently

Though not necessary for salvation itself, when giving the Great Commission Jesus commanded His followers to baptize those who chose to receive the gospel and become disciples. What was so significant about water baptism? Quite simply, water baptism serves the following purposes:

- Water baptism is a **public declaration** of a person's determination to turn from sin in repentance, and their choice to make Jesus both Savior **and Lord** of their lives. *"Whoever acknowledges me before men,"* Jesus promises, *"I will also acknowledge him before my Father in heaven"* (Matthew 10:32).

- Water baptism publically **identifies a person with the new Christian community** of disciples. Neither Jesus nor the apostles treated a commitment to discipleship as an individual or private matter. Christ-following actually finds its greatest expression in community, as Paul demonstrates in Romans 12-13, 1 Corinthians 12-14, and elsewhere.

- Water baptism provides a **dramatic picture of dying to sin and rising again to new life in Christ.** The act reinforces the message of the gospel in a visual, experiential way as Paul describes in Romans 6. Going down under the water reminds believers that their old sinful nature has now died with Christ, and coming up out of the water signifies that they are now risen with Christ to new life as new creations with new natures.

Neglecting water baptism as part of the process in evangelism and missions misses a great opportunity to help new believers and remind veteran believers about who they are in Christ.

"Did They Receive the Holy Spirit?"

No presentation of the "Good News" can be complete without introducing new believers to the person and work of the Holy Spirit. Throughout the book of Acts, Luke presents a clear pattern as the gospel moves from Jerusalem to Judea, to Samaria, and beyond. With each major expansion of the Church, He purposely identifies three parts of the gospel message that were given priority:

1) Repent

2) Be baptized

3) Be filled with the Holy Spirit

Peter's message in Acts 2 includes all three of these components.

When they heard that Samaritans received the gospel and were baptized, Peter and John went to check on the fruit of Philip's work. Discovering the new believers had only believed in Jesus and been baptized, Peter and John prayed they would receive the Holy Spirit (Acts 8).

Likewise, Acts 9 tells of Paul's conversion and baptism, followed by Ananias laying hands on Paul and Paul receiving the Holy Spirit. Luke relates in Acts 10 the story of the house of Cornelius hearing the gospel proclaimed by Peter. They too were filled with the Spirit and baptized in water. Many years later, Paul utilized the same pattern in Ephesus (Acts 19).

One can safely conclude from these five accounts that the early apostles considered repentance, water baptism, and being filled with the Holy Spirit to be three vital first steps in the Christian walk. In their minds, no presentation of the Good News was complete until these three elements had been covered. To repent, be baptized, and be filled with the Holy Spirit became the normative pattern for evangelism and missions in the early Church.

MANDATE MOTIVATIONS – THE GOOD AND THE BAD

Evangelism and missions are active and intentional activities – not passive.

Matthew and Mark both quote Jesus as saying "go" in their recounting of the Great Commission. According to John, Jesus tells the disciples, *"As the Father has sent me, I am sending you"* (John 20:21). The mindset is missional, not attractional. No version of the Great Commission suggests an "if one builds it, they will come" mentality. Jesus instructs His disciples to be proactive, purposeful, and intentional about sharing the Gospel with both people they knew and those they did not yet know.

No one exhibits this intentionality better than the Apostle Paul. Acts tells of Paul's three major missionary journeys and the strategies he uses. What are appropriate motivations for evangelism and missions?

Keeping First Things First

In order to fully embrace the Great Commission as more than a task undertaken dutifully "because Jesus said so," followers of Jesus also make what many call "the Great Commandment" a priority. When asked by one of the Jewish religious leaders what the greatest commandment was, Jesus answered, *"'Love the Lord your God with all your heart and with all your soul and with all your mind.' This is the first and greatest commandment. And the second is like it: 'Love your neighbor as yourself'"* (Matthew 22:37-38). These are the "first things."

In living the Christian life, "keeping first things first" enables one to walk that path more easily and with greater joy. In this case, loving God and loving others first guards one's heart from falling prey to misguided motivations for evangelism. What are some poor motivations?

- Because Jesus said so (better than nothing, but may be lacking in love)
- To feel good about oneself for having fulfilled the evangelistic obligation
- To look good for others (keeping up "good Christian" appearances)
- Anger at people's immoral behavior and lack of respect for God
- To enforce Christian morality
- Legalism (it is what good Christians do)

The Apostle Paul tells the Corinthians that God's love compels him to share the Gospel (2 Corinthians 5:14). He can say this because he loves God first (Philippians 3:7-10). The more one falls in love with God, the more he or she begins to love what God loves. And God loves people! The more intimate people become with the Father, the more they discover how much people matter to God. "If they matter to God," believers conclude, "they now matter to me."

Without a strong enough "why?" to motivate, the Great Commission feels like just another "should" in a long list of Christian obligations. For evangelism to be valued, people must be valued. For most people, the Great Commission by itself is not enough to motivate. But when the love of God penetrates their hearts through time spent in intimacy with Him, these same believers discover a motivation rising from within – a motivation to love the very people God loves. Transformation in the heart always produces better fruit in a believer than obligation.

In summary, observing the Great Commandment first leads quite naturally to a love for people. When love for people compels disciples today as it did the Apostle Paul, the motivation for sharing the Gospel of Jesus Christ becomes simultaneously more urgent and selfless.

Missions is Part of the Church's Identity

Throughout Jesus' ministry and within the New Testament epistles, a variety of terms that reinforce the Church's evangelistic mandate can be found:

- Jesus tells His followers that they are the "salt of the earth" and the "light of the world."

- The disciples are called "apostles," meaning "ones sent."

- Jesus tells His followers that after the Holy Spirit comes upon them they will be "witnesses" (Acts 1:8).

- Paul describes himself and believers as "ambassadors" (2 Corinthians 5:20).

- Paul describes himself and believers as "aliens" and "citizens of heaven." Jesus tells the disciples they are to be "in this world but not of it."

In short, evangelism is not just something believers do. It is part of their identity, their makeup. They evangelize because they *are* salt, light, witnesses, and ambassadors.

The Evangelism and Missions Mindset

In addition to flowing from a God-birthed love for people, evangelism and missions flow from a mindset. This mindset embraces a few important truths, truths which may cause people of this earth to think these believers are *out of their minds* (2 Corinthians 5:13).

The first truth reminds believers that this earth is not their home. They consider themselves aliens in this world. Instead, Christ followers live as citizens of heaven and of God's household, as Paul writes in Ephesians 2:19 and Philippians 3:20. They give allegiance to God and His kingdom rather than to this world and its values. Peter exhorts, *Dear friends, I urge you, as aliens and strangers in the world, to abstain from sinful desires, which war against your soul* (1 Peter 2:11). Even Jesus, during His Last Supper conversation with the disciples, says, *"You do not belong to the world"* (John 15:19). Understanding this truth about their citizenship, participants in evangelism and missions live their lives as though they are here on earth on a short-term mission trip from heaven. Sent by God himself, they long to fulfill their mission – sharing the Good News of the kingdom, the gospel of Jesus Christ. They are now ambassadors of God, commissioned with making God's appeal through themselves. *He has committed to us the message of reconciliation* (2 Corinthians 5:19-20).

Enabling more of lost humanity to become disciples of Christ overshadows any desires they have to amass wealth and material possessions on this earth. Depopulating the kingdom of darkness takes precedence over personal gratification, great accomplishments, and personal notoriety. They invest in eternity by making the Great Commission their personal mission. They identify with Paul when he declares, *Woe to me if I do not preach the gospel!* (1 Corinthians 9:16). *Christ's love compels us* (2 Corinthians 5:14).

Second, these gospel ambassadors view the Good News and their mission to make disciples as a stewardship matter. Like Paul, they say, *We speak as those approved by God to be entrusted with the gospel* (1 Thessalonians 2:4). What God has entrusted to them, they are now responsible to multiply through the power of His Holy Spirit. The message cannot be hoarded; the Good News must be shared!

Finally, people motivated to share the gospel accept the reality of a spiritual world in addition to this physical world. They realize that every evangelistic and missional action equates to an act of war against the kingdom of darkness. They rightly perceive that lost persons are bound by chains of sin and blinded by a strong deception. Satan, the spiritual enemy, actively seeks to deceive unsaved individuals into believing that salvation is unnecessary and that Jesus' call to follow Him is not real.

These ambassadors of God's kingdom join God in His quest to pursue those who don't know Him. They don their armor and live as warriors fighting against the kingdom of darkness and all its deception. What they cannot see with their eyes, they grasp with their minds. Through evangelism and missions followers of Christ wage war for the freedom of lost souls, knowing their fight is not against *flesh and blood, but against the rulers, against the authorities, against the powers of this dark world and against the spiritual forces of evil in the heavenly realms* (Ephesians 6:12). As with the parents of a kidnapped or lost child, all other earthly activities pale in importance compared to the task of reaching the lost one.

A correct mindset deeply motivates Christ followers to action. Right thinking leads to right priorities and right living. Unrenewed minds have difficulty grasping the truths described here; therefore, the importance of renewing one's mind according to God's word is vital.

THE GREAT COMMISSION'S SCOPE

Jesus taught that this *gospel of the kingdom* would be preached throughout the world before the end comes (Matthew 24:14). Mark recalls that Jesus sent the disciples out to preach the gospel to *all creation*. Luke records Jesus highlighting Old Testament affirmations that *"repentance and forgiveness of sins will be preached in his name to all nations"* (Luke 24:46).

Evangelism and Missions Extend to All People

Each reference to the Great Commission in the Bible includes a phrase like "all nations," "all creation," or "throughout the world," indicating the Gospel's scope. No one is to be excluded.

Throughout Scripture, God reveals His heart for the nations. Yes, the Bible identifies Israel as *His chosen people* in the Old Testament and the Church as *His bride* in the New Testament. However, He does not speak specifically to Israel or the Church to exclude the rest of mankind. Rather, He calls them out in order to demonstrate His profound love for *all* people.

The following passages from both the Old and New Testaments demonstrate that God's love extends to all the nations:

- God promised to bless Abraham so that he could be a blessing to all nations (Genesis 12:1-3).
- God sent the prophet Jeremiah to prophesy to nations other than Israel, one of which was Egypt (see Jeremiah).
- God sent Jonah to preach to Nineveh of Assyria (see Jonah).
- *"For God so loved the world"* (John 3:16).
- *"You will be my witnesses in Jerusalem, and in all Judea and Samaria, and to the ends of the earth"* (Acts 1:8).
- The Samaritans received the Good News (Acts 8).
- God called Paul to be an apostle to the Gentiles (Acts 9).
- Cornelius's household (Gentiles) received salvation (Acts 10).
- The Ephesians received the Good News (Acts 19).

Only Those Who Believe Receive Salvation

Jesus states in the Great Commission, *"whoever does not believe will be condemned"* (Mark 16: 16). With this assertion, Jesus affirms that men and women have free will, and they can actually choose to reject God's gracious offer of salvation.

While God's heart beats for *all* people of *all* nations, salvation itself belongs exclusively to those who repent of their sins and make Jesus their Savior and Lord. The invitation to salvation is universal, inclusive, and available to all. God invites men, women, and children from all people groups to enter a relationship with Him. He lovingly offers all the same opportunity.

Sadly, some who receive this gracious invitation from God will choose to reject it. With free will, each person has the ability to respond positively or negatively to God's invitation. Those who respond positively to this universally available invitation will receive salvation and enter a relationship with God. Those who reject this universally available invitation will be condemned by their sin and rejection of God's offer.

Because salvation itself belongs exclusively to those who repent of their sin and make Jesus their personal Savior and Lord, people who reject the invitation to salvation choose eternal judgment and separation from God by default. Thus, salvation is universally offered and available, but not universally accepted and applied. Receiving the free gift hinges upon this condition: One must repent of his or her sins and make Jesus their Savior and Lord. Jesus made it clear that this condition was a prerequisite to becoming His disciple; however, some teachers in the church are teaching a heresy called *universalism*. Universalism holds to the idea that ultimately all people will be saved. No one will end up eternally condemned and separated from God for not accepting His invitation to salvation. After all, they contend, the gift is free and God is a God of love. He would never allow humans to be in such a state.

While such a teaching sounds appealing, Scripture does not support this claim. Jesus told parables which vividly describe the consequences awaiting those who reject His invitation. Jesus taught about two paths from which each person can choose, the "***wide path***" and the "***narrow path***" (Matthew 7:13-14).

Universalism inevitably teaches that multiple paths lead to God in the end. Whether one accepts or rejects God's invitation to salvation does not matter, for in love, God will give salvation to everyone anyway.

Not only does this teaching contradict the Bible and the teachings of Jesus, but this teaching is very risky. If one decides he or she does not need to accept the gift of salvation because in the end he or she will end up saved anyway, that person plays "Russian roulette" with eternity. What if, as Open Bible Churches believes, the person is wrong? That individual gets only one chance to die and find out whether his theology was right or wrong. That is a most dangerous game!

In summary, the scope of the Great Commission includes all people of all nations. Through followers of Jesus, the invitation to salvation goes out to all. Some will receive that invitation to salvation and discipleship with great joy; others will reject it and live their lives apart from God.

WHAT FULFILLING THE GREAT COMMISSION PRODUCES

The commission to "make disciples" includes teaching new believers to observe and do all that Jesus commanded .

The experience of salvation is just the beginning. True, people repenting for the forgiveness of sin points them in the right direction. However, without good teaching these new disciples will flounder. They will be susceptible to false teaching. They will shrink back from persecution. They will fail to pass their faith on to the next generation and so much more.

Those participating in evangelism and missions long to make disciples who can and will live out the commitment they now profess. Therefore, effective plans for evangelism and missions include a strategy for taking new believers beyond the point of decision to follow Jesus. This strategy will include solid grounding in the faith so that new believers can stand firm in the face of opposition and persecution (Ephesians 6 and Philippians 1).

What a Disciple Looks Like

Several authors have written books in an effort to help make the abstract concept of "making a disciple" more concrete and attainable. For example, Josh Hunt elaborates on nine areas to address when making disciples. Andy

Stanley highlights seven, calling them "checkpoints." Bill Hull, another author and pastor, goes into much greater depth on the subject. Hunt and Stanley are referenced below.

Characteristics of a Disciple (*Disciple-Making Teachers,* by Josh Hunt):

D – Disciplined
I – Intimate Family Relationships
S – Self-Esteem (Identity in Christ)
C – Corporate Worship
I – Intimate Friendship
P – Passion for God
L – Lay Ministry Involvement
E – Evangelistic Involvement
S – Sacrificial Giving

Checkpoints (*The Seven Checkpoints for Youth Leaders,* by Andy Stanley):

1) Authentic Faith
2) Spiritual Disciplines
3) Moral Boundaries
4) Healthy Friendships
5) Wise Choices
6) Ultimate Authority
7) Others First

In summary, evangelism and missions work to make fully devoted disciples of Jesus, not just "decisions" for Christ. Therefore, responsible plans for evangelism and missions include strategies for how people will be further discipled after making their decisions to follow Christ.

POWER FOR THE TASK
Holy Spirit-Empowered Evangelism and Missions

Jesus did not give His disciples a commission without giving them the power and authority to fulfill it. After telling them to *go*, Jesus told the disciples to *wait*. They were to wait for the promised Holy Spirit. When the Holy Spirit came, *then* they would be witnesses (Luke 24:49; Acts 1:8).

This provides a good reminder that evangelistic and missional methods should never replace or overshadow the Holy Spirit's role. With so many great approaches taught today, one can easily and unconsciously turn evangelism and missions into activities done primarily in human strength. God never intends for evangelism and missions to be done apart from the Holy Spirit's power.

Through their faith in God and the empowerment of the Holy Spirit, the disciples would do the same works, and even greater works, than Jesus did (John 14:12). God would be with them always (Matthew 28:20). Signs would accompany them (Mark 16:17). The authority and truth of their message would be confirmed by God Himself.

Those sharing the Gospel today should anticipate nothing less. By yielding to the Holy Spirit, disciples can expect the Holy Spirit's gifts to work in and through them. Words of knowledge, words of wisdom, and gifts of discernment can operate today just as they did through the early believers. Words of prophecy, gifts of healing, and more can work through those who surrender to the Spirit.

Throughout his gospel account, Luke shows that Jesus did His ministry completely by the Holy Spirit, not by virtue of His divinity. Acts, then, shared how Jesus' works continued through His disciples by the power of the same Holy Spirit. This truth applies to all people of all times in all places. Jesus' followers will proclaim the Good News of the Kingdom through the power of the very same Holy Spirit.

Similarly, Luke portrays Jesus and the early church leaders as people of prayer. Jesus withdrew from the crowds to pray. Believers were praying together in Acts 2 and 4. In Acts 10, the reader finds Peter in prayer. Paul and Barnabas left on their first missionary journey as a result of fasting and prayer in the Antioch church.

Clearly, prayer and Spirit-empowered evangelism and missions go hand in hand. Through prayer and abiding with the Father, Jesus discovered where His Father was at work and what He was doing so He could do the same thing. Several times, John penned that Jesus says and does only that which He sees the Father doing.

Evangelism and missions find their greatest fruitfulness when conducted by believers devoted to prayer, filled with the Holy Spirit, and following the leading of the Father. Jesus is revealed, His love is experienced, and His power is demonstrated. The Holy Spirit moves with conviction on people's hearts. Individuals, families, and people groups respond to the gospel message.

LIVING THE GREAT COMMISSION EVERY DAY

Christ followers wanting to participate in the Great Commission will find many opportunities. Most Christians engage in outreaches planned and programmed by a local church. The following list highlights some of the most common approaches (not in any particular order):

1) Street witnessing
2) Feeding and benevolence programs
3) Conspiracy of kindness activities (popularized by Steve Sjogren in his book, *Conspiracy of Kindness*)
4) Support groups for single parents
5) Support groups for those experiencing the death of a loved one
6) Support systems for foster parents and adoptive parents
7) Back-to-school supplies and shoes for needy families
8) Thanksgiving food baskets
9) "Toys for Tots" type of outreaches to provide Christmas gifts for needy children
10) Christmas and/or Easter dramas
11) Summer children's and youth camps
12) Ministry and resources for homeless shelters
13) Assistance with local domestic violence women's shelters
14) Assistance with local children's and youth shelters
15) Aid to unwed mothers
16) Art-in-the-park events
17) Adopt-a school projects
18) "Extreme Home Makeovers" for needy families
19) Vacation Bible School
20) "Mother's Day Out" programs
21) Special speakers and/or musical guests
22) Crusade and/or revival services
23) Short-term missions trips
24) Financial support of long-term missionaries
25) Church planting projects

Certainly one could easily list another 25 outreach methods employed by local churches. However, this section will explore ways in which individual believers can be "salt" and "light" (Matthew 5:13-16), witnesses in their daily lives outside of a church-organized program. Opportunities to share and demonstrate the "Good News" abound every day.

Why is living out the Great Commission daily as individuals so important? First, for most people, salvation happens not just as an event, but as a process over time. Paul makes this point when he writes, *What, after all, is Apollos? And what is Paul? Only servants, through whom you came to believe – as the Lord has assigned to each his task. I planted the seed, Apollos watered it, but God made it grow. So neither he who plants nor he who waters is anything, but only God, who makes things grow. The man who plants and the man who waters have one purpose, and each will be rewarded according to his own labor. For we are God's fellow workers; you are God's field, God's building* (1 Corinthians 3:5-9).

So much attention gets focused upon the moment of decision that one easily forgets all that led up to a person's final choice to make Jesus Savior and Lord. Somewhere, sometime, someone plants the seed of the gospel message into a person's mind and heart. From that point forward, God strategically places people in that person's life to water the seed and make it grow. One day, that person makes the decision to follow Jesus official.

With this in mind, the role of individual believers living as witnesses of Jesus each day cannot be underestimated. A Christian may plant the seed of the gospel into someone during the morning, water the seed of the gospel in another person's life that afternoon, and even reap the harvest in the evening by praying with someone to make Jesus Lord of their life. What an exciting way in which to live! Every conversation could be important.

Second, some missiological studies indicate that believers, when surveyed, credit their salvation to a person with whom they had a significant relationship. Even if a believer made the final decision to follow Christ at a crusade or while watching Christian television, the relationship with another believer over time was the critical factor in that person's conversion. Through what may be called *relational evangelism*, seeds of the gospel are planted and receive regular watering over protracted periods of time, often resulting in people's ultimate decision to make Jesus their Savior and Lord.

Thus, the people in Christians' lives that are most likely to accept Jesus are those with whom Christians already have significant relationships: family members, co-workers, neighbors, and others. Most evangelism and missions events planned by the local church target people with whom church members have the fewest relationships and the least amount of influence. While those church-organized methods still have merit, disciples of Jesus cannot neglect the responsibility they have to live out the Great Commission in their own daily lives, in ways not planned and programmed by their churches.

What then does intentional, but unprogrammed evangelism and missions look like when lived out by disciples in the context of their everyday lives? How are seeds of the gospel planted and watered, not by accident, but on purpose? Perhaps the best way to illustrate this would be through some anecdotal stories. The following stories are real examples of real believers planting and watering the seed of the gospel in the lives of non-believers. (Names, places, and some details may have been altered for privacy purposes, but the essence of each story is true.)

Note how these Christians weave their faith into the very fabric of their lives, including work, recreation, social activities, and more. Their love for God does not sit unused in the "church cupboard" until Sunday. Instead, their love for God exudes from them wherever they are. These Christ followers exhibit what evangelism and missions look like when sharing the Good News of the Kingdom becomes more than a church program and instead reflects the inherent DNA of each disciple.

Richard, now 66, plays shortstop and pitcher for at least two recreational, fast-pitch baseball leagues – one for those over 60, and one for those over 50. Baseball has been Richard's passion since he was a child growing up in the East. "I feel closest to God when standing on the pitching mound under a deep, blue sky," he claims.

For more than ten years Richard has made his love for baseball an opportunity to share the gospel with men who might never hear it otherwise. Playing with many of the same men over the years has afforded him opportunities to not only play with them, but to also eat with them, visit their homes, invite them to his home, and even grieve the loss of loved ones with them.

The relationships he built with these men created a foundation of trust and loyalty, a foundation that allows him to openly share the gospel. Richard planted and watered seeds with many unbelievers over the years – Jews, atheists, agnostics, and more. From time to time, he gets to experience the joy of praying with one who decides to make Jesus Savior and Lord.

Linda serves as the chairperson for a miniatures club with which she has participated for many years. Highly respected by the club members for her skills and for her genuine interest in each person's success, Linda gets to use her favorite hobby as a platform for sharing the gospel. The care she expresses in conversations has led to many women sharing their heart issues with her.

At times, she finds herself functioning in an informal pastoral capacity as members seek her out for counsel and encouragement. Despite the secular nature of the club, Linda has full freedom to share her faith and even pray for people as needed. She gets to plant seeds and water them while doing what she loves to do.

As with Richard, Linda did not have to seek these people out or recruit them. They come to the club on their own because of their love for miniatures. Linda, then, functions pastorally while doing what she loves. Common interests and authentic relationships create many opportunities for her to be a witness.

Ethan stumbled into his ripe opportunity by taking a group from his church to one of the local nursing homes to sing, speak, and visit with residents. While speaking to the gathered group, Ethan makes sure to include a clear presentation of the gospel message. Much to his amazement, residents have been quite responsive to the Good News. A number of them have made Jesus their Savior and Lord.

"We get church groups coming through all the time. They sing for us, talk with us, play games with us, but you are the first to tell us so plainly about Jesus," one gentleman told Ethan. Hungry to know more about God, residents asked for a weekly Bible study through which they could be discipled. Ethan's mother, Alison, now meets weekly with a group of elderly new believers, teaching them about their new-found faith.

Bella loves teaching people how to train their dogs. She posts an ad in the local paper and charges people to come to her dog-training classes. Each class meets for 12 weeks, during which time Bella purposes to be a "lay pastor" to the people in her class. Intentional about being a witness, she concludes each week's training time with a brief talk about how the relationship between a dog and his/her master is like the relationship between people and God. Over the years, Bella has led many to Christ through this dog-training class. In fact, a whole group of people sit together in one part of the church she attends, most of whom are fruit from her dog classes.

Testimonies of regular people being "salt," "light," and "witnesses" right where God has planted them abound. Rather than waiting for a church planned activity, they demonstrate and share God's love wherever they are. Christ's love compels them. It's in their DNA.

Regular people in normal everyday situations living out the Great Commission – that is what true discipleship looks like when believers are connected with Him, practicing His presence all day, every day. They purposefully and intentionally look for ways to demonstrate and share the Good News outside of pre-planned, programmed church events. They look for organic opportunities to build relationships with the people they see the most and are most likely to influence. They live their lives as God's ambassadors to a world of lost people.

OPPORTUNITES FOR ENGAGING IN THE MISSION THROUGH OBC

Through an outreach culture, leadership development, and aggressive church planting Open Bible Churches zealously strives to fulfill the Great Commission. Every minister, church, district, region, department, and office is committed to bringing people to Jesus Christ and making them fully devoted followers of His.

Open Bible Churches offers a variety of ways for its constituents to participate in evangelism and missions. What follows represents a sampling of those opportunities. One can gain a more comprehensive understanding by exploring the website links provided.

Pray

Those engaged in fulfilling the Great Commission through Open Bible Churches deeply appreciate the support of faithful prayer warriors. They long to have their ministry endeavors undergirded with intercession. By going to *www.globalmissionsobc.org* one can learn about Open Bible missionaries and their work. He or she can sign up for the Global Link newsletter, which gives updates from around the world regarding Open Bible's Missions efforts.

Receive Training

The School Of Global Leadership (SGL): SGL is a specialized missions training school for young global leaders set in a permission-giving atmosphere. Providing both academic and hands-on training to individuals who have a heart for the world, SGL offers cross-cultural opportunities to use one's gifts, so that his/her God-given dreams can become a reality. To learn more, go to ***www.sgl-trinidad.com***

Inste Bible College: No matter the size of the church, Inste Bible College is a fit for training and discipling local church members. All that is needed to get started is a mature, dedicated leader called to make disciples, whom INSTE trains through a short leader-training program right where he or she is. Inste Bible College supplies the materials – books and tests included – a support system for the group leader, and records and recognition for the courses studied. Learn more at ***www.inste.edu***

New Hope Christian College (NHCC): New Hope Christian College inspires students to become ambassadors for Christ as they are taught and mentored by competent and godly professors who know their students by name and invite them to grow in discipleship. View their website at ***www.newhope.edu***

Take a Short-term Missions Trip

Men Of Vision Evangelize (MOVE): God still performs miracles in the hearts and lives of men who join the annual Men of Vision Evangelize (MOVE) crews in nations around the world. Hundreds of men from our churches in the United States experience God's love for "the least of these" on the mission fields of Open Bible. You can learn more about this ministry at ***www.moveministries.org***

Puente De Amistad (Bridge of Friendship): Puente de Amistad is a short-term mission base in Tijuana, Mexico, that hosts church teams or individuals from the States who want to experience missions. These teams get to display the love of Jesus by helping with orphanages and feeding kitchens, assisting in building projects for the poor, ministering in various churches, and working with other missionaries and local pastors to help meet peoples' needs. Learn more at ***www.puentedeamistad.org***

Plant, Participate In, or Support a New Church Start

The continual addition and multiplication of disciples, leaders, and churches was a hallmark throughout the book of Acts. Church planting continues to be one of the most effective tools God uses to accomplish the Great Commission and build His Church. The future of any church movement is directly tied to its vision and unbending commitment to reproduce disciples, leaders, and churches. Church planting is biblical with evangelism at its core. It develops new leaders, is efficient, and is a means of fulfilling Open Bible's mission.

Become a Global Missionary

Global Missions exists to serve, equip, and resource churches, missionaries, and leaders committed to global evangelism, discipleship, and church planting. Presently Global Missions of Open Bible is ministering in 44 countries. Through the outreaches of Open Bible churches overseas, approximately 20,000 people receive Christ every year. To learn more about Global Missions, go to *www.globalmissionsobc.org*

Give Financially Through MVP (Mission Venture Plan)

Mission Venture Plan (MVP): MVP is a giving emphasis based on designated giving with programmed options. In other words, you decide where you want your contributions to go. You are able to support church planting, disaster relief, and other ministries in the United States and assist missionaries, fund the digging of water wells, and help meet other global ministry needs.

Contributions to the **Global Mission Leadership Fund** are Global Missions' main source of funding. As noted in the information under that option, this fund covers many aspects of Open Bible's outreach around the world. Even that listing is not all-inclusive.

Open Bible's wonderful missionaries raise all their own funds to fulfill the ministries for which God has called and equipped them. Read about each of them on the missionaries' respective pages at *www.missionventureplan.org/ministry-ventures/im*

NO GREATER THRILL

What greater sense of significance can a person live with than knowing he or she plays a vital role in "Good Newsing" this world with the Gospel of Jesus

Christ? What can compare to helping an individual change the course of his or her eternal destiny?

Jesus' call to fulfill the Great Commission invites every believer to live a life of significance and impact for the kingdom of God. Nothing compares to the thrill one experiences when he or she gets to be part of rescuing another person from the kingdom of darkness and bringing that person into the kingdom of God. Furthermore, active involvement in the Great Commission inevitably produces another benefit – increased joy and appreciation for one's own salvation.

Related Scriptures

Psalm 2:8; Proverbs 11:30; Matthew 9:38; Mark 16:15; John 4:35-37; Acts 1:8; Romans 10:13-15; Ephesians 5:16; 2 Timothy 4:1-2; James 5:20; Revelation 5:9

For Further Reading

Hunt, Josh. *Disciple-Making Teachers*. Josh Hunt, 2001

Stanley, Andy. *The Seven Checkpoints for Youth Leaders*. West Monroe, LA: Howard Publishing Co., Inc., 2001

Time to Interact

Take some time to interact with the following questions. Consider writing your answers in a journal and/or discussing them with a fellow believer for deeper reflection and insight.

1. What thoughts and images come to mind when you think of the terms *evangelism* and *missions*? What feelings do each of these words stir in you? In what possible ways do you anticipate these words being associated with your life? Why is that important to you?

2. If you encountered someone today that wanted to "be saved," what would you say to them? What needs to happen in order for you to feel prepared for potential moments like that?

3. How do you perceive the differences between the "gospel of salvation," and the "gospel of the kingdom?" Why do you think this chapter stresses and favors the need to present the latter?

4. How would you define "radical discipleship?" Is it possible to be a true disciple of Christ and not be radical? Why or why not?

Time to Integrate

Evangelism and missions are not spiritual terms that only apply to a few select people. The call to carry the Kingdom into all the world belongs to each of us! Consider how to best act on that call as you work through these final points.

1. Who was instrumental in helping you discover Christ and become a disciple? Write a letter of appreciation and send it to them (or share with a friend if you are no longer able to contact that person). How does God want to use you in similar fashion to communicate the Gospel to someone else? In what ways are a person's actions just as important as their words when it comes to communicating the Gospel?

2. Who do you know right now that desperately needs to come into a saving relationship with Jesus Christ? Make a short list of specific people whom you will lift before the Father in prayer this month, crying out for their redemption. Look for moments and opportunities that the Holy Spirit just might give you in accordance with those prayers.

3. Consider the many ways you can live out the Great Commission from the list of options presented in this chapter. Where do you see yourself? Ask the Holy Spirit to speak to you regarding an area of local outreach ministry. Does your church body also have ministry opportunities beyond what is listed here? What can you do to become actively involved?

4. Is it possible (and even probable) that God may want to work through you in a different global setting? What mission opportunities are available to you? What skills, talents, time, money, or effort could you offer in a foreign field? Ask the Lord to share His heart with you concerning the citizens of a particular nation or people group. Begin to earnestly pray for them. Take steps to obtain your passport. As you depend on God to open up the right doors at His right time, what else can you do to recognize and respond to a God-ordained opportunity?

Glossary

Agape: One of several words in the biblical Greek language which are defined as our English word for "love," commonly used to refer to God's unconditional love towards us.

Alpha: A Greek word referring to the first letter of the alphabet, often referring to Jesus Christ as "the beginning" or "the first."

Amillennialism: An interpretation of the one-thousand-year reign of Jesus Christ on earth (found in Revelation 20) that emphasizes the symbolic nature of this passage of Scripture, rather than the belief in a literal period of one thousand years as a prophecy to be fulfilled.

Angels: Spiritual (non-human) beings created by God to do His bidding in spiritual realms (worshiping around the throne of heaven, battling against demonic entities) and acting on God's behalf in the lives of people on earth.

Anthropological argument: An argument for the existence of God that sees God's existence demonstrated in the consciences of men and women as they yearn for a higher power or something (or Someone) that is beyond their mundane existence.

Apostle: One sent by God for a certain time and to a certain place to establish and oversee the work of God.

Atonement: To make amends for, or to satisfy or make reparations for a wrong or injury (used in the Old Testament to describe what happens during altar sacrifice to cover sins; in the New Testament to describe the sacrifice of Jesus on the cross to forgive our sins).

Baptism in the Holy Spirit: A biblical experience available to all believers that is distinct from salvation, in which persons are overwhelmed with the power of the Holy Spirit, enabling them to speak in tongues/pray in the Spirit, and exercise other spiritual gifts as they are empowered to bear witness to Jesus Christ.

Believer: A person who has had a conversion experience, having confessed Jesus Christ as their Savior and Lord, having received forgiveness of sins, and who can correctly be called a follower of Christ or a Christian.

Breaking of bread: A phrase found in the book of Acts referring to fellowship meals in the early church, which included both a regular sharing of food and also a celebration of the Lord's Supper.

Canon: Referring to Scripture, the body of books (39 in the Old Testament and 27 in the New Testament) which were received by the early church as the authoritative Word of God inspired by the Holy Spirit.

Church: The body of Christ; the people of God called out from the world by Jesus to fellowship in His name and to live for Him.

Church Fathers: The great leaders and theologians of the church, sometimes called "Patristic Fathers," who lived in the first few centuries after the generation of the apostles and the close of the New Testament canon.

Commemoration: The remembrance of Christ's sacrificial death by partaking of the emblems (bread and wine) of the Lord's Supper, which represent and symbolize the body and blood of Christ.

Communion: The celebration of the Lord's Supper, as we participate and "commune" with the Lord and His people in the sharing of the bread and the cup.

Conciliar: Referring to decisions on important matters of doctrine (such as on the humanity and deity of Christ or the Trinity) made by church leaders at early ecumenical (or universal) councils, such as the Council of Nicea in 325 A.D.

Cosmological argument: The argument for God's existence (offered by Aristotle and Thomas Aquinas) that appeals to a first cause or a prime mover, who could be understood to be God, that causes all else to exist.

Day of Atonement: As described in the Old Testament, a holy feast day celebrated by the people of Israel every year during which the High Priest made an atoning sacrifice for the sins of the people, bringing about reconciliation between the people and God.

Day of Pentecost: A feast day celebrated by Jews; this is also the day described in the book of Acts when the Holy Spirit was poured out among all those gathered in Jerusalem for the annual feast, a day often described as the birth of the Church.

Deism: The belief in a "watchmaker God," or the idea that God created the world but has nothing to do with its daily operation, leaving it to run on its own without His involvement.

Demons: Spiritual beings who are described as evil spirits in the Bible, having fallen from heaven due to rebellion and who are currently at work in the world under the direction of Satan, doing his bidding until they experience ultimate judgment after Christ returns.

Depravity: The innate corruption of human nature due to original sin.

Dichotomy: A view of the composition of human beings that describes them as having two parts – a material and spiritual component, or a body and a soul.

Disciple: One who has chosen to repent of sin, turn from sin, make Jesus Lord, and follow Him.

Dispensationalism: An approach to the study of the Bible that emphasizes distinct eras or time periods (dispensations) given by God in history, and interprets the meaning of passages of Scripture according to the particular ways God has chosen to show His grace during those identified time periods.

Distinguishing between spirits: The supernatural ability to understand what kind of spirit is controlling or motivating an individual or situation; a gift of the Holy Spirit often used in ministry as one exercises the authority given believers by Jesus Christ over evil spirits.

Elect: Those who are chosen by God for salvation; in the context of the free will of all human beings, referring to men and women who become followers of Jesus Christ, receive salvation, and become members of God's elect.

Elohim: One of the Hebrew names for God found in the Old Testament, used over 2,000 times in Scripture; a plural form used prominently in the creation account; for example, *"Let us make man in our image"* (Genesis 1:26).

Encouraging: Stimulating the faith of others by giving direction or steps of action; described as a gift of the Holy Spirit in Romans 12.

Eucharist: From the New Testament Greek word meaning "to give thanks," used in the Church to describe the Lord's Supper or Holy Communion.

Evangelism: The process of sharing the gospel with others, inviting them to receive God's invitation to salvation and discipleship.

Evangelist: One gifted to preach the gospel to unbelievers.

Expiation: The work of Christ on the cross which removes the penalty officially imposed by the law of a holy God, which had indicted and proven the sinner guilty.

Feast of Pentecost: The Greek name of the Jewish Feast of Weeks, which celebrates the giving of the Law to Moses on Mount Sinai (celebrated fifty days after the Feast of Passover).

Feast of Tabernacles: Known in Hebrew as "Sukkot," an annual Jewish observance commemorating the forty years during which the children of Israel wandered in the desert wilderness; also a fall festival which celebrates the annual harvest.

Feast of Trumpets: Also known by the Hebrew name Rosh Hashanah, a feast which marks the Jewish New Year and also commemorates the day that God created Adam and Eve.

Fellowship: An English word which is a translation of the New Testament Greek word *koinonia*; the sharing among believers in Christ as they participate and commune with the Lord Jesus and with one another in Christian unity.

Free will: The teaching that even though God is sovereign and accomplishes His purposes on the earth, He has created men and women to be free to choose either to accept His grace or to reject it and that this freedom of the will is an aspect of what it means for us to be uniquely created in the image of God.

Gift of administration: The ability to guide and govern in various settings on behalf of the Church.

Gift of faith: Not saving faith, but a manifestation of supernatural faith related to a particular need.

Gift of giving: Making one's assets available to the kingdom of God.

Gift of healing: The divine impartation of restoration for various types of physical ailments and afflictions.

Gift of helping: Assisting those suffering, in weakness and in need, on behalf of the Church.

Gift of hospitality: The gift of providing a godly welcoming presence and care for strangers and guests on behalf of the Church.

Gift of leadership: Coordinating the efforts of others to accomplish a common goal.

Gift of martyrdom: A special grace by God to follow Christ fully, even to death.

Gift of mercy: An attraction to, understanding of, and ministry to people who are in distress.

Gift of prophecy: The ability to speak forth a message from God.

Gospel: The word in the New Testament that refers to the "Good News" or message of the life, death, and resurrection of Jesus Christ, which all believers are to proclaim to others in their everyday lives.

Gospels: The first four books of the New Testament (Matthew, Mark, Luke, and John).

Haggadah: A Hebrew word meaning "telling"; a text that is read during a Passover Seder that enables Jewish adults to tell their children about the deliverance of the children of Israel from Egypt at the Exodus, in fulfillment of the command found in Exodus 13:8.

Heresy: The name given to a teaching or belief which does not line up in harmony and agreement with the clear teachings of the Bible; the opposite of orthodoxy.

Holy Spirit: The Spirit of God, or the third member of the Trinity, who points persons to Jesus Christ and provides believers with the presence of God until Christ returns at the end of the age.

Immanent: The nearness of God or sense of His being among us, in contrast to God's transcendence or His being beyond our grasp.

Immanuel: An Old Testament prophetic title given to the promised Messiah (Christ), meaning "God with us."

Imminency: The belief that the return of Christ to earth could take place at any time – there are no unfulfilled prophecies that are delaying His return.

Immutable: A biblical attribute of the greatness of God, unique to Him, in which He demonstrates unchangeability and stability.

Imputation: The action of the grace of God the Father that confers upon us the righteousness of Christ through His (Christ's) atoning death on the cross.

Incarnation: The Son of God became human and did so without diminishing His divine nature.

Inerrancy: The belief that the very words of each book of the Bible are the words of God and that these books were delivered to us completely true and without error.

Infallibility: The belief that the Bible is fully authoritative and is intended to guide believers in all matters of faith and practice.

Inspiration: The belief that the books of the Bible are "God-breathed," or that the Holy Spirit enabled the human authors of the Bible to write exactly what God wanted to be said.

Interpretation of tongues: The ability to interpret to a gathering of believers the sense of a message conveyed in tongues.

Justification: The aspect of our salvation that focuses on the work of Christ on the cross, which provides for us to be declared righteous before God on the basis of the righteousness of Christ.

Laying on of hands: A form of prayer in which believers trust God for healing and miracles in the lives of others while they place their hands on the person being prayed for, believing that the power of the Holy Spirit will be released in the process and that the prayer will be answered.

Lent: An annual period of prayer, fasting, and spiritual preparation during the forty days before Easter that Christians from many church denominations observe as part of their worship experience.

Logos: The Greek word for "Word" in the New Testament, used to describe Jesus in the book of John as the living Word of God.

Marriage Supper of the Lamb: The beautiful picture found in Revelation 19 that points to the wedding of Jesus Christ and His Bride (the Church) when believers join together with the Lord in heaven.

Matzah: Unleavened bread, which was (and still is) used by the Israelites during the feast of Passover and was also used by Jesus and the disciples during the Last Supper.

Message of knowledge: Knowledge revealed supernaturally by God about a person or a situation.

Message of wisdom: The ability to have some of God's wisdom as a direct result of the revelation of the Spirit and not through experience or gradual understanding.

Millennium: A word found in the original Greek text of Revelation 20 that means "one thousand years," and refers to a period of time related to the Second Coming of Jesus Christ and His reign over the earth.

Miraculous powers: A spiritual gift which enables a believer to receive grace to operate in the power of God beyond human ability.

Missions: The outreach to others, usually in a cross-cultural setting, to share the gospel and invite them to receive God's invitation to salvation and discipleship.

Nicene Creed: A statement of faith agreed upon by the leaders of the early church in 325 A.D. and affirmed by Christians today, which declares a biblical understanding of and belief in who God the Father is, the person and work of Jesus Christ, and the Holy Spirit.

Omega: The last letter of the Greek alphabet, which is sometimes used to describe Jesus as the greatest or the last or the ultimate Being.

Omnipotence: A biblical attribute of the greatness of God, unique to Him, in which He has unlimited power to do whatever He chooses to do.

Omnipresence: A biblical attribute of the greatness of God, unique to Him, in which He can be anywhere or any combination of places that He chooses to be at any time.

Ontological: An argument for the existence of God which affirms that since we can conceive of a Being which is the greatest being in the world, there must actually be such a Being.

Pastor: One gifted to exercise leadership and care over a local body of believers.

Pentecost: A Greek word meaning "fiftieth"; the name of the Jewish Feast of Weeks, which celebrates the giving of the Law to Moses on Mount Sinai (celebrated fifty days after the Feast of Passover); for Christians also the day of the initial outpouring of the Holy Spirit on the Church, which the Church celebrates fifty days after Easter each year.

Plenary verbal inspiration of Scripture: The belief that the very words which we find in each of the books of the Bible were "God-breathed," or given to us by God, through the individual authors of those books.

Post-millennialism: A belief in the one-thousand-year reign of Jesus Christ on earth (found in Revelation 20) that emphasizes a period of increasing transformation, triumph, and evangelistic success on earth before the Lord returns.

Pre-millennialism: A belief in the one-thousand-year reign of Jesus Christ on earth (found in Revelation 20) that emphasizes both a tribulation period and the Lord's return prior to His one-thousand-year reign.

Prophecy: A message from God delivered by His messenger.

Prophesy: To deliver a message from God to His intended recipients.

Prophesying: Speaking forth a message from God in one's own language to a gathering of believers.

Prophet: One called of God and empowered by the Holy Spirit to speak forth revelations of divine truth.

Propitiation: An understanding of the atoning and sacrificial death of Jesus Christ on the cross for our sins that emphasizes Jesus' death as appeasing or turning away the holy wrath of a just Father towards sin.

Rapture: A term that describes the belief that Christians will be caught up into heaven to be with the Lord Jesus Christ before He returns to earth and establishes a new heaven and a new earth.

Reconciliation: The result of our salvation in Christ, the restoration of right relationship between us and the Father and our adoption as His children.

Redemption: The deliverance from enslavement to sin and condemnation to hell by the ransom paid by Christ's death on our behalf which has set us free to be children of God.

Regeneration: The supernatural act of God whereby the spiritual and eternal life of the Son, the Lord Jesus Christ, is imparted to the individual through faith in Jesus Christ.

Repentance: Recognizing our sin is offensive to God and turning away from it in mind and heart.

Rhema: In the original Greek New Testament, the "word" of God, emphasizing the way in which believers are trained to sometimes hear the voice of the Lord in prophetic ways or in daily life as distinguished from the objective words that are read in the Scriptures.

Salvation: The deliverance from sin and its consequences.

Sanctification: The position and process of being made holy unto the Lord.

Sanctify: To set apart for special use, or to purify.

Scripture: The books of the Old and New Testaments, which are the inspired and authoritative Word of God.

Seder: The annual ritual during the Jewish feast of Passover that includes a meal of matzah (unleavened bread) and other foods, while the story is told of the deliverance of the children of Israel from slavery in Egypt during the time of the Exodus.

Serving: A spiritual gift that enables one to exercise God's grace in meeting the practical needs of others.

Sin: Thoughts, words, actions, attitudes, and dispositions towards God and others which miss the mark, or break God's law, and, apart from His redemption and forgiveness, separate us from Him.

Soteriology: The doctrine of salvation. (The Greek word in the New Testament for salvation is *soteria*.)

Soul: The seat of one's personality; the eternal self that if redeemed will exist forever to dwell rewarded in God's presence or if unredeemed will exist forever to be punished in hell for rejecting His offer of salvation.

Speaking in tongues: The manifestation of an unknown and unlearned language, either as a message to be interpreted in public worship, or as a devotional prayer language used during private worship.

Spirit: Mankind's immaterial self, which discerns and decides to reflect the character of sin, Satan, or the Savior; the seat of human will and cognition; may also refer to the Holy Spirit, the third member of the Trinity.

Spiritual gifts: Gifts of grace from the Holy Spirit to believers, enabling them to build up and encourage one another in the Church and to more effectively bear witness to the life of Christ to unbelievers.

Substitution: An aspect of the atonement, or the work of Christ on the cross, which emphasizes the necessity of the Lord Jesus taking our place and paying the penalty for our sins in order for us to be reconciled to God.

Teacher: One gifted to instruct believers in all righteousness.

Teaching: A spiritual gift which supernaturally enables one to clarify, validate, and present foundational truth about God and the Christian life.

Teleological argument: An argument for the existence of God which looks at the amazing design of the universe, the world and all of creation, and concludes that a Supreme Designer must have been behind it all, and that the Designer is God.

Ten Commandments: These are the ten commands given by God to Moses on Mount Sinai, inscribed on stone tablets, which were to guide the lives of the children of Israel as they followed the Lord in worship and obedience; sometimes called "the Decalogue."

The Great Commandment: Jesus' twofold response to a question, "what is the greatest commandment?" in which He articulated the two commands found in the Old Testament: that believers should love God with all of their hearts, minds, and souls, and that they should also love their neighbors as themselves (Matthew 22:36-39).

The Great Commission: Jesus' command toward the end of His earthly ministry, found in Matthew 28:19-20, that believers are to *"go and make disciples of all nations, baptizing them in the name of the Father and of the Son and of the Holy Spirit, and teaching them to obey everything I have commanded you."*

The Lord's Supper: The participation of Christians in the practice of gathering together and sharing the bread and cup in the same way Jesus and His disciples did at the Last Supper, in remembrance of His broken body and shed blood on our behalf; sometimes referred to as Holy Communion or the Eucharist.

Theophany: A visible manifestation of God (most often occurring in the Old Testament, such as the appearance of the burning bush in Exodus).

Tithe: A tenth of one's income or resources, which is offered to God as a biblical act of worship and obedience.

Tithing: A biblical expression of worship and obedience to God in which His followers offer Him the first-fruits (or literally, a tenth) of their income and resources, in thanksgiving and trust for His blessings in their lives.

Transcendent: An attribute of God which focuses on the fact that God is beyond humanity in His perfection and power; to be distinguished from the immanence, or nearness, of God.

Tribulation: A time period described in the book of Revelation and in other prophetic passages of Scripture, thought to take place near the time of the Second Coming of Jesus Christ and to involve the persecution of Christians.

Trichotomy: A view of the composition of human beings that describes them as having three parts – a body, a soul, and a spirit.

Trinitarian: A view of God that affirms the belief in one God, who exists eternally as the persons of the Father, the Son, and the Holy Spirit.

Trinity: The Christian belief in God the Father, God the Son (Jesus Christ), and God the Holy Spirit, who have existed eternally as One.

Universalism: A belief (without biblical support) that all persons will eventually be welcomed into heaven for eternity; a doctrine which denies the existence of a literal hell.

Unpardonable sin: Considered by some to be a sin of apostasy or betrayal against God that leads to death, for which there is no forgiveness; sometimes referred to as blaspheming or sinning against the Holy Spirit.

Water baptism: A public action taken by believers in obedience to the command of Scripture that symbolizes a washing away of one's sins and declares one's new life in Christ.

Voluntary poverty: Living a life of extreme simplicity by God's grace, for the sake of the Kingdom.

Worship: Ascribing to God the honor and glory that are due to Him alone; declaring His praises here on earth in a way that anticipates our eternity in His presence around the throne in heaven.

Made in the USA
Charleston, SC
20 February 2017